UNLOCKING
THE TORAH TEXT

AN IN-DEPTH JOURNEY
INTO THE WEEKLY PARSHA

SHMOT

SHMUEL GOLDIN

gefen
publishing house   בית הוצאה לאור
JERUSALEM ◆ NEW YORK

Typesetting: Raphaël Freeman, Renana Typesetting
Cover Design: S. Kim Glassman

ISBN 978-965-229-449-4

Edition   3   5   7   9   8   6   4   2

Gefen Publishing House Ltd.   Gefen Books
6 Hatzvi Street, Jerusalem 94386, Israel   11 Edison Place, Springfield, NJ 07081
972-2-538-0247 • orders@gefenpublishing.com   516-593-1234 • orders@gefenpublishing.com

www.gefenpublishing.com

Printed in Israel   Send for our free catalogue

Dedicated, with love, to Barbara

When you choose your life partner, you don't really know what life will bring. All you can hope and pray for is that, come what may, your partner will be by your side.

You have never left my side. Your love, strength, dedication, wisdom and support continue to guide me.

You have encouraged, advised, cajoled and sacrificed beyond measure, all in an effort to enable your loved ones to realize our dreams.

And, through it all, against great odds, you've never let us forget what is really important.

This volume and so much else in my life is much more yours than mine.

I love you.

Shmuel

This set, *Unlocking the Torah Text*,
is lovingly dedicated to the memory of

my parents
Naftali and Lola Goldman
נפתלי בן יוסף הכהן
לאה בת חנניא יום טוב ליפא הלוי

who exemplified love of
תורה, ארץ ישראל ועם ישראל

and my grandparents, aunts and uncles, and great-grandparents
who perished in the Shoah

Josef (Yussel) and Bayla Goldman
Avrum, Ascher and Gittel

Leopold (Lipa) and Rose Weinfeld
Ascher Weinfeld

Yosef and Bina Korn

Shiya and Miriam Weinfeld

and to the memory of
David (Dudek) Fink
אריה דוד בן משה מאיר הכהן
stepfather and *bompa* extraordinaire

JOSEPH (YOSSI) AND GAIL GOLDMAN
NEIL, DANIEL AND MICHAEL

Contents

Acknowledgments

The management and staff at Gefen Publishing House continue to be a true pleasure to work with.

Ilan Greenfield, the publisher at Gefen, has made this project his own. His ready availability, innovative advice, constant encouragement and willingness to explore new ideas prove invaluable every step of the way.

Smadar Belilty, Gefen's project coordinator, supervised the unfolding of this volume with great professionalism from start to finish. She consistently kept me on track and on schedule, in spite of myself.

Kezia Raffel Pride continues to be a writer's dream editor. She not only edited this volume with her usual painstaking wisdom and skill, but patiently adapted her schedule to coincide with my piecemeal submissions.

David Nekrutman, international sales director at Gefen, assumed special responsibility for publicity of this project. His creative energy and imaginative approach were greatly appreciated.

* * *

Raphael and Linda Benaroya, Kenneth and Ruthann Eckstein, Daniel and Thalia Federbush, Jeffrey and Nava Parker, Seena Flechner and her family (on behalf of the Eve Flechner Institute) and Dina Perry and her family (on behalf of the Isaac Perry Beit Medrash) provided generous material assistance and warm encouragement through their sponsorship of this project. I cherish their friendship more than they can imagine.

My administrative assistant, Eileen Gorlyn, is a constant source of support. Her masterful ability to calmly manage the disparate segments of my professional life continues to astound me.

* * *

Few, if any, other settings in the world could have provided me with the rich professional life that I have experienced over the past twenty-five years as rabbi of my extraordinary synagogue, Congregation Ahavath Torah in Englewood, New Jersey. I continue to be amazed by the breadth of human resources that characterizes our community. Sincere intellectual search, genuine warmth, generous giving, devoted activism and a deep love of all aspects of our heritage surround me on a daily basis.

Many of the lessons found within this volume stem from my shared learning with my community. Reflected as well are countless hours of study, discussion and debate with my students at Yeshiva University, the Eve Flechner Institute, the Isaac Perry Beit Medrash and various other venues. I am grateful for our shared exploration.

*   *   *

Although my dear father, Isaac Goldin, of blessed memory, passed away over eleven years ago, I feel his presence in my life every day. The example that he set within his lifetime -of honesty, loyalty, personal responsibility and dedication to the family serves as the standard to which I aspire.

My mother, Pnina (Pearl) Goldin, is a constant source of inspiration. Her remarkable aliya to Israel after a decades-long teaching career in the United States has led to even more learning, deeper religious devotion and an ever-growing commitment to Torah ideals. She is an unassuming family matriarch who, without realizing it, sets an example for us all.

*   *   *

My children, Avi and Rena, Yossi and Shifra, Yehuda, Donny and Rivka and my grandchildren, Isaac, Benjamin, Temima and Jacob (two additions, thank God, since the publishing of the last volume), continue to be a source of tremendous *nachat* and unending pride. Simply put, children, you are "what it's all about."

Special thanks to Yossi and to my mother for, once again, serving as my "in-house proofreaders" for this text.

*   *   *

Most importantly, as indicated above, this book is dedicated with unending appreciation and love to my wife, Barbara. This volume was the real test for me: could I write a book while not on sabbatical? I would have given up ten times over had it not been for her constant encouragement and personal sacrifice. I owe her more than I can express.

Introduction

An unknown (at least to me) observer once remarked, *"In too many Jewish circles today the Torah is perceived as the commentary on the Talmud written by God..."*

The challenge of reclaiming the centrality of the Torah text in Jewish thought and study has become something of an obsession with me over the years. I believe that, too often, the study of God's word is summarily shunted aside in favor of studies perceived as more scholarly and advanced. Chumash has become a subject from which we "graduate" as we move past grade school, rarely to be critically revisited by adults. Our understanding of the text, therefore, remains fixed at a fourth- or fifth-grade level and the significant, sophisticated lessons embedded in the Torah are largely overlooked, to our great detriment.

How deeply gratified I am, therefore, by the response to the first volume of this series, which appeared in print a little over a year ago. While the positive published reviews were certainly encouraging, more meaningful to me were the informal communications from countless readers. Many of you, from many walks of life, shared with me your excitement in our joint exploration of the text. I thank you. You have reinforced my belief that the Torah has much to say to each of us, regardless of our prior level of knowledge, educational background or religious affiliation. This divine, timeless tome yields countless lessons of continued relevance, each with the potential to inspire ongoing study, discussion and debate in every generation.

With great excitement and pleasure, therefore, I invite those of you who have been traveling with us to continue – and those who are beginning now to join – our shared journey through the text. A grand adventure awaits us in the book of Shmot, as together we will explore the events which mark the birth of the Israelite nation. Slavery in Egypt, Moshe's call to leadership, the Exodus, Revelation at Sinai, the construction of the

Sanctuary, the sin of the golden calf; these and other foundational, familiar events will come under our renewed scrutiny as we probe for the lessons embedded within.

First, however, a brief review of the parameters of our search (these guidelines are recorded in greater detail in the introduction to volume 1):

1. While traditional Torah study is based on a fundamental belief in the divine authorship of the text, questioning and challenging the text itself is not only allowed but encouraged. Unless we struggle with the narrative, God's word and God's intent remain distant and unclear and the Torah remains a closed book.

2. The treasures of the Torah can only be uncovered when the narrative itself is seen as the truth, comprised of real events that happened to real people. The heroes of the Bible were human beings, not gods, and the stories of their lives are not fables.

3. No part of the text or its contents will be off-limits to our search. We will explore the motives and actions of the personalities who populate its pages. We will probe God's role in the unfolding narrative and attempt to discern what the Torah reveals about His divine will. We will seek to understand why events took place as they did and how the narrative might inform our lives. And we will explore the deep philosophical currents mirrored in the events described to us.

4. Two distinct approaches to the Torah text are reflected in rabbinic literature: *pshat* and *drash*.

Pshat refers to the straightforward explanation of the text. When we operate within the realm of *pshat*, we search for the literal, concrete meaning of the narrative before us. *Proper understanding of pshat reveals deep, unexpected meaning within the text itself.*

Drash refers to rabbinic commentary serving as a vehicle for the transmission of lessons and ideas beyond the literal narrative. Many authorities maintain that Midrashic commentary is not meant to be taken literally, nor is it meant to be seen as an attempt to explain the factual meaning of a specific Torah passage. The key question in the realm of *drash* is: *What are the rabbis trying to teach us?*

When, as unfortunately often happens, we confuse these two approaches – when we ignore the *pshat* and instead offer *drash* as the literal interpretation of the text – we end up understanding neither of these interpretive realms. In our studies, therefore, we will make every attempt to distinguish between *pshat* and *drash* and to present each approach appropriately.

5. Each of our studies on the parshiot of Shmot will raise a series of questions designed to strike to the core of a particular passage of the text.

Our search for answers to the questions raised will take us on a journey through traditional commentary and original thought. In each study, a sampling of rabbinic opinion on the issues will be reviewed and original approaches will be offered as we humbly continue our own struggle with the text.

Finally, many studies will include a "Points to Ponder" section in which connections are made between the Torah passage and relevant concerns that touch our lives. This section is specifically designed to encourage ongoing thought and debate.

I again close with the hope that our continuing journey will be, for each of us, a passionate one, inspiring continuing exploration and thought, sparking conversation, dialogue and debate each week in homes, synagogues, schools and beyond, as together we unlock the treasures of the Torah text.

Shmot

פרק א:א-ו:א

Parsha Summary

Persecution and promise…

After the death of Yosef's generation, Pharaoh embarks upon a campaign of persecution against the Israelites. His edicts include isolation, degradation, forced labor and the murder of male newborns.

An Israelite male infant, born to a couple from the tribe of Levi, is hidden by his parents who place him in a basket which they release on the surface of the Nile River. When the infant is discovered by the daughter of Pharaoh, she names him Moshe and determines to raise him as her own son.

After years in Pharaoh's palace, Moshe emerges to witness the enslavement of the Israelites. He observes an Egyptian taskmaster striking an Israelite slave and rises to the defense of the victim, slaying the taskmaster and hiding his body in the sand. Afraid of Pharaoh's retribution, Moshe flees to the land of Midian where he encounters and marries Tzippora, the daughter of Yitro, a Midianite priest.

Moshe remains in Midian with Yitro, serving as shepherd for his father-in-law's flocks. One day, as he is performing his duties, Moshe is drawn to the sight of a bush which burns but is not consumed by the fire. When he turns aside to examine this strange apparition, God addresses him from the burning bush. God charges Moshe with the task of returning to Egypt and leading the Israelites to freedom. Overruling Moshe's repeated objections concerning his own worthiness for leadership, God ultimately appoints Moshe's older brother, Aharon, to serve as Moshe's partner and spokesman.

Moshe begins the return journey to Egypt, accompanied by his wife and two sons, Gershon and Eliezer. Along the way, God suddenly threatens Moshe with death. Tzippora circumcises their younger son, Eliezer, and the danger passes.

Moshe arrives in Egypt and, together with Aharon, gathers the Israelite elders and informs them of their people's impending redemption. Moshe *and Aharon then appear before Pharaoh and, as God had instructed at the burning bush, ask the Egyptian king to allow the Israelites to leave Egypt for a three-day period to worship their God. Pharaoh refuses and increases the burden of labor upon the Israelites.*

Moshe turns to God in frustration and questions his own mission to Egypt. God responds by promising that Moshe will now see the Exodus begin to unfold.

1 A Blueprint for Persecution

Context

The Israelites, initially welcomed to Egypt at the end of the patriarchal era,[1] experience a precipitous change of fortune after the death of Yosef and his generation.

A "new" Egyptian king initiates a campaign of persecution against the descendents of Yaakov, transforming them into a subgroup of slaves within the Egyptian population.[2]

Questions

Why does the Torah dedicate twenty-two sentences of text to a detailed, step-by-step description of the enslavement of the Israelites at the hands of the Egyptians?

What eternal lessons can be gleaned from this tragic narrative?

Approaches

— **A** —

The enslavement of the Israelites is not Pharaoh's endgame. While the king clearly intends to benefit from the forced labor the Hebrew slaves will provide, he will ultimately be satisfied with nothing less than this fledgling people's total destruction.[3] *Genocide, however, even when mandated by a mighty Pharaoh, cannot be perpetrated in a vacuum.*

A careful reading of the text, therefore, reveals a frighteningly prescient reality. The first phase of our nation's birth is shaped by a painful pattern.

---

1. Bereishit 45:16–20.
2. Shmot 1:8–22.
3. Ibid., 1:15–16, 22.

We become the targets of a blueprint for persecution which, tragically, will be reused over and over again during the ensuing centuries.

—— **B** ————————————————————————————————

The purpose of Pharaoh's malicious plan is twofold.

On the one hand, as the Ramban explains:

> Pharaoh and his advisers could not attack [the Israelites] by the sword. An unprovoked attack upon a people that had originally come to Egypt at the invitation of the first king would be viewed as great treachery.... The [Egyptian] populace would not have allowed such an abomination.[4]

Instead, Pharaoh realizes, the stage must first be set. A painstaking, detailed plan must be set in motion that will render the destruction of the Israelites "acceptable" to their Egyptian neighbors.

On the other hand, Pharaoh must "prepare" the victims, as well. Slowly and inexorably robbed of their confidence, of any vestige of self-worth, the Israelites will be transformed into unwitting participants in their own demise.

We watch with horrible fascination as the stages of this plan unfold – details that, centuries later, are much too familiar for comfort.

Stage One: Propaganda

> And a new king rose up over Egypt who did not know Yosef. And he said to his nation: "Behold the nation, the children of Israel are more numerous and stronger than we. Come let us be wise to them, lest they become numerous and it will be that if war occurs, they will join our enemies and wage war against us and go up from the land."[5]

Persecution, the Torah testifies, inevitably begins with propaganda, with the verbal isolation of a people from surrounding society.

Clearly Pharaoh's description of the Israelites as "more numerous and

---

4. Ramban, Shmot 1:10.
5. Shmot 1:9–10.

stronger" than the Egyptians is patently false, even ludicrous. And yet the king knows that lies, boldly spoken, will be readily accepted by those who want to believe them.

Pharaoh's evil genius is also evident in his specific accusations against the Israelites. He consciously plays upon his own nation's envy, xenophobia and fear of a fifth column within their borders. *Why should we tolerate,* he asks, *a dangerous separate "nation" in our own land?*

Stage Two: Isolation

> And they appointed taskmasters over them in order to afflict them with their burdens and they built storage cities for Pharaoh, Pitom and Raamses.[6]

Pharaoh's edicts move to the next level with the designation of taskmasters and projects specific to the Israelites. *These people are different,* the Egyptian king proclaims through these actions, *and the problems they create require special treatment.*

The physical and psychological isolation of the Israelites is now complete.

Stage Three: Degradation

> And the Egyptians enslaved the children of Israel with crushing harshness (*b'pharech*).[7]

When the Israelites respond to Pharaoh's initial decrees with resilience, the Egyptians ratchet the process up to the next level.[8]

The biblical term *b'pharech* potentially conveys, according to the commentaries, varied aspects of this new level of persecution:

Rashi leads a number of scholars who, choosing the path of *pshat* (the straightforward explanation of the text), explain that the term refers to labor that crushes and breaks the body.[9] Such toil has no real purpose

---

6. Ibid., 1:11.
7. Ibid., 1:13.
8. Ibid., 1:12.
9. Rashi, Shmot 1:13.

beyond the physical torment and psychological degradation inflicted upon the laborers.

Some Talmudic sages suggest that, in order to mock and demean the slaves, men's work was given to the Israelite women and women's work to the men.[10]

In a brilliant stroke, Rabbi Shimshon Raphael Hirsch connects the term *b'pharech* to the *parochet* – the dividing curtain which, centuries later, separated the Holy of Holies from the rest of the Temple. The purpose of the work placed upon the Israelites, suggests Hirsch, was to further *divide* the Israelites from their neighbors.[11]

Finally, one particularly telling Talmudic source sees the word *pharech* as a consolidation of the two Hebrew words *peh* (mouth) and *rach* (soft). The Egyptians beguiled the Israelites with soft, enticing speech. Through lies and false promises of security, the taskmasters induced the slaves to cooperate in their own enslavement.[12]

Stage Four: Murder

> And the king of Egypt said to the Hebrew midwives…, "When you deliver the Hebrew women, you shall see on the birthing stool, if it is a son you are to kill him, and if it is a daughter, she is to live."
>
> And the midwives feared God and they did not do as the king of Egypt spoke to them….[13]
>
> And Pharaoh commanded his entire people, saying: "Every son that is born – into the river you shall throw him! And every daughter – you shall keep alive!"[14]

Only after the physical and psychological subjugation of the Israelites has reached a critical point can Pharaoh embark upon his true plan, the physical destruction of this fledgling nation.

Murder, however, particularly when carried out in the public arena, must be perpetrated slowly and cautiously. Pharaoh, therefore, opens the

---

10. Talmud Bavli Sota 11b.
11. Rabbi Shimshon Raphael Hirsch, Shmot 1:13.
12. Talmud Bavli Sota 11b.
13. Shmot 1:15–17.
14. Ibid., 1:22.

final devastating stages of his design against the Israelites in a manner that not only attacks the weakest among them but that can be carried out secretly. He commands the Hebrew midwives to kill the male infants in such a way that "even the birthing mothers themselves will remain unaware."[15]

Pharaoh's actions, however, may well be governed by even deeper, more devious motivations. To protect himself, the Egyptian king wants the extermination of the Israelites to begin in territory that carries a degree, however slight, of moral ambiguity. The Talmud postulates that Pharaoh conveyed to the midwives a method of determining the sex of the Israelite children before their birth.[16] Rabbi Shimshon Raphael Hirsch explains that, in this view, Pharaoh is deliberately commanding abortion rather than infanticide.[17] *We are not really murdering the Israelite males. We are only preventing their birth.*

When this subterfuge is thwarted by the righteous midwives, Pharaoh finally proclaims his true intentions and commands that all male infants be cast into the Nile. Even at this point, however, as the king's malicious plan moves into the open, Pharaoh ingeniously shields himself from blame. The Ramban notes that Pharaoh couches this final, devastating edict in language that distances the murder from the official seat of government. The king does not command his army or his officers to carry out this terrible act. Instead, he instructs his "entire people" to murder the Hebrew infants.[18] In retrospect, the king will be able to protest, *What do you want from me? This was not an official action. This was a spontaneous, popular pogrom.*

——— C ———

Pharaoh's ultimate success in manipulating the mindset of both the Israelite victims and Egyptian perpetrators may well be reflected in two telling biblical passages.

---

15. Ramban, Shmot 1:10.
16. Talmud Bavli Sota 11b.
17. Rabbi Shimshon Raphael Hirsch, Shmot 1:16.
18. Ramban, Shmot 1:10.

Concerning the Egyptians

> And Pharaoh commanded his entire people, saying: "Every son that is
> born – into the river you shall throw him! And every daughter – you
> shall keep alive!"

Rashi notes a startling omission in the Egyptian king's directive. The king
does not say, "*Every Israelite son* that is born – into the river you shall throw
him!" He says, "*Every son* that is born…"

Rashi explains the omission by citing the following Midrashic tradition quoted in the Talmud.

Pharaoh's astrologers had predicted to the king that the savior of the
Jewish nation would soon be born. The astrologers also foretold that this
savior would ultimately meet his downfall through water.

Uncertain as to whether this savior-to-be would be born to an Egyptian or to an Israelite family, Pharaoh decrees that all male infants, *including Egyptian infants*, be cast into the Nile. Astoundingly, the Egyptians
comply.[19]

The rabbinic observation quoted by Rashi is profoundly telling. The
omission in the biblical text indicates how completely Pharaoh had influenced his own nation. By the time the king's plan reaches its climax, Egyptian hatred of the Israelites is so great that *the Egyptians are even willing to
sacrifice their own children to the cause.*

Concerning the Israelites

Later in Parshat Shmot, after Pharaoh has increased the burden upon the
Israelite slaves in response to Moshe's initial demands for freedom, the Israelites turn on Moshe and exclaim: "May the Lord look upon you and judge,
for you have made our very scent abhorrent in the eyes of Pharaoh and in
the eyes of his servants, to place a sword in their hands to kill us!"[20]

How astonishing! Pharaoh has subjugated the Israelites, tormented
them physically and psychologically, murdered their children and, yet,

---

19. The Midrash goes on to note that Pharaoh's astrologers had perceived a truth that they
    did not understand. Moshe's fate would, indeed, ultimately be determined through
    water; not the waters of the Nile, but the "waters of strife." See Bamidbar 20:1–13; Tal-
    mud Bavli Sota 12b; Rashi, Shmot 1:22.
20. Shmot 5:21.

these very Israelites now turn to Moshe and, in effect, protest: *Because of you, Pharaoh and his servants won't like us!*

The genius of the Egyptian king is in full evidence. He has successfully robbed the Israelites of their freedom in a way that, nonetheless, maintains their dependence upon him. Unwilling to believe in the total evil that confronts them, the Israelite slaves still harbor a hope that, somehow, with just the right approach, Pharaoh may still relent.

One is reminded of the very sad joke in which two Jews stand before a Nazi firing squad. The German commander orders: "Ready, aim…"

Suddenly one of the Jewish victims shouts out at the top of his lungs, "Down with the Nazis!"

"Mordy!" exclaims the other Jew. "*Don't make trouble!*"

Pharaoh's influence over both the Egyptians and the Israelites is complete. As a result, the Jewish nation finds itself in mortal danger even before it is born.

—— **D** ——————————————————————————————

Finally, a further cautionary message is subtly conveyed by the well-known rabbinic debate concerning the phrase in the text that introduces the subjugation of the Israelites, "And a new king rose up over Egypt."[21]

"Rav and Shmuel [disagreed]: One maintained that the Torah literally refers to a new king, while the other argued that the same king changed his decrees."[22] What is the substance of this debate? The Torah clearly states, "a new king rose up." Why not accept this statement at face value?

Perhaps there is no real debate at all but, rather, a shared warning of the complex potential dangers that will shape the lot of a diaspora people, a people who will remain, for so much of their history, dependent upon the goodwill of others.

Both "new kings" and "new decrees" will affect the descendents of the Israelites across the centuries. Years of careful political cultivation will dissipate in the face of changing regimes. Even more disturbingly, the seemingly strong relationships forged with those around us will often fall prey to the vagaries of changing circumstance. Expedience rather than loyalty will

_____

21. Ibid., 1:9.
22. Talmud Bavli Eruvin 53a.

rule the day as benevolence and generosity are replaced with harsh "new decrees" directed against the Jews, frequently with little or no warning.

Was the Pharaoh who enslaved the Israelites a "new king"? Perhaps, perhaps not… Either scenario, viewed in retrospect through the lens of history, potentially rings true.

Points to Ponder

The uncanny ability of the Torah text to speak across the centuries is nowhere more clearly – nor more frighteningly – evident than in its description of the enslavement of the Israelites at the hands of the Egyptians. Here, openly rooted at the dawn of our history, are the very methods used against us and other innocent victims, to such devastating effect, by enemies in every era, including our own.

From cold, calculating Nazi murderers to zealous Islamic fundamentalists, willing to kill their own children in the pursuit of the destruction of Israel and, now, all of Western culture, the adversaries and tactics we face today are much too familiar. Propaganda, demonization, subterfuge and the teaching of hatred remain the preliminary tools of the murderers' trade as, over and over again, words inexorably lead to deeds.

Constant, as well, is the unwillingness of decent people to accept the reality of the evil that confronts us. We cling to a desperate, illusory hope that somehow, with the right gesture, with the right concession, we will convince our enemies to totally change their ways. After all, we feel, they can't *really* mean what they say…

Laid down at the beginning of time, the painstaking tactics of prejudice and persecution have remained remarkably constant. Evil will be defeated only if these initial tactics are recognized when they first appear and confronted head-on.

2 A Strange Announcement

Context

Into the cauldron of Egyptian slavery, a child is born who is destined, at God's command, to lead the Israelites to redemption and national birth.

The Torah announces the arrival of this child, Moshe, in the following way: "And a man went from the House of Levi and he took a daughter of Levi. And the woman conceived and gave birth to a son."[1]

Questions

What is the meaning of the puzzling, seemingly unnecessary sentence "And a man went from the house of Levi and he took a daughter of Levi"?

Why does the text omit the names of Moshe's parents, Amram and Yocheved, only to reveal these names later?[2]

Approaches

—**A**—

A variety of approaches are suggested by the rabbis as they struggle to explain the strange announcement of Moshe's birth.

Rashi and numerous other commentaries interpret the sentence "And a man *went* from the house of Levi and he took a daughter of Levi"[3] in light of a Midrashic tradition quoted in the Talmud. According to this tradition, the passage actually refers to a second marriage of Moshe's parents which took place at the instigation of their daughter, Miriam: "Amram *went* at the advice of his daughter…"

---

1. Shmot 2:1.
2. Ibid., 6:14–27.
3. Ibid., 2:1.

When Pharaoh decreed the murder of the male infants, Amram, a leading figure in the Israelite community, divorced his wife in order to prevent the birth of a male child. Noting Amram's actions, other Israelites followed suit.

Amram's daughter, Miriam, however, argued with her father's decision:

> "Father, your decree is harsher than Pharaoh's! Pharaoh only pronounced [death] upon the male infants and you have decreed upon the females as well…"
>
> [Upon hearing his daughter's argument] Amram immediately remarried his wife and the Israelites again followed his lead.[4]

With this poignant interpretation, the Midrash underscores the agonizing decisions that must be made by those who live under the shadow of persecution.

— B —

Working within the realm of *pshat* (the straightforward explanation of the text), the Ibn Ezra suggests that, by the time of Amram and Yocheved, the Israelites lived in many cities in Egypt. The Torah is simply informing us that Amram "went" from one Egyptian city to another in order to marry Yocheved.[5]

The Ramban objects to Ibn Ezra's explanation by arguing that the Torah would have no reason to inform us concerning a journey taken by Amram from one city to another. Instead, maintains the Ramban, the phrase in question is actually consistent with the linguistic style of the Torah. The verb *lalechet*, "to go," is often used in the text when an individual or individuals prepare to take new and difficult steps. By stating "*Vayeilech ish*, (And a man went)," the Torah underscores Amram's courageous willingness to marry in spite of Pharaoh's harsh decrees.[6]

The names of Moshe's parents are omitted in the narrative, continues the Ramban, because the text desires to trace the lineage of this great leader in intergenerational fashion. In order to avoid interrupting the dramatic

---

4. Talmud Bavli Sota 12a.
5. Ibn Ezra, Shmot 2:1.
6. Ramban, ibid.

story of Moshe's birth with a lengthy genealogical discussion, however, the text delays the description of his lineage to a later point.[7]

—— **C** ——

Yehuda Nachshoni maintains that the cryptic description of Moshe's birth is meant to convey one overarching fact: *Moshe's origins are human, not divine.*

In clear contradistinction to both pagan mythology and Christian tradition, Judaism views its heroes as mortal beings who aspire to and attain greatness (see *Va'eira 2, Approaches* B; see also *Bereishit: Lech Lecha 2, Questions; Toldot 4, Approaches*).

The Torah thus emphasizes that Moshe, the greatest of our leaders, was fully human – the son of "A man from the house of Levi" who took "a daughter of Levi."[8]

The "Genius of Barshov" (Rabbi David Sperber) goes one step further by suggesting that the text also conveys, in its description of Moshe's birth, the limitations of *yichus* (pedigree). The names of Moshe's parents are omitted to underscore that Torah greatness is not inherited but earned. Moshe will rise to leadership on his own merit, not on the merit of his ancestors.[9] (See *Bereishit: Vayeishev 4.*)

—— **D** ——

Finally, a series of tantalizing possibilities are raised by a striking textual pattern that encapsulates Moshe's life. The story of this great leader is bound in the text by two puzzling phrases, both of which prominently feature the word *vayeilech*, "and he went":

▸ *Vayeilech ish,* "And a man went,"[10] heralding the birth of Moshe
▸ *Vayeilech Moshe,* "And Moshe went,"[11] heralding the approach of Moshe's death

Each of these phrases in context seems unnecessary, its purpose vague and

7. Ibid.; Shmot 6:14–27.
8. Yehuda Nachshoni, *Hagot B'parshiot HaTorah* (Tel Aviv: Zohar Publishing, 1979), p. 209.
9. Michtav l'David, Shmot 2:1.
10. Shmot 2:1.
11. Devarim 31:1.

unclear. Together, however, marking the endpoints of Moshe's life, these passages enable the Torah to subtly convey the remarkable sense of *halicha* (movement) that characterizes the career of this great leader. Moshe's continuous spiritual growth and development is captured in the verb *lalechet* (to go), which encloses his story in the text.

The texture of this phenomenon deepens when we consider that the life of another great biblical figure – the first patriarch, Avraham – is similarly marked at its boundaries by the verb *lalechet*. In Avraham's case this term is twice conjugated as part of divine commandments opening with the words *Lech lecha*, "Go for yourself":

> ‣ *Lech lecha mei'artzecha, mi'moladetecha u'mi'beit avicha*, "Leave your land, your birthplace, and the home of your father,"[12] commencing Avraham's personal journey, the patriarchal era and Jewish history itself
> ‣ *Lech lecha el Eretz HaMoriah*, "Go to the land of Moriah,"[13] announcing Avraham's most dramatic test, *Akeidat Yitzchak*

Not by coincidence, the Torah delineates the lives of both Avraham and Moshe with the term *lalechet*. The personal journeys of these two individuals launch the two major biblical periods of Jewish history, respectively, the patriarchal and national eras. Movement and continued spiritual growth mark their pioneering roles.

—— **E** ——————————————————————————

There are, however, two fundamental differences between Avraham's *lech lecha* and Moshe's *vayeilech*.

1. *Lech lecha* literally means "Go for yourself" and is understood by Rashi to imply, "Go for your own good and for your own benefit."[14]

Vayeilech, on the other hand, is open ended, without the reflexive reference.

Avraham's era, the patriarchal era, unfolded before the Jewish nation was born and was defined by the personal journeys of the patriarchs,

---

12. Bereishit 12:1.
13. Ibid., 22:2.
14. Rashi, Bereishit 12:1.

matriarchs and their families. Theirs was the time of the *yachid*, the individual. Only once the concept of individual value was fully established and entrenched in Jewish thought could the period of the *tzibur*, the national era, begin (see *Bereishit*: Vayechi 4, *Approaches*).

Avraham's life is therefore defined by the individual commandment *lech lecha*, a charge towards personal growth and accomplishment.

With Moshe's birth and the dawn of the national era, however, success becomes measured not only in personal terms but in communal terms, as well. Moshe leads others; that is his primary role. His leadership will emanate, however, not from the sidelines, but from personal example. Moshe will "go" – and others will follow.

2. *Lech lecha* entails response to a commandment from God.

Vayeilech reflects self-motivation and initiative on the part of man.

While one can certainly find examples of personal initiative within the patriarchal era, God "ups the ante" when the national era begins. Over and over again, God conveys the clear message that He will no longer act until man takes the first step.

A series of episodes in Moshe's life underscore this transition:

"And it came to pass in those days that Moshe grew up and went out to his brethren and observed their burdens…"[15] Moshe's trajectory towards leadership is launched when he, of his own accord, leaves the luxury of Pharaoh's palace to view the pain of the Israelites. This voluntary step on Moshe's part changes not only the course of his life but the course of Jewish history.

"And God saw that he [Moshe] turned aside to see and God called to him from the midst of the bush."[16] God does not call Moshe to leadership until he notes that Moshe has turned aside to observe the phenomenon of the burning bush. Had Moshe ignored the bush and continued on his way, God might never have spoken to him at all.

"And Moshe ascended to God and God called to him from the mountain…"[17] When the Israelites arrive at Sinai, the Torah clearly states that Moshe ascends the mountain, and only then does God call to him with the instructions preparatory to Revelation. The order of events is counterintuitive.

---

15. Shmot 2:11.
16. Ibid., 3:4.
17. Ibid., 19:3.

One would have expected Moshe to wait at the foot of the mountain until he is summoned by God. The Torah's message, however, is clear. Revelation itself will wait until Moshe takes the first step up Mount Sinai.

— **F** —

God's willingness to overtly direct the course of Jewish history apparently diminishes as the nation matures. *Lech lecha* is transformed into *vayeilech*. In incremental fashion our own initiative will determine the course of our lives and our nation's history.

How appropriate, therefore, that the verb *lalechet*, which is used in the text to capture the lives of both Avraham and Moshe and to mark the transition from one to the other, eventually becomes the root of the word *halacha*, Jewish law. Across the ages, the descendents of Avraham and Moshe will not wait, paralyzed, for a sign from above to indicate God's design. They will, instead, take the initiative to determine that design through the study, application and observance of God's law, a law that continues to develop through a partnership between God and man. Involvement in the halacha will indicate how "to go," as its adherents are guided along the path of continued spiritual growth and development.

Points to Ponder

This parsha provokes a few thoughts about initiative.

Who knows how different history might have been had Moshe failed to initiate and act at each of the critical moments of his life?

Had he opted to remain in the luxury of Pharaoh's palace, would the Israelites have eventually succumbed to Egyptian persecution and disappeared into the mists of history?

Had he ignored the burning bush would Moshe have, nonetheless, risen to leadership along a different path?

Had Moshe waited at the foot of Sinai for God to summon him, would we still be waiting for Revelation to begin?

These unanswerable questions serve to remind us of the ways in which the course of history can hinge upon the single act of a solitary individual.

For all the opportunities successfully taken across the generations, who knows how many others have been lost? For all we know, full redemption may be at hand – and God is simply waiting for one or all of us to take the first step.

3 First Impressions

Context

While shepherding the flocks of his father-in-law, Yitro, Moshe arrives at Mount Chorev (synonymous with Mount Sinai, destined to become the site of God's Revelation to the Israelites). There, Moshe's attention is drawn by a strange apparition: a bush that burns but is not consumed by the fire.

When Moshe "turns aside" for a closer look, God suddenly begins to speak: "Moshe, Moshe…. Do not come nearer to here. Take off your shoes from your feet for the place upon which you stand is holy ground."[1]

Questions

At face value, God's first words to Moshe are somewhat disappointing. The encounter at the burning bush, after all, marks Moshe's introduction to his own, divinely ordained, historic mission. Even more importantly, this is Moshe's first "meeting" with God.

Couldn't God have chosen a more meaningful opening to His initial dialogue with Moshe? Perhaps God should have immediately begun by introducing Himself (as He does in the very next sentence[2] and again later in the conversation, albeit enigmatically, in response to Moshe's queries[3]).

Or, perhaps, He could have opened the conversation by explaining the historic significance of Moshe's impending journey to leadership.

A general statement concerning man's relationship to God would certainly have been in order, as would have been a description of the global role soon to be played by the newborn Jewish nation.

---

1. Shmot 3:1–5.
2. Ibid., 3:6.
3. Ibid., 3:14–15.

Why, then, does God open His relationship with Moshe with the strange commandments "Do not come nearer…. Take off your shoes"?

Is there deeper meaning to these seemingly arbitrary directives?

Approaches

— **A** —

The Ramban maintains that a stark contrast emerges between Moshe's two encounters with God at Sinai, a contrast that reflects Moshe's growth in the realm of prophecy. At the inception of his career, Moshe is commanded not to approach the burning bush. Later, however, when Moshe returns to Sinai with the Israelites following the Exodus, the text states, "And Moshe approached the thick darkness where God was."[4] Moshe's ability to approach God does not emerge full bloom but, rather, develops over the course of his spiritual journey.

Moshe is commanded to remove his shoes, continues the Ramban, because the entire mountain is sanctified at this point by God's presence and shoes may not be worn on hallowed ground. The Ramban does not offer, however, any rationale for this prohibition.[5]

— **B** —

While agreeing that on the level of *pshat* Moshe is commanded to remove his shoes in response to the holiness created by God's presence, numerous commentators go on to suggest other, symbolic interpretations for this commandment, as well.

Rabbeinu Bachya, for example, posits that the removal of Moshe's shoes represents Moshe's obligation to "remove" the physical aspects of his existence which serve as an impediment to prophecy. "Just as an individual can remove his shoes," claims Bachya, "so, too, he has the power to remove from himself the physical dimensions of his existence in order to be prepared for prophetic vision."

God's first words to Moshe are thus a summons to leave the physical and enter the spiritual realm.[6]

---

4. Ibid., 20:18.
5. Ramban, Shmot 3:5.
6. Rabbeinu Bachya, ibid.

Rabbeinu Bachya's approach would seem to stand in stark contrast to the approach of the Sforno and others who see Moshe's greatness specifically in light of his ability to prophesy while remaining in full control of his physical faculties.[7]

—— **C** ——————————————————————————————————

Rabbi Shimshon Raphael Hirsch, in a brilliant stroke, connects God's two initial commandments to Moshe: the admonition not to approach the burning bush and the commandment that Moshe remove his shoes.

The bush represents that aspect of God's existence which remains incomprehensible to man.

God, therefore, commands, "Do not come nearer to here… Take off your shoes…" *Instead of trying to find out about the phenomenon that lies beyond and outside your sphere, understand the high destiny of the ground on which you already stand and give yourself up entirely to that.*[8]

A holy space, explains Hirsch, has the potential to reflect directly back upon the personality of the ministrant. The removal of one's shoes represents a willingness to give oneself up entirely to such a place.

Centuries after Moshe's encounter with God on Sinai, the Kohanim (priests) in the Temple will similarly perform their functions barefooted to symbolize their desire for direct contact and connection with the Temple's holiness.[9]

Moshe is thus commanded by God to stay in his own realm and experience the holiness of Chorev, the sanctified place in which he finds himself right now.

—— **D** ——————————————————————————————————

If we go one step beyond Hirsch's approach, a powerful new possibility emerges.

Far from arbitrary, God's first instructions to Moshe are the perfect introduction, not only to the monumental events that are about to unfold, but to the eternal challenge that God is about to issue to Moshe and his people.

——————————

7. Sforno, Shmot 19:9, Bamidbar 12:8.
8. Rabbi Shimshon Raphael Hirsch, Shmot 3:5.
9. Ibid.

God commands Moshe: "Do not come nearer to here." *Do not search for me in esoteric visions of a burning bush.*

"Take off your shoes." *Root yourself to the ground, to the physical world in which you live.*

"For the place upon which you stand is holy ground." *Kedusha, sanctity, is to be found wherever you stand, wherever you are. You and your people are about to become partners with me in the creation of holiness in this world. You will be challenged to be "mekadesh Shem Shamayim," to sanctify God's name in your everyday lives. The Divine Presence will be discovered not in a realm of mystery but in your daily activities and in your ongoing interactions with each other.*

Search for holiness, Moshe, "where you stand."

—— **E** ——————————————————————————————————

Understood this way, God's opening words to Moshe are neither extraneous nor arbitrary. These directives, in fact, capture the overarching message that will soon be reiterated on this very spot, to a nation standing at the foot of Sinai, precluded from climbing the mountain by divine decree.[10]

God, the Israelites will learn, is not to be found in the mists on the summit of the mountain but at its base. There, rooted in their own world, they will experience Revelation and receive the Torah. There, they will be challenged to create holiness as they discover, through the application of God's law, the Divine Presence in their own daily lives (see Yitro 2, *Approaches* C, D).

———————————

10. Shmot 19:12–13.

4 A Brief Vacation?

Context

Speaking from the burning bush, God commands Moshe to return to Egypt and deliver the following message to Pharaoh: "The Lord, the God of the Hebrews, has encountered us. And now please let us go on a three-day journey in the wilderness and we will bring offerings to the Lord, our God."[1]

Questions

God's instructions to Moshe at the burning bush threaten to undermine our understanding of the entire Exodus narrative.

Where is the ringing, powerful demand for freedom, *Let my people go*? Why do we find in its place the seemingly tepid request, *Please let my people go on a three-day journey to the desert to worship God*? What could be more central to the Exodus story than the demand for complete freedom?

And…if Pharaoh had agreed to Moshe's request, would the Israelites have returned after three days? If so, what would have been accomplished by their brief departure? If they would never have returned, if a three-day journey was not a truly viable option, why would God instruct Moshe to lie to the Egyptian king? Is the Jewish nation to be born through deceit? As the Abravanel exclaims: "How could the Almighty have commanded Moshe to lie in His name? It would have been better to clearly demand, 'Release my nation from under the burdens of Egypt.'"[2]

Finally, in the aftermath of the Exodus, after Pharaoh has released the Israelites from bondage, the text relates: "And it was told to the king of Egypt that the [Israelite] nation had fled."[3]

---

1. Shmot 3:18.
2. Abravanel, Shmot 3:18.
3. Shmot 14:5.

How are we to understand this bewildering statement? Clearly Pharaoh knows that the Israelites have left Egypt. The king himself, broken by the last of the ten plagues, ordered the slaves out of his country![4] Why must he now be told that the Israelites have fled? Can it be that Pharaoh, even after the devastation of the plagues, still believes he has released the Israelites only for a three-day religious holiday? Is that why the Egyptian king leads his army in pursuit of the Israelites three days after the Exodus, when the king concludes that the slaves are not returning? Has the entire Exodus been divinely structured, through the three-day request, to lead Pharaoh and his army inexorably to their deaths in the Sea of Reeds?

Approaches

—— **A** ——————————————————————————————————

The classical commentaries are divided in their approach to the limited request for a three-day journey from Egypt.

Some scholars, including Abravanel[5] and the Akeidat Yitzchak,[6] view the request as an exercise meant to test and expose the limits of Pharaoh's obstinacy. As the Abravanel puts it, "The Almighty proffered this request in order to demonstrate to the world the extent of Pharaoh's stubbornness and to justify the divine judgment and punishment about to be brought upon Pharaoh and Egypt."[7]

This position implies that the request for a three-day journey was offered as a serious option. Had the Egyptian king shown flexibility by agreeing to this first request presented to him, the Israelites would indeed have returned and the Exodus might well have unfolded in a different, less painful, fashion.

Once Pharaoh refuses to accede even to this reasonable appeal, however, the three-day option is removed from the table and replaced with the demand for total freedom.[8]

———————————————

4. Ibid., 12:31.
5. Abravanel, Shmot 3:18.
6. Akeidat Yitzchak Shmot, sha'ar 35.
7. Abravanel, Shmot 3:18.
8. Shmot 6:11.

—— **B** ————————————————————————————————

Other commentaries maintain that the limited journey was never really presented as a viable option at all. God certainly had no intention of allowing His people to return to Egypt after three days of freedom.

What, then, can possibly justify the request? Why would God order Moshe to deliberately deceive the Egyptian king?

On this point, two contrasting schools of thought emerge:

1. Some authorities simply refuse to accept the possibility that God – and upon His orders Moshe as well – could be deceitful.

Rabbi Yaakov Mecklenberg, for example, maintains that, notwithstanding the implied commitment to return to Egypt, Moshe never clearly verbalizes a pledge to come back. He was therefore not guilty of an outright falsehood.[9]

The Chizkuni goes one step further and claims that the request for a three-day journey was factually truthful. He points to the fact that on the second day after the Exodus the Israelites encamp at Eitam in the "edge of the wilderness,"[10] effectively halting their flight from Egypt.[11]

2. The Midrash, on the other hand, embraces, without apology or excuse, God's deliberate deception of Pharaoh and the Egyptians.

Commenting on the puzzling phrase "and it was told to the king of Egypt that the nation had fled," Rashi, quoting a Mechilta, relates that Pharaoh sends spies with the departing Israelite slaves. When the third day after the Exodus arrives, the day on which the Israelites had promised to return, the spies see that no such return is imminent. These agents therefore report to Pharaoh, "The Israelites have fled."[12]

The idea of a three-day journey, according to the Midrash, was never truly abandoned by Pharaoh. Even after the devastation wrought upon his land, the Egyptian king fully expects the Israelites to return. When he realizes that he has been deceived, he immediately takes off in pursuit of the "fleeing" slaves. Numerous other commentaries mirror this Midrashic approach.[13]

From this point of view, the three-day request emerges as an integral

————————————————

9. *Haktav V'hakabala*, Shmot 3:18.
10. Shmot 13:20.
11. Chizkuni, Shmot 3:18.
12. Rashi, Shmot 14:5.
13. Ibn Ezra (Hakatzar), Shmot 11:4, 14:5; Chizkuni, Shmot 14:5.

part of God's planning from the outset. The Exodus is designed, from its earliest stages, to ultimately lead Pharaoh and his army to the banks of the Reed Sea. The Israelites will never truly be free of their taskmasters unless they witness the total destruction of Egyptian power in the roiling waters of that sea.

Concerning the moral issues raised by this divinely ordained deceit, Shmuel David Luzzatto (Shadal) argues: "[The deception] was justified by the fact that Pharaoh would certainly have enslaved Israelites upon their return to Egypt. We should not be surprised, therefore, that God commanded the Israelites to give Pharaoh a taste of his own medicine."[14]

As Rabbi Yehuda Nachshoni essentially argues in his discussion of an earlier moral quandary raised by the Torah narrative (see *Bereishit: Toldot 4, Approaches* C), "All is fair in love and war." If we are obligated to kill on the battlefield in order to defeat evil, it stands to reason that we are obligated to use subterfuge, when necessary, to accomplish the same goal.[15]

— C —

One final approach to the three-day request is offered by Rabbeinu Bachya, who views God's instructions from the perspective of the Israelite slaves. Abrupt, total change in the human condition is impossible. Consequently, the Israelites would have been unable to even conceive of an immediate transition from slavery to freedom. God, therefore, proceeds slowly. He approaches the Israelites with a proposal that they can accept. In this way, God orchestrates the entry of the Israelites into the realm of responsibility through measured steps.[16]

Points to Ponder

What if...?

What if, as some of the sources quoted above maintain, the three-day request of Pharaoh was not a ruse at all, but a serious offer? And, what if Pharaoh had agreed to the request? Upon the return of the Israelites, how might the path of the Exodus have been altered?

While it is impossible to answer this question with any degree of cer-

---

14. Shmuel David Luzzatto, Shmot 3:18.
15. Nachshoni, *Hagot B'parshiot HaTorah*, p. 107.
16. Rabbeinu Bachya, Shmot 3:18.

tainty, we can suggest the one variable that would have changed: the Israelites themselves.

Granted a taste of freedom after decades of carefully orchestrated slavery and degradation, the Israelites would have returned to Egypt, in some measure, a changed people. Pharaoh knew this. He knew that he could not allow even a glimmer of hope to illuminate the lives of his slaves. Only through unremitting subjugation could he maintain their physical and spiritual servitude. A holiday from slavery, no matter how brief, could simply not have been countenanced. As the Exodus unfolds, a fundamental truth is mirrored in the depth of a demagogue's fear – a truth that will be proven over and over again across the span of Jewish history. Even the most powerful subjugation and degradation cannot totally destroy the spark of human spirit burning deep in the hearts of the oppressed. Let the smallest glimmer of hope enter, and that spark will be quickly fanned into a rising flame.

5 A Tough Time Talking

Context

From the very onset of God's call to leadership at the burning bush, Moshe objects on the basis of an apparent speech impediment. He describes himself as "heavy of mouth and heavy of speech."[1] On further occasions Moshe refers to himself as an individual with "sealed lips."[2]

Questions

What was the source and extent of Moshe's speech impediment?

Why doesn't God respond to Moshe's objections by granting him a miraculous cure? Certainly such a response would have been more direct than appointing Moshe's brother, Aharon, as his spokesman.

Why does God appoint an individual with a speech impediment to a position so dependent on public speaking? Is there deeper significance to this counterintuitive selection?

Given the nature of Moshe's disability, how does he eventually manage to emerge as one of the most powerful orators in history (as can be evidenced in his magnificent farewell addresses in the book of Devarim)?

Approaches

—A—

A well-known Midrashic tale traces the source of Moshe's speech impediment to an event in his early childhood. As a toddler in Pharaoh's palace, Moshe's behavior led the king's sorcerers to suspect him of preternatural abilities so great that they posed a threat to the monarchy. To determine

---

1. Shmot 4:10.
2. Ibid., 6:12, 6:30.

26

Moshe's suspected skills, a test was devised. A plate containing a glowing coal and shining gold was placed before the toddler. Knowing that a normal child would be attracted to the glowing coal rather than the precious metal, the sorcerers waited to see if Moshe actually possessed the extraordinary knowledge to reach for the gold. Such an act, they decided, would result in his summary execution. Moshe actually began to reach for the gold when, suddenly, the angel Gabriel moved Moshe's hand to the coal in order to save his life. Moshe grabbed the hot coal and, in pain, placed his hand with the coal into his mouth, burning his tongue. This act caused Moshe to become "heavy of mouth and heavy of speech."[3]

Through this tale, the Midrash vividly portrays the ever-present dangers that must have surrounded Moshe – the man destined, as God's agent, to bring Egypt to its knees – as he spends his early years under the watchful eyes of the royal court.

— **B** —

Whatever its actual source, the majority of traditional commentators view Moshe's speech impediment as a real, physical disability.[4]

Why, then, doesn't God simply grant Moshe a miraculous cure?

The Ramban claims that God does not alleviate Moshe's disability because Moshe, hoping that God will choose someone else, fails to pray for a cure. Absent such prayer, no heavenly healing is forthcoming. Man must work with God, as a partner in the determination of his own fate. God will, therefore, not grant miraculous intervention on Moshe's behalf until Moshe solicits such intervention.[5]

Rabbi Yaakov Skili, in contrast, argues that Moshe does implicitly ask for his disability to be removed. God fails to do so because fulfilling that request would require suspension of the natural laws that govern the world. Almost all the miracles performed during the Exodus and beyond, Skili maintains, remain on some level within the bounds of nature. Those exceptional wonders that do move beyond the borders of natural law are already woven into the fabric of existence, as evidenced by the rabbinic claim that ten miraculous phenomena were fashioned by God at twilight

---

3. Midrash Rabba Shmot 1:26.
4. Rashi, Shmot 4:10; Ramban, ibid.; Ibn Ezra, ibid.
5. Ramban, ibid.

on the last day of creation.[6] A person's makeup, however, is determined in utero. Changing that framework would require the suspension of natural law, a step that God generally resists.[7]

In a dramatic move, the Ran takes the striking position that *Moshe's speech impediment actually serves as a leadership qualification.* God wants the message, rather than the eloquence of the messenger, to drive the events of the Exodus. As history has proven, powerfully articulate and naturally persuasive orators can hypnotize their audiences into believing that even lies are true. In Moshe's case, however, the truth was accepted not because of eloquence but because of substance.[8]

— C —

The Rashbam, who always adheres to his perception of *pshat* (straight-forward explanation of the text), claims that Moshe's supposed "speech impediment" was not physical at all. Moshe's insistence that he is "heavy of mouth and heavy of speech" is simply a reference to the fact that he is no longer adept in the language of Egypt and its nuances. *I left Egypt as a young man,* Moshe argues, *and I am now eighty years old. Surely you can find a better candidate for leadership.*[9]

Centuries later, Rabbi Shimshon Raphael Hirsch bridges the gap between the Rashbam and his colleagues.

Hirsch distinguishes between the two sets of terms that Moshe uses when he describes his own inability to speak. "Heavy of mouth and heavy of speech" refers to a physical defect of the organs of speech and to clumsiness of the tongue. "Sealed lips," on the other hand, alludes to Moshe's inability to find the right words even if he were to temporarily overcome his disability.[10]

— D —

Once we embark upon the path suggested by the Rashbam and accept the possibility that Moshe might not have been afflicted by a physical disability, another approach to Moshe's "impediment" emerges.

---

6. Pirkei Avot 5:6.
7. Torat Hamincha, Va'eira 21.
8. Drashot HaRan 3:5.
9. Rashbam, Shmot 4:10.
10. Rabbi Shimshon Raphael Hirsch, Shmot 4:10; 6:12.

Perhaps Moshe is protesting his appointment not on the basis of ability but on the basis of style: *You know me, God. I am a poor choice for this job. I am simply not one to mince words or to hold back from honest confrontation. I speak my mind and I call things the way that I see them. I possess no diplomatic skills whatsoever. Why would you send me to speak to a king or to influence a people?*

This argument references not only Moshe's speaking style but his life philosophy. According to Talmudic tradition, Moshe's motto was "Let the law cut through the mountain!"[11] The picture of Moshe we glean from the text is of a man who is blunt and honest almost to a fault, a man who believes that "what's right is right" and that the truth must be pursued at all costs. Moshe would seem to be a poor candidate, indeed, for a diplomatic mission.

God's selection of Aharon to accompany Moshe can now be seen in a fuller light, as well. Aharon is everything that his brother, Moshe, is not, and vice versa.

Kind, sensitive and soft, Aharon is a man who "loves peace, pursues peace and creates peace between man and his friend."[12] Aharon serves not only as Moshe's spokesman but as a counterbalancing influence in the leadership of the people. God clearly values both Moshe's forthrightness and Aharon's softness. Together, they forge a balance that serves as the prototype for effective leadership across the ages. (For a fuller discussion of the partnership between Moshe and Aharon, see Mishpatim 4, *Approaches* B3; Tetzave 2, *Approaches* E2.)

—— **E** ——————————————————————————————

One additional thought might be offered to round out our discussion.

If we return to the traditional position – that Moshe's disability was indeed physically based – we can suggest yet another reason for his selection: *God wants Moshe's personal struggle to serve as an eternal example for his people.*

If the Israelites see a leader who is flawed, they will come to realize that perfection is not a prerequisite for accomplishment. If they witness, in addition, Moshe's successful struggle to overcome his limitations, they will

---

11. Talmud Bavli Sanhedrin 6b.
12. Ibid.

learn of the indomitable nature of the human spirit. As Moshe journeys, with effort and persistence, from "heavy of mouth and heavy of speech" to the eloquence of the book of Devarim, he sets an example for us all.

Points to Ponder

The greatest leader our people have known was a man with a disability. Through God's selection of Moshe, therefore, we are taught never to "write someone off" because of a perceived shortcoming or weakness.

This point assumes critical significance when we consider the education of our children. In too many communities, Jewish education has become the inalienable right of only the best and the brightest. Students with learning disabilities are frequently lost in the system, struggling to keep up with the rigors of a dual curriculum. Selective admission standards of yeshiva high schools often lead to the rejection of even students with "B" averages, as these schools strive to build their reputations as elite institutions.

Due to increased awareness and sensitivity, strides are being made in existing schools and through the creation of new programs and educational settings. True progress in this area, however, will be dependent upon the recognition that Jewish education is a right, not a privilege, for every child in our community; and upon the realization that surprising accomplishments can often be attained from the least expected quarters.

Had Moshe's selection been based upon community approval, he probably would have been rejected out of hand. Who among us, after all, would knowingly choose someone with a speech impediment for a job so dependent on public speaking? Thankfully, however, God did the choosing. By selecting Moshe, God reminds us of the vast ranges of human potential that often lie hidden from view.

6 Almost Over before It Begins?

Context

Moshe, together with his family, departs the land of Midian for Egypt as he prepares to assume his leadership role and initiate the events that will lead to the Exodus. Along the way he stops at an inn where God suddenly threatens to kill him. Recognizing the immediate danger, Moshe's wife, Tzippora, takes a stone and circumcises their newborn son, Eliezer. Apparently as a result of Tzippora's actions, the danger passes and the journey to Egypt resumes.[1]

Questions

No incident within the Torah is more frighteningly bewildering than Moshe's divinely ordained brush with death as he travels back to Egypt.

After selecting Moshe and charging him with leadership at the burning bush, why does God, abruptly and without any warning at all, now threaten him with death?

Why doesn't the Torah clarify the reasons for Moshe's sudden vulnerability?

Why does Eliezer's circumcision, carried out by Tzippora, remove the threat to Moshe?

At risk is much more than Moshe's life. How could God threaten to end Moshe's leadership before it even begins, thereby endangering the entire Exodus of the Israelites from Egypt?

Approaches

—— **A** ——

Classical rabbinic interpretation of this event is rooted in the premise that

---

1. Shmot 4:20–26.

the source of the danger is revealed, in retrospect, by Tzippora's response. The threat dissipates upon her circumcision of Eliezer because *the circumcision, itself, is at issue.*

Three approaches, based upon this premise, are recorded in the Talmud.

1. Rabbi Yehoshua ben Korcha accepts the obvious, yet troubling, possibility that God moved to punish Moshe simply because Moshe was lax in circumcising his son.

2. Rising to Moshe's defense, Rabbi Yossi argues that Moshe was actually justified in delaying Eliezer's circumcision.

As he prepares for the return journey to Egypt, Moshe finds himself facing a difficult quandary: *If I circumcise Eliezer and then leave for Egypt immediately I will be endangering the child's welfare. If, on the other hand, I perform the circumcision and wait three days for the child to recuperate, I will be disobeying God's commandment to return without delay to Egypt.*

Moshe correctly determines to postpone the circumcision and return to Egypt at once.

Why, then, was Moshe punished? Because when he arrived at the inn, he busied himself with his own needs, failing to perform Eliezer's circumcision as soon as it became possible to do so.

3. Finally, Rabbi Shimon ben Gamliel maintains that Moshe was never the intended victim of the divinely ordained directive. The target was, instead, his uncircumcised son, Eliezer.[2]

—— **B** ——————————————————————

Most later authorities approach the text with variations on the theme suggested by Rabbi Yehoshua ben Korcha and Rabbi Yossi: Moshe was the intended target of the divine threat because he delayed Eliezer's circumcision.[3] A minority position does persist, however, agreeing with Rabbi Shimon ben Gamliel that the potential victim was Eliezer.[4]

Some scholars, including Rashi, echo Rabbi Yossi's suggestion that Moshe becomes vulnerable only when he arrives at the inn.[5] Rabbi Eliyahu Mizrachi, a commentary on Rashi, explains that the inn was located so close to

---

2. Talmud Bavli Nedarim 31b–32a.
3. Rashi, Shmot 4:24; Ramban, Shmot 4:20; Ibn Ezra, Shmot 4:24; Sforno, ibid.
4. Rabbi Saadia Gaon, ibid.; Rabbeinu Chananel, ibid.
5. Rashi, ibid.

Egypt that Moshe and Tzippora could have easily performed the circumcision and continued on their way without endangering Eliezer.[6]

The Ramban and Ibn Ezra rework the chronology of the event by suggesting that Eliezer reached the age of circumcision only during the journey and therefore could not have been circumcised before the departure. By the time Moshe and his family arrive at the inn, however, Eliezer has reached the eighth-day milestone and his circumcision has become obligatory.[7]

—— C ——

Standing alone, the Rashbam offers a strikingly different approach to the narrative. Moshe is faulted by God, not for delaying Eliezer's circumcision, but for failing to respond to his newly ordained leadership role with appropriate diligence. Moshe was meant to travel to Egypt alone, without his family. By bringing Tzippora and their sons on the journey, Moshe inevitably compromises his own ability to act with due speed and dilutes his total focus upon the tasks before him.[8]

In stark contrast, the Midrash portrays Moshe defending his decision to bring his family to Egypt. He does so to ensure that they will be present, following the Exodus, when God reveals himself to the Israelites at Sinai.[9]

The Ramban further justifies Moshe's decision to bring his family to Egypt by noting that the presence of Moshe's wife and children could only serve to encourage the Israelites slaves. Obviously Moshe would not endanger his family's freedom unless he was certain of the immediacy of the impending Exodus.[10]

The Ibn Ezra goes on to note, however, that Moshe's wife and sons mysteriously disappear from the narrative after the incident at the inn. They reappear only months later at Sinai, when they are brought to the Israelite camp by Tzippora's father, Yitro. Perhaps, suggests the Ibn Ezra, Moshe's plan to bring his family to Egypt goes awry when Tzippora is forced to circumcise Eliezer at the inn. At that point, Moshe leaves his family and they return to Midian upon Eliezer's recuperation.[11] The Ramban ultimately

---

6. Mizrachi, ibid.
7. Ramban, Shmot 4:20; Ibn Ezra, Shmot 4:24.
8. Rashbam, Shmot 4:24.
9. Midrash Rabba Shmot 4:4.
10. Ramban, Shmot 4:19.
11. Ibn Ezra, Shmot 4:20.

rejects the Ibn Ezra's contention and maintains that Tzippora and the children descend to Egypt with Moshe, only to return to her father's home when it becomes clear that the Exodus will take time to unfold.[12]

—— **D** ————————————————————————————————————

Whichever approach we take to explain this puzzling event, serious problems with the narrative remain.

Why doesn't God warn Moshe before suddenly and without explanation threatening him with death? Why would God risk the entire Exodus from Egypt without giving Moshe a chance to correct the errors he might be making? Is Moshe's sin so unforgivable? Moshe has just reluctantly accepted the mantle of leadership. How could God reasonably demand that he be totally error free from the outset?

There are times in Moshe's career, it would seem, when a particular idea is so potent that God wants Moshe to arrive at the realization of that idea on his own. Outright articulation of the message would diminish its impact (see Yitro 3, *Approaches* C).

If we return to the interpretation (accepted, as we have seen, by the vast majority of authorities) that Moshe becomes culpable for failing to circumcise Eliezer in a timely fashion, the message that emerges from this event is significant, indeed.

God wants Moshe to recognize that *communal leadership cannot be used as an excuse for the abdication of personal responsibility.* In fact, within Jewish thought, the opposite is true. *The higher you rise on the ladder of public leadership, the greater the private standard to which you are held.* Moshe learns through bitter experience, even as his journey towards leadership is just beginning, that he will not be excused from fulfilling his own obligations. This lesson, conveyed by God in the most powerful way possible, sets the standard for Jewish leadership for centuries to come.

Points to Ponder

People who assume the mantle of leadership in our time often seem to consider themselves above the rules of their own societies. This phenomenon, of course, is not new. Power has frequently corrupted those who have attained it throughout history.

———————————

12. Ramban, ibid.

By now, however, we might have hoped for more. We might have hoped that the democratic reforms of the last two centuries would have created real change in the nature of leadership. Such change, however, has not been consistently achieved. Even in the most enlightened of countries (including, unfortunately, the United States and Israel) the blight of corruption often strikes at the loftiest leadership levels, engendering a high level of cynicism within the entire population.

As the phenomenon of leadership begins to emerge within the national era of Jewish history, God forcefully projects a different model. He teaches us that leadership must be marked by the highest level of personal conduct. Far from being excused from the rules that govern others, a true leader exemplifies loyalty to those rules. Only then can he "lead" – through example – in an enduring fashion.

Va'eira

CHAPTER 6:2–9:35

 וארא
פרק ו:ב-ט:לה

Parsha Summary

A turning tide…

God continues to encourage Moshe and instructs him to inform the Israelites that the journey towards full redemption is at hand. The Israelites,
however, are unable or unwilling to heed Moshe's words due to the burdens
of their servitude.

In spite of Moshe's objections that he is not capable, God commands the
leader to return to Pharaoh and demand the release of the Israelite slaves.

The text digresses to present a genealogical table delineating Moshe and
Aharon's ancestry.

When Moshe's audience with the king fails to produce results, God begins to inflict a series of plagues upon the Egyptians. One after another, the
plagues of blood, frogs, lice, wild beasts, pestilence, boils and hail rain down
upon Egypt.

Although Pharaoh relents during some of the afflictions, he returns to his
initial position of refusal over and over again after each plague ends.

1 Glimpses of God

Context

Parshat Shmot closes with Moshe standing in frustration before God, complaining that his return to Egypt has only resulted in increased misery for the Israelites. God responds with assurances that the Exodus is about to unfold.

As the conversation continues in Parshat Va'eira, God proclaims: "I am A-do-nai. And I appeared to Avraham, to Yitzchak and to Yaakov as E-l Shad-dai but through My name A-do-nai I did not make Myself known to them. And also, I established My covenant with them to give to them the land of Canaan, the land of their sojourning, in which they sojourned."[1]

God then informs Moshe that He has heard the cries of the Israelites and that He has remembered His covenant. He instructs Moshe to tell the Israelites that they will soon be fully redeemed.[2]

Questions

Why does God suddenly digress, in the midst of His reassurances to Moshe, to discuss the quality of divine revelation to the patriarchs? Why would this information be of significance to Moshe at this critical moment?

What does God mean when He says that He was revealed to the patriarchs as E-l Shad-dai but not as A-do-nai?

Even on a factual level, God's claim is problematic. The text repeatedly refers to God by the name A-do-nai during the narrative of the patriarchal era. On two occasions God directly says to the patriarchs "I am A-do-nai."[3]

---

1. Shmot 6:2, 3.
2. Ibid., 6:2–8.
3. Bereishit 15:7, 28:13.

How, then, could God assert that He was not known to the patriarchs by that name?

Approaches

The rabbis maintain that, by contrasting the names E-l Shad-dai and A-do-nai, God references a qualitative distinction between two different aspects of His own being. Until now, God appeared to man only as E-l Shad-dai. The name A-do-nai was known to the patriarchs but the divine aspect which that name represents was not realized in their time. With the birth of the Jewish nation, however, all is about to change as E-l Shad-dai becomes A-do-nai.

The scholars, however, are not uniform in their understanding of the different aspects of God represented by these two titles.

—**A**——————————————————————

An early Midrashic tradition maintains that the name E-l Shad-dai refers to God in His role as a "promise maker," while the name A-do-nai refers to God in his role as a "promise keeper."

God's message to Moshe at this critical moment, says the Midrash, is far from benign: "Woe concerning those who are lost and are no longer to be found!" *Where is your faith, Moshe? You fare poorly when compared to the patriarchs. How many promises did I make to them which remained unfulfilled? I commanded Avraham to walk the length and breadth of the land of Canaan for it would eventually be his.*[4] *Upon Sara's death, however, he was forced to buy a plot of land for her burial.*[5] *I instructed Yitzchak to dwell in the land that would be his and his children's.*[6] *Yet he was forced to strive with those around him for water.*[7] *I pledged to Yaakov that the land upon which he lay would be given to him and his children.*[8] *Yet, he, too, did not own the land until he purchased a section from the sons of Chamor, the king of Shechem.*[9]

In spite of all these disappointments, the patriarchs never questioned My

---

4. Ibid., 13:17.
5. Ibid., 23:3–20.
6. Ibid., 26:3.
7. Ibid., 26: 15–23.
8. Ibid., 28: 13.
9. Ibid., 33:19.

ways nor asked Me My name (inquired into the nature of My being). You, on the other hand, immediately asked Me My name at the burning bush and, now, with the first setback you experience, you doubt your mission. Your faith pales in comparison to the faith of those who came before you.[10]

—— **B** ——————————————————————

While accepting the Midrashic contention that the titles E-l Shad-dai and A-do-nai respectively refer to God in the roles of "promise maker" and "promise keeper," Rashi maintains that the midrashically suggested rebuke of Moshe does not fit the flow of the text.

The Rashbam, Rashi's grandson, following his grandfather's lead, explains God's message to Moshe as follows: *Moshe, you are about to experience momentous events. I made numerous promises to the patriarchs which, nevertheless, remained unfulfilled in their time. Now you and the Israelites will experience the fulfillment of those very promises.*[11]

—— **C** ——————————————————————

Other scholars offer alternative explanations for the distinction between the titles E-l Shad-dai and A-do-nai.

Both the Ibn Ezra and the Ramban maintain that these titles are used by God to reflect a change that is about to occur in the quality of His interface with the physical world. Throughout the patriarchal era, God, as E-l Shad-dai, worked His will within the laws of nature. Now, however, as A-do-nai, God will transcend the boundaries of natural law.[12]

The Sforno carries this thought one step further by asserting that the name E-l Shad-dai refers to God as *Creator* of the universe, while the name A-do-nai refers to God as *Sustainer* of that creation.

God tells Moshe: *Because I have not changed the course of creation until now, I have only been perceived as E-l Shad-dai, the Creator. Now, however, as I work the miracles of the Exodus and Revelation, all will know that I am A-do-nai, that I continuously sustain the world and can change the course of nature, at will.* (See *Bereishit*: Bereishit 1, *Approaches* A for a fuller discussion of this distinction.)

————————————

10. Midrash Rabba Bereishit 6:4; Talmud Bavli Sanhedrin 111a.
11. Rashi, Shmot 6:3; Rashbam, ibid.
12. Ibn Ezra, ibid.; Ramban, ibid.

--- **D** ---

While the specific distinction between the titles E-l Shad-dai and A-do-nai is the subject of dispute, almost all major commentaries agree that the differing names for God reflect a phenomenon of partial revelation. Through the use of these titles, God reveals, in limited fashion, specific aspects of His being to man. This phenomenon of partial revelation is not unique, however, to the conversation between God and Moshe at the beginning of Parshat Va'eira. According to rabbinic tradition, various titles used for God throughout the Torah reflect different dimensions of His character.

The Midrash explicitly lists four biblical titles for God and explains the meaning conveyed by each:

> The Holy One Blessed Be He said to Moshe: "You wish to know My name? I am called according to My acts…. When I judge My creations, I am called E-lo-him. When I wage war upon the wicked, I am called Tze-va-ot. When I examine the sins of man, I am called E-l Shad-dai. And when I show mercy upon My world; I am called A-do-nai."[13]

Other titles are used in our tradition, as well.

We have already noted, for example, that the title *HaMakom* represents God when He is hidden and distant from man (see *Bereishit*: Bereishit 3, *Approaches* F).

--- **E** ---

The fundamental question, however, remains: Why are these partial revelations necessary in the first place? Why can't the Torah consistently use one title to portray all aspects of God's being in a unified fashion?

The most familiar example of this phenomenon of partial revelation can provide the clearest answer. As indicated by the Midrash, the title A-do-nai is used in the text to represent God's attribute of mercy, while the title E-lo-him is used to convey God's attribute of justice.

In our world, justice and mercy are, in their purest forms, mutually exclusive. One simply cannot be all-just and all-merciful at the same time. If you show mercy, you are, by definition, bending justice. If you are totally

---

13. Midrash Rabba Shmot 3:6.

just, mercy has no place. For these concepts to coexist, each must sacrifice a bit of its purity.

This mutual exclusivity of mercy and justice in the human realm is codified, on a practical basis, in Jewish law. Commenting on the Torah's statement "You shall not favor the poor and you shall not honor the great,"[14] the rabbis proclaim that the application of law should be swayed neither by pity for the destitute nor by concern for the reputation of the wealthy.[15] Elsewhere, the Mishna records the emphatic pronouncement of Rabbi Akiva: "We are not merciful in deciding the law!"[16]

The rules are different, however, in the heavenly realm. Although we cannot comprehend how, *God is all-just and all-merciful at the same time.* These concepts coexist in the dominion of the divine without either losing any of its strength.

To convey the undiluted purity of the Godly attributes of justice and mercy, the Torah singles out one quality at a time, dependent upon circumstances. Only through this singularity can the Torah express the full force of each particular characteristic. To us, it appears as if God is acting solely through the attribute being mentioned.

In similar fashion, other divine attributes are singled out in the Torah through the use of God's various names, each title allowing us to focus on one specific aspect of God's being.

We are then challenged, however, to put the pieces together and gain a view, albeit distant, of the whole of God's essence, to recognize that in the realm of the divine, conflicting forces combine without a weakening effect.

By using God's names to reveal pieces of His essence in partial fashion, the Torah ironically underscores the complexity of the whole. In the final analysis, the glimpses of God provided to us by the Torah text only serve to heighten His mystery.

---

14. Vayikra 19:15.
15. Torat Kohanim, ibid.
16. Mishna Ketubot 9:2.

Points to Ponder

Two final points from two disparate realms:

A. Tantalizingly, the physical world at its most basic level may well mirror the mysterious nature of the divine.

In very rudimentary terms, the current scientific theory of quantum mechanics maintains that, at the subatomic level, *classically accepted laws of the universe begin to erode because of the following phenomena*:

1. Electrons, protons and neutrons act, in contradictory modes, as both particles and waves.

2. Particles must be viewed as existing in numerous locations at once because the accurate position and momentum of a moving particle cannot be simultaneously fully predicted.

3. External measurement of a particle suddenly causes that particle to act in predictable, one-dimensional fashion.

In this subatomic world which serves as the foundation for our own, we find *coexisting contradictory forces, infinite potential, and a shift to predictable behavior upon external measurement.* The very building blocks of creation, like God Himself, defy our rules yet become consonant with those rules when they enter our realm.

Is it possible that aspects of God's mystery are built into the most elemental level of His creation?

Who knows what other divine secrets are woven into the fabric of the universe?

B. Through the phenomenon of partial revelation, God may be transmitting an ethical lesson as well.

Just as we are only able to glimpse pieces of God's essence at any one time, so, too, we perceive much of human life piecemeal. Man, created in the image of God, is a complex and contradictory being, replete with deep currents coursing beneath the surface. We must be careful, therefore, not to make judgments and decisions about ourselves or others based on the partial information that we perceive.

In the personal sphere, life should be seen as a continual journey towards self-definition. Our true capabilities inevitably lie hidden from view, beyond the limitations that we often place upon ourselves. "This is who I am," we defensively proclaim upon being challenged, when we really mean,

I have no desire to test my limits or challenge the life compromises that I have made. Yet, only when we push past those limits can we truly approach our God-given potential.

Concerning others, our tradition urges us to be sparing and cautious in judgment, sensitive to the vast array of life variables that simply lie beyond our ken. Who knows what pressures may cause our neighbor to act in a specific way on any given occasion? When the rabbis emphatically state, "Do not judge your fellow until you have reached his place,"[17] they are effectively prohibiting us from judging those around us at all. We can never truly "reach the place" of others. We should, therefore, never rush to judge them.

What we perceive concerning both God and man is not whole. Our actions and attitudes should reflect that fact.

---

17. Pirkei Avot 2:5.

2 Belated Introductions

Context

When Moshe's birth was chronicled in Parshat Shmot, the text deliberately omitted any description of his lineage, choosing instead to preface his birth with the mysterious sentence "And a man went from the House of Levi and he took a daughter of Levi."[1]

This omission of Moshe's bona fides is now addressed in Parshat Va'eira.

God commands Moshe to return to Pharaoh and again demand the release of the Israelite slaves. When Moshe objects, citing his speech impediment, God repeats the directive, this time to both Moshe and Aharon.

The Torah then abruptly digresses to present a genealogical table listing the descendents of Yaakov's oldest sons, Reuven, Shimon and Levi. The listing concludes with a detailed description of the lineage of Moshe and Aharon's family within the tribe of Levi.

Upon completion of this genealogical record, the Torah returns to the narrative of the Exodus with the words "This was Aharon and Moshe…. They were the ones who spoke to Pharaoh…. This was Moshe and Aharon."[2]

Questions

Once again we are confronted with a strange and abrupt digression within the Torah text.

Why does the Torah specifically choose this dramatic moment to detail the lineage of Moshe and Aharon? Why interrupt the historical narrative

---

1. Shmot 2:1.
2. Ibid., 6:10–27.

midstream? This genealogical table would clearly have been more appropriate at the beginning of the story, when Moshe is first introduced.

Amram and Yocheved, the parents of Aharon and Moshe, are mentioned here for the first time by name. Given the reasons for the omission of their identities when Moshe is born (see Shmot 2, *Approaches* B, C), why does the Torah see fit to reveal those identities now?

Approaches

—**A**——————————————————————————

Most of the classical commentaries are strangely silent concerning the most perplexing aspects of this passage, choosing to comment only briefly.

Rashi, for example, states that because the Torah mentions Aharon and Moshe at this time, the text feels compelled to tell us more fully of their birth and lineage.[3] He fails to explain, however, why this information was not given in conjunction with the earlier appearances of Moshe and Aharon in the text.

The Sforno and Abravanel both maintain that the genealogical table is presented to show that the choice of Aharon and Moshe was not arbitrary. God begins His search for worthy leadership with the descendents of Yaakov's first- and second-born, Reuven and Shimon. Only when He proceeds to Levi, the third tribe, does God find the quality He is searching for in Moshe and Aharon.[4]

Once again, however, neither of these scholars explains why this information must be shared with us abruptly, at this point in the text.

The Malbim, in contrast, does offer a solution concerning the placement of the genealogical record. He explains that the passage in Va'eira marks the first time that Moshe and Aharon are clearly appointed by God as full partners concerning all aspects of the Exodus. Only once this partnership of brothers is firmly established does the Torah digress to chronicle their familial credentials.[5]

Rashi finally notes that, as the Torah closes the genealogical table and returns to the historical narrative, the text identifies Moshe and

---

3. Rashi, Shmot 6:13.
4. Abravanel, Shmot 6:14; Sforno, Shmot 6:14–25.
5. Malbim, Shmot 6:13–23.

Aharon twice and reverses the order of their names: "*This was Aharon and Moshe…. They were the ones who spoke to Pharaoh…. This was Moshe and Aharon.*"[6]

Quoting the Mechilta, Rashi explains that, throughout the text, the Torah will variably list each brother first in order to demonstrate that Aharon and Moshe were equivalent to each other in greatness.[7]

The premier halachic authority of the twentieth century, Rabbi Moshe Feinstein (known throughout the Jewish world simply as Reb Moshe), objects, however, to the Mechilta's explanation: "Moshe was the greatest of the prophets, the teacher of the world, and the Torah was given by his hand. How can it be claimed that Aharon was his equal?"[8]

Reb Moshe answers that at this juncture in the text, even as the public leadership of Moshe and Aharon is firmly established, the Torah conveys an essential truth concerning the worth of every human life. Moshe and Aharon each fulfilled his personal role to the greatest extent possible. They are, therefore, in the eyes of God, considered equal. *God judges each of us against ourselves and not against anyone else.* Someone of lesser ability, who reaches his full life potential, towers over someone of greater talent who does not – even if, on an objective scale, the latter's accomplishments seem grander.[9]

How telling that one of the most brilliant, accomplished leaders in recent Jewish memory views this text as conveying the value inherent in each individual – skilled or unskilled, public or private!

— **B** —

The most extensive treatment of the genealogical passage at the beginning of Parshat Va'eira, however, is offered by Rabbi Shimshon Raphael Hirsch. Hirsch insists that the placement of this section specifically conveys a critical lesson concerning the nature of leadership throughout the Torah.

At this moment in the text, says Hirsch, we confront a major turning point in the careers of Moshe and Aharon. Until now, their efforts have been marked by frustration and failure. From this point onward, however, their triumphal mission – marked by powerful miracles and supernatu-

---

6. Shmot 6:26–27.
7. Rashi, Shmot 6:26.
8. Drash Moshe, Shmot 6:26.
9. Ibid.

ral events – begins. The Torah, therefore, feels compelled at this juncture to make one fact abundantly clear for all time. Moshe and Aharon are of "absolutely human origin and the absolute ordinary human nature of their beings should be firmly established."[10] So important is this message that the Torah abruptly interrupts the historical narrative midstream to clearly delineate the ancestry of Moshe and Aharon.

As we have noted before (see *Bereishit*: Lech Lecha 2, *Approaches*), whereas pagans deified their heroes, and Christians returned to such deification, Judaism insists upon seeing its heroes as human beings. When your heroes are gods you can worship them, but you cannot emulate them. As long as we see the characters of our Torah as human beings, their greatness may be beyond our reach, but we can, nonetheless, aspire to that greatness.

On the other hand, Hirsch continues, a critical balance is struck in the passage before us. While the genealogical record clearly establishes the mortal origins of Moshe and Aharon, it also serves to counter the notion that every human being is suitable to prophecy. God's choices are far from arbitrary. Aharon and Moshe were men, but they were "picked, chosen men." God could have chosen from any tribe and any family. His specific selection of Aharon and Moshe serves to underscore that one who serves in a divinely ordained leadership role merits the appointment because of his own innate character.

The text thus captures the exquisite tension between the mortal origins of our biblical heroes and their overarching character and accomplishments.[11]

— C —

Finally, the passage before us, with its extensive genealogical information, clearly serves as a contrasting companion piece to the earlier section in Parshat Shmot which chronicled the birth of Moshe. There, as noted in an earlier study (Shmot 2), the narrative is singular in its lack of information. Even the names of Moshe's parents are deliberately omitted.

This omission is now apparently addressed and rectified in Parshat Va'eira.

---

10. Rabbi Shimshon Raphael Hirsch, Shmot 6:14.
11. Ibid.

Why, however, when all is said and done, are these two sections necessary? If the Torah eventually reveals the genealogy of Aharon and Moshe, why not do so immediately as soon as Moshe is first introduced in the text?

An approach can be suggested if we view these two passages as delineating a balance that shapes the life of every human being.

On the one hand, the glaring omission of Moshe's ancestry in Parshat Shmot serves to remind us that the most important aspects of our lives are self-determined. While God decides to whom we are born, when and where we are born, our genetic makeup, etc., we determine, through our own free will, who we will become (see *Bereishit*: Bereishit 4, *Approaches* A).

Moshe ascends to leadership because of the choices he makes. The Torah, therefore, omits his parentage at the moment of his birth. *Yichus* (pedigree) does not determine the quality of Moshe's life.

On the other hand, while pedigree is neither the sole nor the most important determinant of a person's character, an individual's family background certainly contributes to the formation of that character. Our ancestry creates the backdrop against which we weave the tapestry of our lives. Moshe's story would have been incomplete if his family had not been mentioned. The genealogical table presented at the beginning of Parshat Va'eira is provided to fill in the gaps.

The omission of the names of Moshe's parents and relatives on the occasion of his birth reminds us that Moshe achieves greatness on his own. The inclusion of those names in Parshat Va'eira reminds us of the role his family background plays in enabling him to succeed in his quest.

3 Pharaoh's Free Will

Context

At the core of Jewish theology lies a taut balance between three components which define the very parameters of our lives. While the details of this balance have been debated across the centuries, the majority approach can be summarized in the following three points.

1. *Free will*: The belief that man freely chooses his way and defines the quality of his life is central to Jewish thought. Without free will man cannot be an independent being, responsible before God for his actions.

2. *Prescience*: Almost all classical Jewish scholars maintain that God is aware of all future events, including man's personal choices. God's prior knowledge, however, does not affect man's freely made choices.

3. *Predestination*: Judaism recognizes that elements of our lives are clearly predetermined. On an individual level, predetermined elements include our genetic makeup, when and where we are born, and to whom we are born. On a national level, our belief in Mashiach and a messianic era reflects our conviction that our history is moving towards a definite, predefined goal. In spite of these predetermined elements of life, however, the quality and details of both our personal and national journeys remain in our hands.

As long as the above components stay firmly within their boundaries, the philosophical balance between them remains understandable. Turmoil results, however, when the balance is upset.

Even before Moshe returns to Egypt, God predicts, "And I will harden [Pharaoh's] heart and he will not let the people go."[1] On a number of occasions, as the Exodus narrative continues, the Torah

---

1. Shmot 4:21.

states that God makes good on His promise and actually "hardens the heart" of the Egyptian king.[2]

Questions

The Torah seems to indicate that God robs Pharaoh of his rightful free will. By "hardening Pharaoh's heart" doesn't God unfairly predetermine both Pharaoh's choices and his (and his nation's) resulting fate? Jewish tradition views *tshuva* (repentance or return) as an inalienable right granted by God to every individual. How can God deny that right to Pharaoh?

The textual record is inconsistent. After each of the first five plagues the Torah states that Pharaoh "hardens" his own heart, apparently of his own free will.[3] Only in conjunction with the sixth through tenth plagues does God fulfill His prediction by "hardening the heart" of the Egyptian monarch.

What causes the change in Pharaoh's mindset and in God's response?

Approaches

The rabbis were well aware that the issues surrounding the apparent suspension of Pharaoh's free will strike to the very core of Jewish belief.

Thus, Rabbi Yochanan ben Zakkai is quoted in the Midrash Rabba as stating, "[The textual testimony concerning Pharaoh] provides an opening for heretics to say: '[Pharaoh] was not allowed to repent.'"[4]

And, centuries later, both the Ramban and the Ibn Ezra wonder aloud, "If God hardened Pharaoh's heart, then what was [Pharaoh's] sin?"[5]

Rising to the obvious challenges raised by these concerns, the authorities suggest a wide array of approaches.

—A—

At one end of the spectrum lie those, such as Shmuel David Luzzatto (Shadal), who find the problems so troubling that they feel compelled to claim that the questions are not questions at all:

---

2. Ibid., 9:12; 10:1, 20, 27; 11:10.
3. Ibid., 7:22; 8:11, 15, 28; 9:7.
4. Midrash Rabba Shmot 13:3.
5. Ibn Ezra, Shmot 7:3; Ramban, ibid.

Know that all acts can be ascribed to God, for all are caused by Him – some through absolute decree and others through man's free choice which has been granted by Him…. It can therefore be said that [God], as the author of all acts, hardened Pharaoh's heart.[6]

Pharaoh's choices are made totally of his own free will. These very choices, however, like all events in the world, ultimately trace back to God Who is the One Who grants Pharaoh and all mankind free will in the first place. The assertion that God "hardens Pharaoh's heart" is simply the text's way of indicating a fundamental connection between Pharaoh's independent choices and the divine source of his free will.

This circular reasoning, however, raises an obvious question: How, then, can the Torah ever speak of actions independently performed by individuals? Why doesn't the text attribute every decision made by each of its characters, as it does in the case of Pharaoh, to its ultimate source, God?

Luzzatto addresses this objection by maintaining that only actions that defy logic, such as Pharaoh's obstinacy in the face of the plagues, are actually ascribed in the text to God.[7]

—— B ——

Other scholars, unwilling to dismiss the overwhelming textual evidence that God actually "hardens Pharaoh's heart," attempt mightily to reconcile that fact with Judaism's fundamental view on free will and repentance.

Two intriguing alternatives, for example, are offered by the Abravanel.

1. Different sins warrant different paths towards absolution.

Sincere contrition, prayer and remorse can effect full atonement for sins committed against God. Crimes against one's fellow man, however, will not be forgiven as long as the ledgers remain open in the human sphere.

Atonement cannot, for example, be attained for the crime of thievery until the theft is returned or replaced and appropriate fines are paid. An individual guilty of murder must be punished in an earthly court before he can be cleared in the heavenly realm.

Pharaoh and the Egyptians are guilty of horrendous crimes against the

---

6. Shmuel David Luzzatto, Shmot 7:3.
7. Ibid.

Israelites – crimes which, by definition, give rise to requisite physical punishment. By hardening Pharaoh's heart, God ironically clears the way for the atonement of Pharaoh and his people. The punishment of the plagues is the first, necessary step along the Egyptians' path of repentance.

2. The "hardening of Pharaoh's heart" was directly caused by the methodology of the plagues.

Had God afflicted the Egyptians with one unending plague, Pharaoh would have eventually relented. In order to demonstrate His own power to the world, however, God specifically visits a series of plagues upon Egypt. As each calamity ends, the Egyptian king rationalizes that the event had occurred of natural causes. Clearly, he reasons, had the plague been divinely ordained, it would not have been lifted until the Israelites were freed.

The "hardening of Pharaoh's heart" is not an independent phenomenon but an inevitable outgrowth of the manner in which God orchestrates the plagues.[8]

— C —

A number of commentaries, including the Sforno, insist that God's actions vis-à-vis Pharaoh do not impede but actually enhance the king's free will. Had God not "hardened the king's heart," they claim, Pharaoh would have been "forced" to choose a path for all the wrong reasons:

> Had it not been for the "hardening of his heart," Pharaoh would have certainly released the Israelites; not, however, because of a sincere desire to repent and submit to divine will, but because he could no longer bear the suffering caused by the plagues…. God, therefore, "hardened Pharaoh's heart" and fortified his ability to endure the plagues, so that the king would not release the Israelites simply because of fear of the impending calamities.[9]

According to these commentaries, God certainly seeks the repentance of Pharaoh and the Egyptians, but only if that repentance is sincere. God launches the plagues, therefore, hoping that the Egyptians will be moved by His power and His merciful insistence upon freedom for all.

8. Abravanel, Shmot 7:3.
9. Sforno, ibid.

True repentance, however, cannot take place under duress. God, therefore, hardens Pharaoh against the physical and mental effects of the calamities. By doing so, He affords the king and his subjects the opportunity to repent of their own free will, not because of the pain of the plagues, but because of their message.

— D

The most revolutionary approach to the issues before us, however, actually emerges from an early source. In contrast to the positions cited above, the Midrash cites an opinion which accepts the suspension of Pharaoh's free will and right to repentance. The Talmudic scholar Rabbi Shimon ben Lakish (Reish Lakish) maintains that if an individual fails to return to God after repeated warnings, God then closes that individual's heart to repentance in order to "exact punishment for his sin."

God, continues Reish Lakish, gives Pharaoh five chances to repent: the first five plagues. On each of these occasions, however, the Egyptian monarch hardens his own heart, refusing to bend to God's will. At that point God intervenes, suspends Pharaoh's free will and closes the door to his spiritual return.[10]

This opinion acquires greater poignancy when we recognize that its author, Reish Lakish, was himself no stranger to the path of repentance. Living in the wilderness where he made his livelihood as a bandit, Reish Lakish was swayed to turn his life around through a chance encounter with the man destined to become his scholarly colleague and brother-in-law, Rabbi Yochanan.[11]

Perhaps Reish Lakish felt himself nearing the point of no return before fate played a hand and pulled him back from the brink.

— E

Numerous commentaries are unwilling to accept the Midrash at face value, refusing to believe that God would deny even Pharaoh the right to repentance. The Rambam, however, clearly codifies Reish Lakish's position in his laws of repentance:

---

10. Midrash Rabba Shmot 13:3.
11. Talmud Bavli Bava Metzia 84a.

It is possible that a man may commit a sin so grave, or so many sins...
that repentance is denied to him and he is not given the opportunity
to turn away from his evil...

Therefore the Torah states "and I [God] will harden the heart of
Pharaoh." Because Pharaoh initially sinned of his own volition, divine
judgment was rendered that he be denied the possibility of repentance
so that he would pay for his crimes.[12]

The Rambam's assertion brings our discussion full circle. In contrast to
the attempts to explain away the apparent suspension of Pharaoh's free will,
Maimonides himself is willing to accept what at first seemed unthinkable.
*The ability to repent, itself a gift from God, is not an inalienable right under
all circumstances. This gift will be denied to the perpetrators of the most hei-
nous crimes, to ensure that they receive the justice they deserve.*

Points to Ponder

Even our most basic assumptions must sometimes be reexamined.

This study opened with the contention that the whole fabric of Jewish
tradition begins to unravel if free will and repentance are denied to any
individual. That assumption, in the main, certainly remains correct. There
are, however, according to some authorities, exceptions to the rule. Some
crimes are so unforgivable that God will suspend the perpetrator's basic
rights in order to ensure that justice prevails.

How, however, does this assertion fare in the moral realm? If God
denies even the most evil their rights, can these individuals ever be held
culpable for their crimes?

We can, perhaps, better address this question by moving the issue into
more familiar territory.

If, God forbid, Adolf Hitler stood before us today and proclaimed true
remorse for his crimes, would God grant him absolution? Should the opportunity for repair be available to all or should certain individuals, through
the nature of their crimes, lose that very opportunity?

Which of these possible approaches captures the moral high ground?

Here, it would seem that, according to the Rambam, Jewish and Cath-
olic traditions part company. For while fundamental Christian theology

---

12. Rambam, *Mishneh Torah*, Hilchot Tshuva 6:3.

preaches that repentance remains available to all under all circumstances, the Rambam maintains that repentance is a right which can be lost. Actions speak louder than words. No amount of remorse, contrition, confession or prayer can truly erase the crimes of a Pharaoh, a Hitler or a Stalin. The mobster who confesses to his priest after scores of murders cannot, according to the Rambam, wipe the slate clean.

There comes a point when even a merciful God is unwilling to forgive.

This realization causes the concept of *tshuva* to become substantially more fragile within our own lives. While, please God, none of us will even come close to the point where the right of repentance is totally denied to us, who knows whether such denial might be applied piecemeal? Perhaps a particular failure can become so habitual, so embedded in our lives, that the opportunity to turn away from that failure is lost.

Who knows where the tipping point might be? The gifts of free will and *tshuva* should never be taken for granted; we never know the exact moment when those gifts might be taken away.

4 Plagues: Patterns and Purpose

Context

In response to Pharaoh's repeated refusal to allow the Israelites to leave Egypt, God afflicts the Egyptians with a series of devastating plagues. In all, ten afflictions rain down upon Egypt: blood, frogs, lice, swarms of wild beasts (or flies), pestilence, boils, hail, locusts, darkness, the plague of the firstborn.[1]

Questions

Why were the plagues necessary? God could certainly have orchestrated the Exodus in any way that He chose. Why not bring the Egyptians to their knees in one fell swoop with a single, overwhelming, enduring affliction? Or, conversely, why not simply redeem the Israelites miraculously without causing any plagues at all?

A close reading of the text reveals a series of patterns embedded within the litany of the plagues. Is there any significance to these patterns?

Approaches

Central to our understanding of the plagues is recognition of the momentous historical backdrop against which they occur. The birth of the Jewish nation is a formative moment in the development of God's relationship with all of mankind, providing a vehicle through which God proclaims not only His existence but His involvement in human affairs.

God declares to Moshe before the plagues begin, "And Egypt shall know that I am the Lord,"[2] a declaration which He reiterates, in various forms, no fewer than nine more times as the afflictions unfold.[3]

---

1. Shmot 7:14–12:31.
2. Ibid., 7:5.
3. Ibid., 7:17, 8:6, 8:18, 9:14, 9:29, 10:2, 11:7, 14:4, 14:18.

Elsewhere God states that the plagues are sent "so that you [the Israelites] may relate in the ears of your son and your son's son that I made a mockery of Egypt, and My signs that I placed among them – *that you may know that I am the Lord.*"[4]

Finally, God declares to Pharaoh that the plagues are designed "so that My name shall be spoken of throughout the land."[5]

Far from arbitrary, the plagues and the patterns within are clearly meant to educate the Egyptians, the Israelites and, through them, the world.

What, however, are the specific lessons of the plagues and how are they conveyed?

—A—

One of the earliest and most well-known observations on the plagues is offered by the Mishnaic sage Rabbi Yehuda, who cryptically divides the afflictions into three groups through the creation of the mnemonic *dtzach adash bachav* (three words constructed out of the first letters of the Hebrew terms for each plague). So significant is this mnemonic that it finds its way into the Seder service, recited each year on the first night(s) of Pesach.[6]

Rabbi Yehuda himself, however, offers no explanation for his proposed formula. Is he simply creating a tool for memorization or is there deeper significance to his division of the plagues into three distinct groups?

—B—

One of the first scholars to interpret Rabbi Yehuda's division of the plagues is the Abravanel. Based upon hints within Pharaoh's initial reaction to Moshe, the Abravanel identifies three basic principles rejected by the Egyptian monarch: the existence of God, Divine Providence (the involvement of God in the life of man) and God's ability to control nature.

The three groups of plagues are specifically designed to respond to Pharaoh's denials, as God's introduction to each set indicates.

Before the first plague God proclaims, "With this you shall know that

---

4. Ibid., 10:2.
5. Ibid., 9:16.
6. Passover Haggada.

I am the Lord,"[7] indicating that the plagues of blood, frogs and lice are meant to counter Pharaoh's denial of God's existence.

The fourth plague is preceded by the proclamation "That you may know that I am the Lord in the midst of the land."[8] This assertion specifies that the afflictions of beasts, pestilence and boils are designed to prove the reality of Divine Providence.

Finally, before the seventh plague God announces, "And you may know that there is none like Me in all the land."[9] The plagues of hail, locusts and darkness demonstrate God's ability to control nature.

The tenth and final plague of the firstborn joins all three elements together in one devastating blow.[10]

A different tack is suggested by the Maharal of Prague. The first grouping of plagues – blood, frogs and lice – represents an attack upon the Egyptians from below, as the land and sea turn against them. The second cluster – beasts, pestilence and boils – consists of an assault upon the Egyptians originating on their own level. Finally, the third set – hail, locusts, darkness and the plague of the firstborn – comprises an attack on the Egyptians from above. Through the plagues God demonstrates His total mastery of the world as each level of existence is turned against the Egyptians.[11]

Rabbi Shimshon Raphael Hirsch, for his part, sees in the structure of the plagues measure-for-measure punishment meted out against the Egyptians for their crimes. The persecution of the Israelites in Egypt progressed through three phases: *gerut* (estrangement within their adopted land), *avdut* (enslavement) and *inui* (torment). The first plague of each group, says Hirsch – blood, beasts and hail – is structured to make the Egyptians feel like strangers in their own land. The second affliction in each set – frogs, pestilence and locusts – conveys the emptiness of pride and masterfulness. The third plague in each cluster – lice, boils and darkness – is designed to torment the Egyptians as they tormented the Israelites. Finally, the last plague of the firstborn brings the process to a climax and accomplishes the redemption.[12]

---

7. Shmot 7:16.
8. Ibid., 8:18.
9. Ibid., 9:14.
10. Zevach Pesach (Abravanel's commentary on the Haggada).
11. Maharal's commentary on the Haggada 117.
12. Rabbi Shimshon Raphael Hirsch, Shmot 7:15.

Numerous other explanations are suggested by scholars as they strive to interpret the overall pattern within the plagues.

— **C** ——————————————————————————

A careful reading of the text reveals another level of design embedded within the progression of the plagues. Rabbi Yehuda's groupings mirror a consistent internal structure. In each set, the first plague is preceded by a public warning to Pharaoh, the second plague by a private notice to the monarch, while the third plague carries no warning at all.

The Abravanel views this internal pattern as a reflection of God's desire to forestall the tragedies confronting the Egyptians. First God warns Pharaoh in the presence of his court, affording the king's powerful retinue the opportunity to object. Recognizing, however, that the monarch might balk at a public warning, God then instructs Moshe to serve notice before the next plague to the king in private. When both of these cautions are ignored, God initiates the third plague of each set in full view of the Egyptian population without any warning at all. He hopes, by doing so, to educate the populace to the moral bankruptcy of their royal leadership.[13]

The Ramban suggests that the plagues of lice, boils and darkness are not preceded by warnings simply because these are the only afflictions that do not carry a mortal threat to the Egyptians. The cautions issued by God were an indication of divine mercy and were therefore only necessary in connection with plagues that could directly result in death.[14]

— **D** ——————————————————————————

A striking yet easily missed anomaly appears when we consider the disposition of the Israelites during the course of the plagues. The testimony of the text is strangely inconsistent. When discussing the plagues of beasts, pestilence, hail and darkness, the Torah goes out of its way to indicate that the Israelites were spared any suffering. During the plague of the firstborn, the Israelites who follow God's instructions are also saved.

In conjunction with the other plagues, however, no such distinction is made in the Torah between the Egyptians and the Israelites.

————————————

13. Abravanel, Shmot 7:26.
14. Ramban, Shmot 8:15.

This textual variance gives rise to a remarkable disagreement between the commentaries.

The Ramban maintains that the Israelites are not affected by any of the plagues. The Torah, however, only mentions their protected status in conjunction with the plagues that are by nature "spreading" afflictions. Since we would have assumed that these plagues affected the Israelites in Goshen as well, the Torah clearly tells us otherwise.[15] The plague of hail, descending from the skies, might also give rise to confusion since there is no clear demarcation in the airspace over Egypt and Goshen. The text again, therefore, feels compelled to inform us that the Israelites are spared.[16]

The Ibn Ezra, in stark contrast, maintains that the majority of the plagues afflict the Israelites together with their Egyptian masters. Only those plagues clearly indicated in the text actually leave them unscathed. God spares the Israelites from the afflictions that carry the greatest potential for enduring pain and mortal danger: beasts, pestilence, hail, darkness and, of course, the plague of the firstborn. [17]

At first glance, the Ibn Ezra's position seems deeply puzzling. Why should the Israelite victims of Egyptian slavery suffer even a measure of the punishment meted out against their taskmasters? The Avi Ezer, a commentator on the Ibn Ezra, is so troubled by this notion that he claims it was erroneously incorporated into the text of the Ibn Ezra by a "mistaken, poor student."[18]

Two rationales, however, might be suggested in support of the Ibn Ezra's recorded position that the slaves are affected by a number of the plagues.

1. The Israelites bear a measure of culpability in their own enslavement.

The descent of Yaakov's family to Egypt was meant to result only in a temporary sojourn. Yosef's brothers emphatically proclaim in their meeting with Pharaoh, *Lagur ba'aretz banu*, "We have come to *dwell* in the land."[19] Yet, in the very next breath they reveal a subconscious desire for perma-

---

15. Ibid., 8:18–19.
16. Ibid., 9:26.
17. Ibn Ezra, Shmot 7:24.
18. Avi Ezer, ibid.
19. Bereishit 47:4.

nence by requesting, *v'ata yeishvu na avadecha b'eretz Goshen*, "And now please allow your servants to *settle* in the Land of Goshen."[20]

Eventually the Israelites "settle and secure a permanent foothold" in the land of Egypt.[21] Clearly the children of Yaakov become too comfortable with the exile from the land of their fathers.

Another measure of blame can be leveled against the Israelites for their attempt to assimilate into Egyptian society. Upon his family's descent to Egypt, Yosef carefully manipulates their settlement in Goshen, thereby orchestrating a clear separation from the Egyptians.[22] The text, however, later testifies: "And the children of Israel were fruitful, multiplied, increased, and became strong...*and the land became filled with them*."[23] The Netziv comments, building upon an earlier Midrashic tradition[24]: "They filled not only the land of Goshen which had been especially assigned to them, *but the whole land of Egypt*.... Wherever they could purchase a dwelling, there the Israelites went.... They wanted to be like the Egyptians."[25]

For these failings, the Israelites deserve partial punishment along with the Egyptians. (For a full discussion of the above events see *Bereishit*: Vayigash 3, and for a discussion of the difference between the biblical terms *lagur* and *lashevet* see *Bereishit*: Vayeira 2, *Approaches* c.)

2. God does not want the Jewish nation to become a people so callous that they are capable of ignoring the pain of others, even their sworn enemies. As the nation is about to be born, therefore, God conveys a necessary, painful lesson. The Israelites cannot remain untouched while surrounded by a sea of agony. They must endure a number of the plagues together with their taskmasters in order to feel a measure of their pain.

—— **E** ——

A final approach to the overall purpose of the plagues emerges if we consider the events from the perspective of the Israelites.

Before the plagues begin, God instructs Moshe to describe the impending redemption to the Israelites through a series of four proclamations:

20. Ibid.
21. Bereishit 47:27.
22. Ibid., 46:31–34.
23. Shmot 1:7.
24. Yalkut Shimoni, Shmot 1.
25. Ha'amek Davar, Shmot 1:7.

1. *v'hotzeiti etchem mitachat sivlot Mitzraim*, "And I will take you out from under the burdens of Egypt."

2. *v'hitzalti etchem mei'avodatam*, "And I will rescue you from their labor."

3. *v'ga'alti etchem bi'zroa netuya u'vishfatim gedolim*, "And I will redeem you with an outstretched arm and with great judgments."

4. *v'lakachti etchem li l'am*, "And I will take you to Me for a people."[26]

These proclamations, referred to in numerous sources as the "four languages of redemption,"[27] are deemed particularly significant by the rabbis. They serve, in fact, according to many, as the basis for the four cups of wine at the Pesach Seder service.[28] (A fifth pronouncement, *v'heiveiti etchem el ha'aretz*, "And I will bring you to the land," may well be the source for the symbolic cup of Elijah.[29])

A return to the Talmudic source discussing these terms, however, reveals a fascinating nuance. The Talmud actually refers to the pronouncements not as the "four languages of redemption" but rather as the "four redemptions."[30]

This distinction is more significant than it might seem. The phrase "four languages of redemption" indicates that the Torah uses four terms to describe a single phenomenon. "Four redemptions," on the other hand, connotes four separate phenomena or four stages in the redemption process. Building upon this latter possibility, numerous commentaries struggle to delineate four concrete steps in the redemption of the Israelites from Egypt, with each step corresponding to one of the four terms used in the text.[31]

These rabbinic sources reflect, as they so often do, the seriousness with which the biblical narrative is meant to be approached. Far from imaginary tales, the Torah describes real events involving real human beings. Redemption is a process that requires both time and gradation. As the world has since learned through bitter experience, a servile population cannot make the transition to freedom and responsibility in one single step.

---

26. Shmot 6:6–7.
27. Yalkut Shimoni, Vayeishev 147; Rashi, Bamidbar 15:41; Rashbam, Talmud Bavli Pesachim 99a and elsewhere.
28. Talmud Yerushalmi Pesachim 10:1.
29. Torah Temimah, Shmot 6:6.
30. Talmud Yerushalmi Pesachim 10:1.
31. Sforno, Shmot 6:6–7; Ha'amek Davar, Shmot 6:6.

In light of the challenges confronting the Israelites at the time of the Exodus, therefore, the plagues acquire new significance. To truly become free, the slaves must witness the total decimation of all that has previously held them in thrall. Only if Egypt, its citizens, its royalty, its sorcerers and its gods are laid low in full view can the participants in the Exodus even begin their journey towards full freedom.

Step by step, the plagues destroy all that the Israelites have learned to fear. As the shackles are broken, the promise of freedom begins to emerge.

So difficult will the transition prove to be for the Israelites, however, that a full generation must pass before that promise is realized. In spite of the plagues, the parting of the Reed Sea, the Revelation at Sinai and all the accompanying miracles, the generation that leaves Egypt never fully leaves Egypt behind. Unable to realize their potential, they die in the desert. Only their children, who never knew slavery, inherit the Land.

Bo

בא

CHAPTER 10:1–13:16

פרק י:א–יג:טז

Parsha Summary

Slavery's end, new beginnings…

    The last plagues rain down upon Egypt, as Pharaoh wavers but repeatedly refuses to allow the Israelites to depart.

    As the final plague approaches, God informs Moshe of the imminence of the Exodus and tells him to have the Israelites prepare for their departure by accumulating wealth from their Egyptian neighbors. God further commands Moshe to launch the transmission of Jewish law with the first mitzva of Kiddush Hachodesh and to instruct the people concerning the Pesach offering and the Pesach festival itself.

    Moshe conveys God's instructions to the Israelites, who proceed to perform the rituals surrounding the Pesach offering.

    At midnight on the fifteenth day of Nisan, as the Israelites sit in their homes consuming the Paschal Lamb, God strikes Egypt with the final devastating blow: the tenth plague, the plague of the firstborn. Buffeted by the calamity, Pharaoh orders Moshe and Aharon to lead the Israelites out of Egypt. As they prepare to depart, the Israelites fulfill God's prior request by turning to their Egyptian neighbors, who willingly give them gold, silver and garments.

    At midday on the fifteenth of Nisan, centuries of slavery come to an end as the Israelites begin their journey, accompanied by a mixed multitude from other nations. So tumultuous are the events surrounding this departure that the dough of the Israelites' bread does not have time to rise.

    The parsha closes as God transmits additional laws concerning the Pesach offering, the redemption of the firstborn and the Pesach festival.

1 Unnecessary Roughness?

Context

As the intensity of the afflictions increases over the course of the plagues, Pharaoh offers three compromise positions to Moshe and the Israelites: worship your God in Egypt,[1] depart Egypt temporarily with some of the people while others remain,[2] depart Egypt temporarily with the entire nation but leave your cattle behind.[3]

Moshe emphatically rejects each compromise in turn.

The second of these potential compromises appears towards the beginning of Parshat Bo, in the following puzzling conversation between Moshe and Pharaoh:

Pharaoh: "Go and worship your Lord! Who are they that shall go?"

Moshe: "With our young and with our old we will go! With our sons and with our daughters! With our sheep and with our cattle! For it is a festival of the Lord for us!"[4]

Questions

How can Pharaoh ask, after all that has taken place, "Who are they that shall go?" Hasn't God made it abundantly clear that He demands the release of the entire people?

Why, in addition, does Moshe answer Pharaoh in such confrontational fashion? He could simply have said, *We all must go*. Why risk further antagonizing the king with the unnecessarily detailed proclamation "With our young and with our old we will go…"?

---

1. Shmot 8:21.
2. Ibid., 10:8.
3. Ibid., 10:24.
4. Ibid., 10:8–9.

Approaches

—**A**—

Much more is taking place in this conversation than initially meets the eye. The negotiation between Moshe and Pharaoh overlays a monumental confrontation between two towering civilizations, as Pharaoh and his court begin to face, with growing understanding, the true nature of the new culture destined to cause Egypt's downfall.

—**B**—

Pharaoh is, in reality, being neither deliberately obtuse nor intentionally confrontational when he raises the question "Who are they that shall go?" His response to Moshe is, in fact, abundantly reasonable in light of Moshe's original request of the king.

As we have already noted, God did not instruct Moshe to demand complete freedom for the Israelites. From the very outset, the appeal to the king was, instead, to be, "Let us go for a three-day journey into the wilderness that we may bring offerings to the Lord our God."[1] (See Shmot 4.)

In response to that request Pharaoh now argues: *All right, I give in! You have my permission to take a three-day holiday for the purpose of worshipping your Lord. Let us, however, speak honestly. Moshe, you and I both know that religious worship in any community remains the responsibility and the right of a select few. Priests, elders, sorcerers – they are the ones in whose hands the ritual responsibility of the whole people are placed.*

Therefore I ask you, "Who are they that shall go?" Who from among you will represent the people in the performance of this desert ritual? Let me know, provide me with the list and they will have my permission to leave.

—**C**—

Moshe's emphatic response is now understandable, as well: *You still don't get it, Pharaoh. There is a new world a-borning and we will no longer be bound by the old rules. No longer will religious worship remain the purview of a few chosen elect. A nation is coming into existence that will teach the world that religious participation is open to all.*

"*With our young and with our old we will go, with our sons and with*

---

1. Ibid., 5:3.

our daughters...." No one and nothing is to be left behind; our "festival of the Lord" will only be complete if all are present and involved.

—— **D** ————————————————————————

Moshe's ringing proclamation reminds us that the Exodus narrative chronicles not only a people's bid for freedom, but the beginning of a new chapter in the relationship between God and man. Step by step, a nation is forged that will be based upon personal observance, study and spiritual quest – a nation that will teach the world of every human being's right and responsibility to actively relate to his Creator.

With the Exodus and the subsequent Revelation at Sinai, the rules will change forever. The birth of Judaism will open religious worship and practice to all.

2 Conspicuous Consumption

Context

Finally, Moshe receives the news for which he has waited. "One last affliction shall I bring upon Pharaoh and upon Egypt," says God. "After that he shall send you forth from here."

Immediately, however, God continues with the following instruction: "Speak, please, in the ears of the people and let each man request from his [Egyptian] friend and each woman from her [Egyptian] friend *vessels of silver and vessels of gold.*"[1]

The Torah later attests to the successful fulfillment of God's directive: "And the children of Israel did as Moshe had directed; they requested from the Egyptians *vessels of silver, vessels of gold and garments.* And God granted the people favor in the eyes of the Egyptians and they granted their request – and they [the Israelites] despoiled Egypt."[2]

Questions

God's instructions to Moshe at this powerful moment are deeply troubling. One would expect the birth of the Jewish nation to be heralded by lofty principles and ideas. Why, then, does God specifically ask the Israelites to mark the first footfalls of their national history with the accumulation of material wealth? Is this what the slaves should be thinking of as they prepare for their journey to freedom?

The very idea seems not only out of place, but contrary to the creation of a people for whom spiritual search and religious ideal should be more important than material acquisition.

Compounding the problem is the fact that the theme of wealth is

---

1. Shmot 11:1–2.
2. Ibid., 12:35–36.

apparently foundational, woven into the fabric of the Exodus story from the very outset.

Centuries earlier, during the first reference to exile in Egypt, God promises the patriarch Avraham that the exile will end and "after that, they [your descendents] will leave with great wealth."[3]

At the burning bush, during his initial conversation with Moshe, God again predicts: "And each woman will ask of her neighbor and from the one who lives in her house *vessels of silver, vessels of gold and garments*; and you shall put them on your sons and your daughters, and you shall despoil Egypt."[4]

Clearly then, the directive to Moshe on the eve of the final plague does not represent a new idea but marks the fulfillment of a prophetic theme fundamental to the Exodus story. We ask again, therefore, with even greater bewilderment, why is the accumulation of wealth so critical to the Exodus and to the birth of the Jewish nation?

To complicate matters even further, additional questions emerge from the very structure and language of God's instructions to Moshe:

Daber na, "*Speak, please,* in the ears of the people..."[5]

Why is this directive couched in terms of a request rather than a commandment? If God wanted the people to leave Egypt with possessions, why involve the Israelites in their acquisition? God could have miraculously bestowed riches upon the departing slaves in any number of ways.

v'yishalu ish mei'eit rei'eihu, "And let each man request from his [Egyptian] friend..."[6] The verb *lishol* means either to ask or to borrow, depending upon context. Could God have been instructing the Israelites to deliberately mislead the Egyptians into thinking that the gold and silver was a loan, to be returned?

Approaches

Two classical rabbinic sources clearly reflect an awareness of the philosophical tension created by the divinely ordained transfer of wealth at the dawn of Jewish history.

---

3. Bereishit 15:14.
4. Shmot 3:22.
5. Ibid., 11:2.
6. Ibid.

1. The Talmud explains that God tells Moshe: "Speak, please, in the ears of the people…" because God must actively convince the Israelites to assist Him in the fulfillment of His promise to Avraham: "After that, they will leave with great wealth."[7]

The Israelites' reluctance to participate can be compared to a person languishing in prison who receives a promise: "Tomorrow you will be released and you will be given a great deal of money." "Release me today," answers the prisoner, "and I do not ask for anything more!"[8]

With the moment of liberation at hand, the Israelite slaves care little about material wealth. All that matters is their impending freedom.

Why, the rabbis implicitly ask, *does God redirect the attention of the Israelites, at this moment of deliverance, towards material gain?*

2. Elsewhere, the Talmud records a fascinating event. Centuries after the Exodus, the Egyptians bring a legal case against the Jews to the court of Alexander the Great. "Return to us," they demand, "the gold and silver which you took from us."

Gaviha ben Pasisa defends the honor of the Jews by responding that the Egyptians are responsible for the back wages of the six hundred thousand Israelites they had enslaved. The Egyptians can offer no rejoinder.[9]

With striking candor, the rabbis acknowledge that the transfer of wealth from the Egyptians to the Israelites raises moral questions that necessitate response.

These sources and others mirror the rabbinic struggle with the message God seems to transmit to the Israelites and with the moral questions raised by the instructions themselves.

So difficult are these issues that the Ibn Ezra sums up his approach to the event as follows: "There is no purpose in asking why; God created everything, He gives wealth to whom He desires and He takes it from the hand of one and gives it to another."[10]

— **B** —————————————————————————————————

Other scholars, however, unwilling to accept the unquestioning approach of the Ibn Ezra, wrestle with every aspect of this strange episode.

---

7. Bereishit 15:14.
8. Talmud Bavli Brachot 9a–b.
9. Talmud Bavli Sanhedrin 91a.
10. Ibn Ezra, Shmot 3:22.

Many focus, for example, on the word *v'yishalu*, "and they shall request," in an attempt to determine the moral underpinnings of God's directive to the Israelites.

Was the wealth transferred to the departing slaves freely given, they wonder, or did the Egyptians view the transaction as a loan which they expected to be returned?

Critical, of course, to this question is the answer to another question: were Pharaoh and the Egyptians, at the time of the Exodus, still operating under the presumption that the Israelites were only leaving for a three-day journey or was it clear by that time that the Exodus was meant to be complete and final? (See Shmot 4.) If the Egyptians believed that the Israelites were planning to return, the possibility that they considered the wealth a loan becomes more pronounced.

Rabbeinu Bachya, quoting the position of Rabbeinu Chananel, emphatically rejects the possibility that God commanded the Israelites to deceive the Egyptians: "Heaven forbid that the Holy One Blessed Be He would have sanctioned fraud, that they should borrow vessels of silver and vessels of gold and not return them."

Rather, continues Rabbeinu Bachya, the verb *lishol*, in this context, means to ask for the items as a full gift with no expectation of return.[11]

Numerous other commentaries, including Rav Saadia Gaon, the Rashbam and the Chizkuni, mirror the same position, supporting their claim with other instances in Tanach where the verb *lishol* is used analogously.[12]

Other commentaries assert, however, that the wealth was, indeed, given by the Egyptians to the Israelites as a loan with full expectation of return.

Some, such as the Netziv, go so far as to claim that God's intent is to further entrap the Egyptian population. The Egyptians fully expect the Israelites to return after a three-day holiday. To further ensure that the Egyptians will pursue the departing slaves when they fail to return, God instructs the Israelites to "borrow" wealth from their erstwhile masters. Angered by the apparent deceit and anxious to retrieve their possessions, the Egyptians will have an additional reason to follow the Israelites to the banks of the Reed Sea. This aspect of the Exodus, like so many others, is

---

11. Rabbeinu Bachya, Shmot 3:22, 11:2.
12. Saadia Gaon, Shmot 3:22, 11:2; Rashbam, ibid.; Chizkuni, ibid.

designed to lead the Egyptians to their unavoidable rendezvous with destiny in the roiling waters of that sea.

Noting the questionable morality of such deceit, the Netziv asserts that the Egyptians had earned, through their own actions, to be treated in this fashion. He then closes his comments, however, with the statement "The mind of God remains beyond our ken."[13]

— C —

The Malbim, for his part, posits two separate transfers of wealth from the Egyptians to the Israelites.

When God speaks to Moshe at the burning bush He mentions assets that will be directly conveyed to the Israelites by "neighbors and those who live in your house."[14] Here, God refers to wealth that will be given to the Israelites in exchange for their own possessions. As the Israelites leave Egypt, they will be forced to leave their homes and many of their belongings behind. Transferring ownership of those assets to their neighbors, they will receive, in return, "silver vessels, gold vessels and garments."[15]

Now, however, before the final plague, God instructs the Israelites to accumulate additional wealth in advance by approaching Egyptians who are not their immediate neighbors in order to "borrow" their gold and silver vessels. In agreement with the Netziv, the Malbim maintains that at this point, before actual Exodus, the Egyptians fully expect the Israelites to return after a three-day journey. They will, therefore, lend their vessels freely. Once the plague of the firstborn strikes Egypt, however, the status of these "borrowed" possessions changes. In reaction to the devastation, Pharaoh determines to permanently drive the Israelites from the land. At that point, the Egyptians, in their desire to be "free of the Israelites," decide of their own free will to release all claims to their belongings.[16]

An additional layer to the narrative is further suggested by the Vilna Gaon and the Malbim. They note that, throughout the Torah, the word *rei'eihu*, "friend," used here in God's instructions to Moshe, invariably refers to fellow Jews. To convince the Egyptians to lend their belongings, the Israelites first openly borrowed from each other in preparation for their

13. Ha'amek Davar, Shmot 3:18, 11:2.
14. Shmot 3:22.
15. Ibid.
16. Malbim, Shmot 3:22, 11:2.

journey. Witnessing these transactions, Egyptians believed that the items were necessary for the Israelites' religious holiday in the desert and they felt comfortable lending their wealth, as well.[17]

— **D** —

The fundamental questions, however, remain: Why is the transference of wealth from the Egyptians to the Israelites so critical to the Exodus? Why, as well, must the Israelites request that wealth from their former taskmasters?

Central to the rabbinic approach to these questions is recognition of the moment of the Exodus as a powerfully formative moment for the Jewish people. The Israelites' self-perception as they leave Egypt is of vital importance to the development of their national character. God does not want the departing slaves to sneak out of Egypt in the darkness of the night. Theirs is to be a triumphal march, befitting a divinely chosen nation.

Numerous scholars, therefore, building on the argument of Gaviha ben Pasisa (see above), argue that the wealth accrued by the departing slaves is actually payment for their years of service and servitude. The Kli Yakar asserts:

> Even though no obstacle prevented God from bestowing great wealth upon the Israelites without their having to take from the Egyptians through borrowing and subterfuge, nonetheless, the God of justice orchestrates events in order to redeem from the Egyptian population the wages owed to the Israelites for their labor.[18]

The wealth of the Egyptians cannot be given to the Israelites as a gift from God. They must, instead, receive these riches directly from their taskmasters so that they will understand that their past labor had value for which they must be paid.

— **E** —

Rabbi Zalman Sorotzkin, in his commentary on the Torah, offers an additional poignant insight concerning the events before us. The initial

---

17. Hagra al Haparshiot, Shmot 12:35–36; Malbim, Shmot 11:2.
18. Kli Yakar, Shmot 11:2.

reluctance of the Israelites to accept the wealth of the Egyptians, he says, can only be truly understood in light of the experiences of our own time.

During the decades since the Holocaust, debate has raged within the Jewish community concerning the acceptance of reparations from the Germans and their allies. Some have argued "Shall our murderers also inherit our wealth?" Others have countered: "We should have nothing to do with them. Can we accept atonement-money as payment for the souls of our brothers and sisters whose blood was spilled like water?"

This same dispute raged at the time of the Exodus, as well. Many Israelites were reluctant to accept wealth from the Egyptians, lest those riches be perceived as restitution for the many souls, particularly the children, murdered during the years of servitude. Others argued that the funds were certainly fairly earned payment for their labor during the years of slavery.

Recognizing the sensitivity of the issue, God does not force a decision. Instead of issuing an outright commandment, He turns to Moshe and says: *The people must accrue this wealth for many reasons. I cannot, however, in good conscience command them to do so. Please, therefore, speak to the people.*[19]

—— **F** ——————————————————————————————————————

A final, additional dimension to the episode before us can be discerned if we consider the eventual use to which the wealth received from the Egyptians is put.

The gold and silver of Egypt is ultimately applied by the Israelites to two projects that could not be more vastly different: the construction of the golden calf and the creation of the Mishkan (the portable sanctuary that traveled with the Israelites through the desert). The acquired riches thus become the medium through which the Israelites actualize their choices for good and for bad.

Freedom is only meaningful if you have something to lose. If the Israelites had left Egypt with nothing precious, nothing that they truly saw as their own, their liberation would have been incomplete. They would have had no way to actualize their responsibilities, to concretize their independent decisions.

---

19. Oznaim LaTorah, ibid.

God, therefore, directs the departing slaves to acquire wealth. He does not grant these riches as a gift. The Israelites must see them as earned.

The true challenge of an independent nation then faces the erstwhile slaves: how will they use their own prosperity, which they have earned through the sweat of their brow? The choices they make determine the very quality of their freedom.

3 Time in Our Hands

Context

As the Exodus approaches, a momentous event takes place. God begins the transmission of mitzvot (eternal divine commandments) to the Israelites with the directive of Kiddush Hachodesh, sanctification of the new moon: "This month shall be for you the beginning of the months; it shall be for you the first of the months of the year."[1]

Contained within this statement are the instructions that the *beit din* (court) shall consecrate the beginning of each month and that the month of Nisan is to be considered the first month of the year.

Questions

Why does God choose to begin the transmission of mitzvot with the technical obligation of Kiddush Hachodesh?

Would it not have been more appropriate to launch Jewish law with a more meaningful commandment such as the observance of Shabbat, kashrut, "love thy neighbor" or the like?

Approaches

As is so often the case, the full wisdom and beauty of God's decisions lie just beneath the surface of the text, waiting to be discerned through analysis and study. In this case, we will see that no other mitzva could have been a more suitable choice for the launching of Jewish law than the mitzva of Kiddush Hachodesh.

The appropriateness of this selection emerges simultaneously on multiple levels.

---

1. Shmot 12:2.

—— **A** ————————————————————

The first mitzva given to the Israelites rests upon the central foundation of *man's partnership with God*. As first established, the commandment of Kiddush Hachodesh was not simply one of sanctifying the new moon but, rather, of *establishing* the new moon.

In the days of the Sanhedrin, Kiddush Hachodesh began with the appearance of witnesses before the High Court, testifying that they had observed the "new moon" in the heavens. Based upon examination of their report, the court determined whether or not the new month should be declared.[2] *Only once the court declared the new moon sanctified did the next month actually begin.*[3]

This monthly decision was of overwhelming significance not only in setting the course of the months, but in determining the holiday calendar. As each festival was observed on a set calendar date, the actual celebration of that holiday obviously depended on when the month began. The *beit din's* judgment as to when the month of Tishrei commenced in a specific year, for example, would determine the day on which the fast of Yom Kippur would be observed that year.

While God, therefore, continues to direct the cycle of the moon in the heavens, through the mitzva of Kiddush Hachodesh, He hands over the application of that cycle to man. The Sanhedrin, from the very moment of our nation's birth, assumes control of the determination of Jewish time.

—— **B** ————————————————————

Numerous rabbinic sources, on the level of both *pshat* and Midrash, attest to the full partnership that lies at the core of the mitzva of Kiddush Hachodesh. They include:

1. "This month shall be *for you*" – [the determination of the new moon] is *given over to you* (i.e., to the Sanhedrin).[4]

2. "*This month* shall be for you" – Moshe was unable to understand the point in the moon's cycle at which sanctification should take place. God,

---

2. The extent of the calendar variation that could take place on a monthly basis was one day, depending on whether or not the previous month would be seen as "full" (thirty days) or "missing" (twenty-nine days).

3. Rambam, *Mishneh Torah*, Hilchot Kiddush Hachodesh 1:5.

4. Talmud Bavli Rosh Hashana 22a.

therefore, turned Moshe's attention heavenward at the appropriate moment and said, "When the moon reaches this phase, see it and sanctify it."[5]

3. "To *beit din* the matter is given; when *beit din* sanctifies and establishes a specific day as Rosh Chodesh, that is the day which is Rosh Chodesh."[6]

4. "The heavenly angels approach the Holy One Blessed Be He and ask: 'Master of the world, when is Rosh Hashana?' God responds: 'Why are you asking me? You and I must inquire of the earthly court.'

"If the earthly court declares: 'Today is Rosh Hashana!' the Holy One Blessed Be He proclaims to the angels: 'Erect a podium! Call the prosecuting attorneys; call the defense attorneys! My children have declared: Today is Rosh Hashana!'

"If the earthly court determines to delay the holiday, the Holy One Blessed Be He declares to the heavenly angels: 'Remove the podium! Remove the prosecuting attorneys; remove the defense attorneys! My children have decided to postpone the holiday for a day.'"[7]

[Historical note: Due to the exigencies of Jewish history, the process of testimony in *beit din* concerning Kiddush Hachodesh was ultimately set aside in favor of a fixed calendar. The laws of Kiddush Hachodesh, however, continue to be studied and the lessons therein remain fully relevant.]

— C —

God's message to the Israelites still languishing under Egyptian domination could not be clearer or more profound: *See yourselves no longer as powerless slaves but as an infinitely powerful people whose reach extends to the heavens themselves. While still in the land of your servitude, gaze up to the moon which seems so far beyond your grasp.*

Today we contract a partnership which grants you control over that celestial sphere. As you "control" the moon, so too, through our partnership, you will be granted the ability to exert control over every aspect of your lives and your world. No longer will others define your destiny. Even in other "Egypts," in times of difficulty and persecution, you will ultimately determine the quality of your lives.

---

5. Mechilta, Shmot 12:2; Rashi, ibid.
6. Rambam, *Mishneh Torah*, Hilchot Kiddush Hachodesh 1:5.
7. Talmud Yerushalmi Rosh Hashana 1:3.

This message, however, only scratches the surface of the mitzva's depth.

———— **D** ————————————————————————————————————

Rabbi Yosef Soloveitchik suggests that the fundamental distinction separating the free man from the slave is *control of time*:

> Time-awareness is the singular faculty of the free man, who can use or abuse it. To a slave, it is a curse or a matter of indifference. It is not an instrument which he can harness to his purposes. The free man wants time to move slowly because, presumably, it is being employed for his purposes.[8]

Not by accident, therefore, the first mitzva transmitted to our ancestors focuses on time. On the eve of their release from physical bondage, God prepares the Israelites for their spiritual transition to freedom: *I grant you control over time itself. Your time will now be your own: to be used as you wish. Recognize the responsibility that such newfound control brings. As free men, endeavor to use your time wisely, filling your lives with meaning.*

Rabbi Yitzchak Mirsky, in his thoughtful work *Hegyonei Halacha*, sees the liberating nature of time-awareness as the basis of a puzzling hypothesis recorded in the Pesach Haggada.

The author of the Haggada wonders: *Yachol mei'Rosh Chodesh…*, "Perhaps the mitzva of retelling the Exodus narrative should begin with Rosh Chodesh Nisan (the beginning of the month of Nisan) and not with Pesach Eve…"[9]

Numerous commentaries explain that this suggestion is based on the belief that Rosh Chodesh Nisan marks the onset of the redemption from Egypt.[10]

In what way, however, asks Mirsky, does liberation commence with the arrival of the month of Nisan? The Exodus does not occur until a full fifteen days later.

The mitzva of Kiddush Hachodesh, he responds, transmitted on Rosh

———————————

8. Abraham R. Besdin, ed., *Reflections of the Rav* (Jerusalem: Alpha Press, 1979), pp. 201–202.
9. Passover Haggada.
10. Rashbam, Haggada; Rashbatz, ibid.

Chodesh Nisan, marks the true start of deliverance from Egypt. Once the Israelites gain control over their own time, their transition from slavery to freedom has begun.[11]

E

The trial of time-awareness and control, however, is not limited to slaves on the eve of their physical liberation. To this day, in our own lives no task is more challenging or more important than the task of "controlling" time.

Time, after all, is the one, universal, precious commodity over which we seem to have no influence at all. Even more, time laughingly mocks our very attempts at control by moving in ways antithetical to our desires. When we want time to move "fast" it moves "slowly"; and when we desperately wish to slow time down, it quickly speeds up. We are all, it would seem, slaves to time.

God, however, demands that we learn to master time. *By choosing how to use our moments – by investing those moments with quality and significance – we break our servitude to time and become its masters.*

Critical to this task, maintains Rabbi Soloveitchik, particularly for the Jew, is the recognition of three dimensions of time, each of which is part of the time-experience:

> *Retrospection* refers to man's ability to re-experience the past, to feel deeply that which is only a memory, to transport an event of the distant past into a "creative living experience" of the present.
>
> *Anticipation* is man's projection of visions and aspirations into the future. Indeed, his present life is regulated in expectation of the fulfillment of these dreams. His present is shaped by his vision of the future.
>
> *Appreciation* embraces the present as a precious possession, as inherently worthy…. Retrospection and anticipation are significant only insofar as they transform the present. In every fraction of a second, visions can be realized or destroyed.[12]

---

11. Yitzchak Mirsky, *Hegyonei Halacha*, vol. 2 (Jerusalem: Rotner Publishing House, 1997), pp. 189–191.
12. Besdin, *Reflections of the Rav*, pp. 200–202.

From the beginning of his national journey, through the medium of the mitzvot, the Jew learns to perfect the art of merging past, present and future within his life moments. Each day resonates to historical experience; each day is touched by future hopes and visions. Great sages, teachers and heroes who lived long ago are not simply figures of the past but companions and advisers in the present, while the march towards a glorious future spiritual destination shapes our actions today. The present itself is seen in perspective, essential to the flow of our people's history, each era meeting its unique challenges and making its specific contribution to our nation's story.

When past, present and future combine, each moment moves outside the boundaries of time's flow and becomes eternal. At that point we truly conquer time.

— **F** —

The first mitzva given to the Israelites also sets the stage for the entirety of Jewish law which is to follow. With uncanny accuracy, the mechanics of the calendar create a paradigm for the functioning of halacha across the ages.

Just as Rosh Chodesh (the beginning of the month) is determined by the earthly court, so too, all of halacha rests upon the principle that divine law is handed over to man for interpretation and application, with the understanding that God will agree to the decisions that are made. Truth within halacha is defined not by the decisions themselves but by the loyalty shown to the law during the decision-making procedure. (See Yitro 5 for a fuller discussion of halachic process.)

While the spiritual partnership between man and God is open to all, however, the application of law requires expertise. Only those sages versed in both the substance and procedure of halacha are equipped to determine its course. Under the guidance of those trained to direct its flow, the law is applied to constantly changing circumstances and situations.

The comments of the Rambam concerning Kiddush Hachodesh could well, therefore, be referring to all of Jewish law:

The sighting of the moon is not handed over to every man.... Rather, the matter is handed to the *beit din*; only once the court sanctifies and establishes a particular day as Rosh Chodesh shall that day actually be Rosh Chodesh.[13]

——— **G** ———

A series of additional, ancillary lessons embedded in the mitzva of Kiddush Hachodesh are also underscored by the commentaries.

Rabbi Yehuda Halevi and Rabbi Shimshon Raphael Hirsch, for example, both maintain that the correlation of the Jewish calendar to the lunar cycle is far from accidental. The moon is the only celestial sphere that undergoes an apparent cycle of renewal in the heavens. This monthly regeneration is meant to serve as a model for our own behavior. Our relationship with God should never become static. Each Rosh Chodesh, as the moon begins its celestial journey, we on earth should examine and reestablish our connection with our Creator. The Hebrew word for month, *chodesh*, thus reflects its origin in the term *chadash*, new, with Rosh Chodesh emerging as a day of personal renewal at the beginning of each month.[14]

The *Aruch Hashulchan* perceives within the observance of Rosh Chodesh an allusion to the miraculous survival of the Jewish nation.

The month is sanctified at the beginning of the moon's celestial journey, at a time of darkness when scarcely a sliver of lunar light can be seen in the heavens. We celebrate, however, in the knowledge that soon the heavens will be illuminated by the brilliance of the full moon.

In similar fashion, our nation's history has been marked by periods of deep darkness when all seemed lost. We have, however, even at those darkest moments, never lost faith in our destiny. We always believed that the time would come when the light of our heritage would, once again, illuminate the world, as surely as the moon shines in the heavens.[15]

Other lessons, as well, can certainly be gleaned from the symbolism of the lunar calendar. The fact that the moon's light is a reflection of the sun's, for example, reminds us that our accomplishments as a people are a "reflection" of God and His Torah. The phases of the Moon sensitize us to the value of life's passages. By marking Rosh Chodesh at the beginning of

---

13. Rambam, *Mishneh Torah*, Hilchot Kiddush Hachodesh 1:5.
14. Hakuzari 3:5; Rabbi Shimshon Raphael Hirsch, Shmot 12:2.
15. Aruch Hashulchan, Orach Chaim 422:6.

the lunar cycle rather than at its height, halacha underscores that the journey towards a goal is often more important than the goal itself.

— **H** —

Finally, the second half of the Kiddush Hachodesh directive, the designation of the month of Nisan as the first of the months, also carries tremendous import.

This designation creates a dichotomy within the Jewish year. We celebrate two major Rashei Shana – New Year commemorations: the Rosh
Hashana of Tishrei and the Rosh Hashana of Nisan. (Other, minor New
Year commemorations, such as Tu B'Shvat, the New Year of the trees, are
found in the calendar as well.)

The Rosh Hashana of Tishrei, popularly known within Jewish tradition simply as Rosh Hashana, is a celebration with universal overtones. On
that occasion, we mark the creation of man as we focus on the collective
human task of *tshuva* (repentance and return). The Rosh Hashana of Nisan,
on the other hand, heralding the holiday of Pesach, is a uniquely Jewish
celebration commemorating national birth and singularity.

Evidence of the philosophical distinction between these two Rashei
Shana is seen in a technical Talmudic mandate. Legal contracts that are
dated according to the reign of non-Jewish kings, say the rabbis, must reflect the universal Rosh Hashana of Tishrei. Contracts, on the other hand,
that reference the reign of Jewish kings are dated according to the Jewish
Rosh Hashana of Nisan.[16]

The very existence of these two Rashei Shana within the Jewish calendar conveys a powerful message: *The establishment of the Rosh Hashana
of Nisan does not render the Rosh Hashana of Tishrei obsolete. The birth of
the Israelites' singular national identity does not cancel their role as citizens
of the world community.*

Jewish time begins with a message from the past. As the Israelites
take their first steps towards independence, the words of self-definition
declared centuries earlier by their ancestor, Avraham, echo across the ages
to shape the new nation's calendar: *Ger v'toshav anochi imachem*, "I am a

---

16. Talmud Bavli Rosh Hashana 2a, 3a.

stranger and a citizen together with you."[17] (See *Bereishit*: Chayei Sara 1, *Approaches* E, F.)

Our world mission is forged upon the balance we create between insularity from and involvement with those around us.

---

17. Bereishit 23:4.

4 A Night to Remember

Context

God commands the Israelites to retreat to their homes on the night before the Exodus. There, in extended family groups, they are to consume the *Korban Pesach* (the Pesach offering).[1]

This event serves as the basis for the Pesach Seder commemorated within Jewish homes on Pesach Eve to this day.

Questions

With the onset of their national journey looming on the morrow, why does God command the Israelites to spend the night before the Exodus within their homes, participating in what amounts to a ritual family meal? Wouldn't the interests of the Israelites have been better served through communal meetings laying the groundwork for their nationhood or, conversely, couldn't the time have been used more wisely in personal preparations for the Exodus?

One can imagine the Israelites, after years of slavery, protesting to God, *Lord, first redeem us and then we will gladly perform all the rituals that You command!*

What is the significance of the many rites associated with the *Korban Pesach*? How do these rituals speak to the powerful historical backdrop against which they are observed?

Why is this event memorialized each year on the first night(s) of Pesach while the actual moment of the Exodus, midday of the following day, passes unmarked?

Approaches

The detailed rituals commanded by God throughout the Torah are often

---

1. Shmot 12:3–11.

designed to convey powerful, specific ethical and moral lessons. At times, these lessons can be difficult to decipher. In the case of the *Korban Pesach*, however, obvious treasures lie just beneath the surface: essential messages transmitted to the Israelites, through practical observance, on the very eve of their emancipation.

———**A**———

The first instructions concerning the *Korban Pesach* are communicated to Moshe on Rosh Chodesh Nisan, immediately following the laws of Kiddush Hachodesh (see Bo 3):

> Speak to the entire assembly of Israel saying: On the tenth of this month they shall take for themselves, each man, a lamb for each father's house, a lamb for the household. And if the household shall be too small for a lamb, then he and his neighbor who is near to his home shall take according to the number of people; each man according to his ability to eat shall be counted for the lamb.[2]

A careful reading of the text reveals that the *Korban Pesach* develops in three stages, ritualistically mirroring the three fundamental foundations upon which Jewish society will rest.

1. "A lamb for each father's house, a lamb for the household."[3]
The first and foremost pillar of Jewish society is the family unit.

God deliberately refrains from marking the birth of the Jewish nation with constitutional conventions, mass rallies or declarations of independence. Each Israelite is, instead, commanded to return to the privacy of his home where he is to participate in the family meal that is the *Korban Pesach*.

By insisting upon a retreat to the home as a prelude to our nation's birth, God delivers a simple yet powerful message: *As you prepare to begin your historic journey, stop and mark this evening within the societal unit that will be most critical to your success. Remember always that your survival will depend upon the health of the family. If the family is strong, if the home fulfills*

———

2. Ibid., 12:3–4.
3. Ibid., 12:3.

its educational role, your people will be strong and your nation will endure
(see *Bereishit*: Vayechi 4, *Approaches* B and *Points to Ponder*).

Not only the nuclear family, but the extended family, as well, will enrich Jewish experience across the centuries. God, therefore, insists that the Paschal Lamb shall be "for each father's home" as well as "for the household."

2. "And if the household shall be too small for a lamb, then he and his neighbor who is near to his home shall take…"[4]

Moving beyond the family unit, the text arrives at the second foundation of Jewish society: the community.

The family unit, as important as it is, cannot operate in a vacuum. Each household will be required, at times, to reach beyond its walls, either to ask for or to offer assistance and support.

God, therefore, instructs any family that cannot perform the Pesach rituals on its own to turn outward. If neighbors work together, creating communal institutions of mutual support, the nation they build will survive and thrive.

An apparent redundancy in the text underscores the mindset that must characterize these shared communal endeavors. A neighbor is, by definition, an individual who lives in close proximity to another. Why, then, does the Torah state that the Paschal Lamb should be shared with "his neighbor who is *near to his home*"?

The text stresses that we should adopt an attitude towards our neighbors which defines them as "near to our home." By recognizing the vulnerabilities, the rights and the dreams that we and our neighbors share, we will be moved to assist those around us to reach their goals even as we strive to achieve our own.

3. "Each man according to his ability to eat shall be counted for the lamb."[5]

Finally, the Torah reminds us that no individual can escape the obligations raised by the third societal foundation: personal responsibility.

Strong families and communities can, at times, serve as a refuge for those who wish to escape the burdens of their own obligations. After all, if there are others to "do the job," why should we?

Such an attitude clearly robs our people of essential human resources.

---

4. Ibid., 12:4.
5. Ibid.

Each and every individual has a unique and invaluable contribution to make to our nation's story; a contribution that is solely his own. God, therefore, symbolically demands that the computation concerning the size of each *Korban Pesach* be based upon the full participation of all involved in that *korban*.

Our national aspirations will be fully met only if "each man" performs "according to his ability."

The very structure of the *Korban Pesach*, consumed on the eve of our nation's historical journey, underscores the foundations necessary to make that journey enduring.

—— **B** ————————————————————

The timing of the *Korban Pesach* carries additional fundamental significance. God's insistence that the ritual be performed on the night before the physical Exodus from Egypt highlights the difference between two dimensions of freedom in Jewish thought:

1. *Dror* (liberty) – the removal of external constraints, physical or otherwise, that impede an individual's personal choice and independent action. *Dror* is either conferred upon an individual by an outside force or attained by an individual through severance from that force.

2. *Cheirut* (freedom) – the injection of positive purpose and value into one's life. The individual who enjoys *cheirut*, by choosing to pursue a higher goal, actively frees himself from servitude to the surrounding world and its potentially enslaving forces. *Cheirut* cannot be granted by another but must be attained by an individual himself.

One can be at liberty and yet not be free. One can be free even though he is not at liberty.

While still surrounded by the darkness of Egyptian servitude, even before their liberty is achieved, the Israelites are commanded to declare their *cheirut*. By setting aside a lamb, the god of Egypt,[6] on the tenth day of Nisan, by publicly waiting four days and then slaughtering and consuming that lamb on Pesach Eve, the Israelites demonstrate that they are already free from Egypt and the Egyptians. *On the night before the Exodus, through the* Korban Pesach, *the Israelites attain their freedom.*

How many times, through their long and arduous history, will the de-

—————————————
6. Midrash Rabba Shmot 16:2.

scendents of the Israelites be forced to relive this scene? How many times, against the backdrop of encroaching darkness and persecution, will the Jewish people be pushed to find the strength, against all odds, to declare their spiritual and philosophical freedom from their persecutors? *The ability to achieve* cheirut, *even in the absence of liberty, will be a component crucial to the survival of the Jewish nation.*

At the same time, the requirement of the *Korban Pesach* reminds us of the emptiness of liberty without freedom. Had the Israelites left Egypt without first experiencing the rituals of the previous night, their emancipation would have been incomplete. Liberty only has meaning when the removal of external constraints is accompanied by the injection of positive purpose.

How many of us or those around us, living at liberty in a free society, nonetheless find ourselves enslaved to the pressures of an outside world? The rabbis, thus, declared with frightening accuracy: *Ein lecha ben chorin ela mi she'oseik ba'Torah*, "No one is truly free except for he who involves himself in Torah." [7]

Only through belief in and pursuit of a higher cause do we truly attain *cheirut*.

─── C ───────────────────────────────

Central to the observance of the *Korban Pesach* is the notion of ritualized haste and urgency: "And so shall you consume it: your loins girded, your shoes on your feet and your staff in your hand. *And you shall eat it in haste*; it is a Pesach offering to God." [8]

At face value, however, this sense of haste seems totally unnecessary. The Exodus is not a sudden, unexpected event. The conclusion of Egyptian exile was clearly predicted as far back as the days of Avraham (see *Bereishit*: Lech Lecha 4; Vayeishev 3). [9] The Israelites themselves have been waiting and planning for this moment over centuries of servitude. To further complicate matters, when Pharaoh finally urges the Israelites to leave Egypt during the night, Moshe refuses and insists that the departure take place in broad daylight, midday of the following day.

───────────────

7. Pirkei Avot 6:2.
8. Shmot 12:11.
9. Bereishit 15:13–16.

Why introduce a sense of urgency into the *Korban Pesach* when the departure for Egypt could well have been experienced in a calm, ordered fashion?

Once again, through ritual, the Torah conveys an idea that cannot be ignored: *Great opportunities are often presented in swiftly fleeting moments.*

While it is true that the moment of the Exodus had been predicted and anticipated for centuries, when that moment finally arrives, an instantaneous decision on the part of each Israelite is required. Hesitation will prove fatal. Only those individuals, decisive and courageous enough to leave a known existence for the unknown, will merit becoming part of the glorious story of their people. Those who miss this small temporal window of opportunity will be too late and will disappear into the mists of history. The difficulties inherent in the choice to leave Egypt are reflected in the rabbinic tradition that only a small percentage of the Israelites ultimately departed.[10]

——— **D** ———————————————————————————————

The challenges raised by fleeting opportunities are further ritualized in another familiar symbol associated with the *Korban Pesach*: matza – unleavened bread.

"You shall not eat leavened bread with [the *Korban Pesach*], for seven days you shall eat matzot…, bread of affliction, for with haste you departed the land of Egypt…"[11]

The symbol of matza, at face value, seems inherently contradictory. On the one hand, matza is born at the moment of the Exodus, when the Israelites leave Egypt with such speed that their dough does not have time to rise.[12] On the other hand, matza clearly predates the moment of the Exodus as God commands the consumption of the *Korban Pesach* together with matza and bitter herbs.[13]

On the Seder night we refer to matza twice. At the beginning of the service we call the matza "the bread of affliction which our fathers ate in

---

10. Midrash Tanchuma Beshalach 1.
11. Devarim 16:3.
12. Shmot 12:39.
13. Ibid., 12:8.

the land of Egypt,"[14] a clear indication that the unleavened bread is a symbol of slavery. Later in the Seder service, however, matza is referenced as a symbol emerging at the moment of freedom: "What is the reason for the matza that we eat? It is because the dough that our fathers prepared did not have sufficient time to rise before the Supreme King of Kings, the Holy One Blessed Be He, revealed Himself to them and redeemed them."[15]

What, then, does the matza represent: slavery or freedom?

The answer lies in the one criterion that differentiates matza from its polar opposite, *chametz* (leavened bread), prohibited on Pesach. Strangely enough, these two ritually antithetical phenomena are physically almost identical. They are made from the same ingredients. The law mandates, in fact, that matza can only be created from ingredients which could have become *chametz* if left unbaked too long.[16] *The one and only thing, therefore, that differentiates* chametz *from matza is a split second of time.* Flour and water baked within eighteen minutes of their mixing become matza while the same components baked a moment later have already become *chametz.*[17]

Matza is physically defined by an instant of time; philosophically, this symbol also depicts a moment of time. *Matza reflects both slavery and freedom because it captures the moment of transition from one state to the other.* By catching and ritualizing this historic instant, with all of its overwhelming import, the symbol of matza reminds us of the potential significance embedded in every passing moment.

Like the *Korban Pesach*, consumed in haste, the symbol of matza reminds us of opportunities that may be presented at any instant of our lives – opportunities that must be noted and pursued before they disappear forever.

— E —————————————————————

Finally, we consider the strikingly strange instruction "And so shall you consume [the *Korban Pesach*]: your loins girded, your shoes on your feet and your staff in your hand."[18]

---

14. Pesach Hagadda.
15. Ibid.
16. Talmud Bavli Pesachim 35a.
17. Mishna Berura Orach Chaim 459:15.
18. Shmot 12:11.

Why must the Israelites eat the *Korban Pesach* already prepared for the journey which will only begin on the morrow? Certainly there will be time to dress appropriately and pick up staffs after the ritual is concluded. Is this detail simply a demonstration of ritualized haste (see above) or is there a deeper lesson to be learned?

Commenting on this extraordinary scene, the rabbis only seem to muddy the waters further: "Rabbi Yossi Hagalili stated: 'Here the text comes to provide good advice for travelers, that they should be energetic.'"[19]

What, exactly, is Rabbi Yossi adding to the mix? Are the rituals of the first *Korban Pesach* to be reduced to "good advice for travelers," conveying a lesson that is already clearly self-evident?

Upon consideration, however, Rabbi Yossi's observation emerges as a brilliant example of rabbinic methodology, which often couches complex, critical lessons in easily remembered tales and pictures. According to Rabbi Yossi, the Torah proposes that, from the moment of the *Korban Pesach*, all Jews become "travelers" in the journey of our people across the face of history. As we travel along that long and arduous road, one talent becomes critical to our survival – a talent captured in the image of the Israelites dressed for tomorrow's journey the night before. *Somehow, we have to learn to be prepared for tomorrow's challenges today.*

In generation after generation, in society after society, the descendents of the Israelites will confront ever-changing circumstances and challenges. At times, change may occur so rapidly and so totally as to seem impossible to predict. Most often, however, the seeds of these transformations will be visible in advance to those perceptive and energetic enough to notice.

At the dawn of their national history, in the darkness of the night, a people gather in groups to eat a family meal while fully prepared for a journey that will only begin on the morrow. From that time on, that people's ability to determine and prepare for changes before they emerge full-blown will be central to their success and survival.

"Who is truly wise? He who sees that which is a-borning."[20]

---

19. Mechilta, Shmot 12:11.
20. Talmud Bavli Tamid 32a.

Points to Ponder

The story is told of the Jewish optician who lives in Berlin in the 1930s. Noting the events taking place around him, he decides to emigrate to Israel. To inform his patients of his departure, he places a sign outside his office: "For all of you who are nearsighted, there is a doctor around the corner. For all of you who are farsighted, follow me."

While the story is poignant, it is also, of course, simplistic. How can we judge, from the safety of our own environment, the issues that must have confronted the Jewish community of Europe in the years leading up to World War II? Would we have believed, had we been there, that countries such as Germany, representing the height of civilization at the time, could possibly commit the unspeakable atrocities that were to come? Are we so certain that, ensconced comfortably in homes that had been ours for decades, we would have been able to pick up and leave?

And yet…the facts remain. Had we been more intuitive, had we listened to what was being said by the Nazis, had we mobilized in the face of impending danger – who knows how many would have been saved?

We must also ask: Are we any better equipped today? Would we see the danger signs looming on the horizon of our own exiles in time to make a difference? Are some of those signs already appearing? Are we sensitive not only to the open physical threats against us but also to the subliminal philosophical dangers that so often lie beneath our radar screen? Have we, without even noticing, begun to worship the societal gods around us?

We would do well to keep the image of the first Pesach table before us as we continue our travels. The lessons learned around it continue to inform our journey to this day.

Beshalach

CHAPTER 13:17–17:16

Parsha Summary

Triumphs and trials...

God leads the Israelites on a circuitous route from Egypt in order to avoid confrontation with the Philistines.

Moshe fulfills a centuries-old vow, by ensuring that the remains of Yosef are carried out of Egypt as the people depart.

The journey of the Israelites is marked by a divinely sent cloud of glory during the day and a pillar of fire by night.

God, instructing the nation to backtrack towards Egypt, informs Moshe that Pharaoh will pursue the people, an act that will ultimately lead to the further glorification of God.

Pharaoh, upon hearing that "the nation has fled," experiences the divinely predicted change of heart and pursues the departing slaves to the banks of the Reed Sea. When the Israelites, apparently trapped at the edge of the sea, sight the approaching Egyptian horde, they turn to Moshe in despair. Moshe assures them that they are about to experience divine redemption as "the Lord fights on their behalf."

God commands Moshe to tell the nation to advance and to raise his staff over the Sea, causing it to split. When Moshe complies, the waters of the Reed Sea miraculously part, allowing the Israelites to cross in safety. God, however, closes the waters upon the pursuing Egyptians and they drown in the Sea.

Moshe and the nation mark their full redemption from Egypt with celebratory song on the banks of the Reed Sea. Miriam leads the women in dance and song.

After a three-day journey without water, the nation arrives at Marah, the site of a non-potable pool of water. When the people complain, God instructs Moshe to throw a specific tree into the pool, miraculously rendering the water drinkable.

As their journey continues, the people complain over lack of food and recall with regret "the fleshpots" that they left behind in Egypt. God responds by granting the Israelites daily rations from the heavens. This miraculous sustenance, which the Israelites call "manna (man hu? – what is it?)," will ultimately provide for the people over a forty-year period in the wilderness. God also issues instructions concerning the daily collection of the manna and the prohibition of collecting on Shabbat.

When the nation arrives at Refidim and complains over lack of water, God instructs Moshe to strike a specific rock, miraculously causing water to flow.

The nation of Amalek attacks the Israelites without warning and Moshe instructs Yehoshua to lead a counterforce in battle. Moshe then ascends to high ground where, with the assistance of Aharon and Chur (the son of Miriam and Calev[1]), he raises his arms in full view of the Israelites. As long as Moshe's arms are raised, the Israelites prevail. In this fashion, they emerge victorious from the battle. God commands Moshe to record a mandate authorizing perpetual struggle against the Amalekites until God "erases their memory from under the heavens."

---

1. Talmud Bavli Sota 11b–12a.

1 The Long Way Around

Context

No sooner do the Israelites depart Egypt than they are confronted by a divinely ordained detour.

"And it was when Pharaoh sent out the people, and God did not lead them by way of the land of the Philistines, *ki karov hu* (as it was near), for God said: 'Lest the people reconsider upon seeing war, and return to Egypt.'"[1]

Questions

Two sets of questions emerge as we consider this strange passage.

Textually, the sentence does not seem to flow. What does the phrase "*ki karov hu* (as it was near)" mean? Proximity would seem to *recommend* rather than *discourage* the choice of a path. Should the text not have said that God bypassed the way of the Philistines *although* it was near?

Conceptually, why is this detour necessary? God, after all, has just decimated the Egyptian empire on behalf of the Israelites. Can He not do the same to the Philistines or, at the very least, protect the Israelites from the effects of an outbreak of hostilities?

Approaches

—**A**———————————————————

The textual difficulty presented by this passage centers around the Hebrew word *ki* in the phrase "*ki karov hu* (as it was near)." The word *ki*, according to the Talmud, translates variably in the Torah, dependent upon the

---

1. Shmot 13:17.

context: "Reish Lakish said: '*Ki* serves four possible meanings – if, perhaps, however, because.'"[2]

Of these four translations, only "because" fits our passage. That interpretation, however, leaves us with the basic question, why would God avoid a specific path "*because* it was near"?

— **B** —

Numerous commentaries, including Rashi and the Ibn Ezra, offer a straightforward *pshat* approach to this sentence which preserves the translation of *ki* as "because." God avoids taking the Israelites through Philistine territory *because* the proximity of this path to Egypt would have encouraged and facilitated the Israelites' retreat from battle. At the first hint of hostilities, the nation would have returned to Egypt. The "nearness" of this path was thus not a potential benefit, as we might have assumed, but a drawback.[3]

Raising issues of syntax, both the Ramban and Rabbi Moshe Hakohen (quoted by the Ibn Ezra) refuse to accept the straightforward solution proffered by Rashi and the Ibn Ezra. The Ramban maintains that the phrase *ki karov hu* is to be translated as "*which* was near,"[4] while Rabbi Moshe understands it to mean "*although* it was near."[5] The objection can be raised, however, that neither of these approaches translates the word *ki* in a fashion consistent with the list suggested by Reish Lakish.

The Rashbam, for his part, explains that God's concern for the Israelites transcended the possibility of war with the Philistines alone. The path through Philistine territory was "near" – the most direct route to the land of Canaan. The Israelites, however, were not prepared for all the battles that would face them in the conquest of the land. God, therefore, diverts them from the shortest route to Canaan and leads them on a circuitous path in order to prevent a disheartened retreat to Egypt.[6]

— **C** —

In stark contrast to the above suggestions, which reflect struggle with the

---

2. Talmud Bavli Gittin 90a.
3. Rashi, Shmot 13:17; Ibn Ezra, ibid.
4. Ramban, ibid.
5. Ibn Ezra, ibid.
6. Rashbam, ibid.

pshat of the text, are a series of creative Midrashic alternatives. Two such explanations are quoted by the *Da'at Zekeinim Miba'alei Hatosafot*:

1. The phrase *ki karov hu* is not to be translated "because *it* was near" but, rather, "because *He* was near." The Torah refers to the fact that God was "near" to the Israelites. Because of their preciousness to Him, God refuses to endanger the departing slaves by taking them along a path that could lead to war.

2. The phrase refers to the Philistines themselves, not to their territory. The Philistines were "near" to the Egyptians in that they shared common ancestry.[7] God does not want the Israelites, upon their departure from Egypt, to encounter the Philistines because he knows that the Philistines will attack in order to uphold the honor of their relatives, the Egyptians.[8]

Numerous other approaches, including a tradition chronicling an earlier failed attempt by the tribe of Ephraim to escape Egypt through Philistine territory,[9] can be found in Midrashic literature.

—— **D** ——————————————————————

While the textual problems surrounding this passage are certainly intriguing, of greater concern are the conceptual issues. Why does God feel compelled to lead the Israelites on a circuitous route upon their departure from Egypt? Could He not have fought the battle for them or, at least, miraculously protected them from the ravages of warfare? Two possible approaches can be suggested; each carrying overarching eternal lessons:

1. God does not punish nations undeservedly.

As noted previously (see *Bereishit*: Noach 4, *Approaches* A), God includes a striking message to the patriarch Avraham in the Covenant between the Pieces. After predicting that Avraham's descendents will be strangers in a land not their own, where they will be made to work and suffer for four hundred years, God states: "And the fourth generation will return here [to the land of Canaan] for the iniquity of the Emorites will not be complete until then."[10]

Do not assume, Avraham, because you and your descendents are chosen, that I relate to you alone. The legitimate rights of all nations continue to be

7. Bereishit 10:13–14.
8. Da'at Zekeinim Miba'alei Hatosafot, Shmot 13:17.
9. Midrash Rabba Shmot 20:11.
10. Bereishit 15:16.

My concern. Your fate will, therefore, be determined not only by your own merit but by the rights of others. You will not return to this land until its inhabitants have become so corrupt that they deserve to be expelled.

The very same principle may well be driving God's decisions during the days immediately following the Exodus. God punished the Egyptians because their acts warranted such penalty. The Philistines, however, have done nothing to this point to earn divine retribution. God, therefore, will not act against them even to protect His "chosen people." He instead leads the Israelites on a circuitous route in order to avoid the confrontation.

2. The Israelites have to learn to fight their own battles.

With the Exodus, the rules begin to change. Until now, before His people set out upon their journey towards freedom, God fought on their behalf. Now, the transition to independence requires that the Israelites must learn to fend for themselves. Even later, when the last act of the Exodus unfolds and God does intervene to complete the destruction of Egyptian might in the waters of the Reed Sea, God does not act until the Israelites take their destiny into their own hands and begin to move into the sea.[11]

Had God waged a divine battle against the Philistines, had He even miraculously protected the Israelites from attack, the wrong message would have been transmitted. The time has come for the Israelites to begin fighting their own battles. They are ill prepared for such challenge, however, at this moment. God, therefore, moves to avoid the confrontation.

— **E** —

A final lesson can be gleaned if we view this episode in a larger context. The endpoints of Parshat Beshalach chronicle a striking transformation. While the parsha opens with God shielding the Israelites from the mere possibility of conflict, it closes, ironically, with the Israelites victorious in battle. The final scene of Beshalach describes the unprovoked attack upon the Israelites by the nation of Amalek and the ensuing battle from which the erstwhile slaves emerge triumphant.[12]

The band of Israelite slaves, ready to retreat at the first hint of hostilities, has evolved, by the end of Beshalach, into a successful fighting force. The march towards nationhood has begun in earnest.

---

11. Rashi, Shmot 14:15.
12. Shmot 17:8–13.

2 Scenes at the Sea

This study departs from the usual structure. We will not focus on one passage in depth through a series of questions and answers. Rather, in order to capture the rising sense of urgency as the Israelites approach and reach the banks of the Reed Sea, we will explore the rapid series of events unfolding at this point in the Torah. The total picture created by the text is dramatic, indeed.

Context

With short strokes, the Torah describes the swiftly moving events that bring both the Israelites and their Egyptian persecutors to the banks of the Reed Sea. There, the final chapter of the Exodus is written as God parts the sea for the fleeing slaves, only to close the waters upon the pursuing Egyptians.[1]

So powerful are these events, so immanent is God's presence during the culminating moments of the Exodus, that, centuries later, the rabbis will declare: "That which the maidservants saw at the [Reed] Sea was not seen by [the Prophet] Yechezkel and all the other prophets."[2]

Approaches

Pshat and Midrash intertwine to paint a fascinatingly complex picture of the road leading to the Reed Sea. What follows is a sampling of the events described.

---

1. Shmot 14:1–31.
2. Mechilta, Shmot 15:2.

—**A**—

"And it was told to the king of Egypt *that the nation had fled*; and the heart of Pharaoh and his servants changed concerning the people, and they said: 'What is it that we have done that we have sent Israel from serving us?'"[3]

How are we to understand this puzzling passage? Why does Pharaoh need to be told that "the nation had fled"? Did he not himself demand their departure on the night of the plague of the firstborn?[4]

As noted previously (see Shmot 4) our understanding of this sentence depends on our position concerning a deeper question: does Pharaoh still believe that the Israelites are planning to return to Egypt after a three-day holiday in the desert, as per their original request?

1. Rashi, quoting a Mechilta, maintains that Pharaoh fully intends to hold the Israelites to their initial request. He therefore sends spies with the departing slaves. When three days pass and no return is imminent, the spies return to Pharaoh with the news: "The nation has fled."[5]

According to this approach, we now witness the culmination of God's plan. From the beginning at the burning bush, God instructed Moshe to ask for a three-day journey from Egypt in order to ensure this very eventuality. The entire Exodus saga is structured to lead Pharaoh and his army to their inevitable demise in the waters of the Reed Sea.

2. While many classical commentaries agree with the fundamental thesis of the Midrash, numerous other commentaries explain the sentence differently.

Rabbi Shimshon Raphael Hirsch, for example, maintains that, after the ten plagues, Pharaoh "sent the people away from his country with the full idea *of their not returning.*" God, however, misleads the Egyptian king by instructing the Israelites to backtrack in the direction of Egypt.[6] When the king hears "*that the nation had fled* – that the Israelites have turned back in the desert as if lost," he interprets this event as a defeat of the God of Israel at the hands of an Egyptian God. He therefore changes his mind and determines to pursue the Israelites.[7]

The Ramban, for his part, explains that Pharaoh still believes that the

---

3. Shmot 14:5.
4. Ibid. 12:31.
5. Rashi, Shmot 14:5.
6. Shmot 14:1–3.
7. Rabbi Shimshon Raphael Hirsch, Shmot 14:5.

three-day journey agreement is in place. Traumatized, however, by the plague of the firstborn, he determines not to pursue the Israelites *even if they fail to return as expected.* As the text indicates, however, God hardens the heart of the Egyptian king to ensure that he will reconsider and give chase when the Israelites show no sign of returning to Egypt.[8] The Ramban goes on to argue, based once more upon textual evidence,[9] that the Egyptians would never have entered the Reed Sea after its parting had it not been for the fact that God hardens Pharaoh's heart yet again.[10]

God will simply not allow Pharaoh and his army to escape their deserved punishment. (For a fuller discussion of the phenomenon of God's hardening of Pharaoh's heart see Va'eira 3.)

—— **B** ————————————————————————

"And Pharaoh drew near; and the children of Israel raised their eyes and behold! *Egypt was journeying after them*; and they were very frightened and the children of Israel cried out to God."[11]

The Sforno and the Malbim, among others, maintain that a careful reading of this and other surrounding sentences fully reveals the terrifying scene that confronts the Israelites on the banks of the Reed Sea.

First, says the Malbim, "Pharaoh drew near."

Upon seeing the Egyptian king approaching with his army, the Israelites remain steadfast in the faith that God will yet redeem them.

Then, however, "the Israelites raise their eyes" and see *"Egypt journeying after them* [i.e., after the Egyptian forces]."

The Israelites observe, following Pharaoh's army, a vast, enraged horde – the entire Egyptian populace prepared to wreak vengeance upon their former slaves. "And they were very frightened..." This latter scene frightens the Israelites beyond measure and destroys their faith.

Interestingly, while the Malbim seems to accept this fear as understandable, the Sforno views it as further reflection of the ill preparedness of the Israelites for battle. Someone versed in the ways of warfare, claims the

8. Shmot 14:4, 8.
9. Ibid., 14:17.
10. Ramban, Shmot 14:4.
11. Shmot 14:10.

Sforno, would have known enough to be more afraid of Pharaoh's trained army than an unruly mob.[12]

— **C** —

"And Moshe said to the people: 'Do not fear! Stand fast and witness the redemption of God which He will perform for you today; for as you have seen Egypt today you shall never see them again! God will make war for you, and you shall remain silent.'"[13]

The Talmud describes a tumultuous scene as Moshe confronts the people:

> Four groups formed from within our forefathers at the banks of the sea. One group exclaimed, "Let us fall into the sea." The second group argued, "We must return to Egypt." The third group maintained, "We should engage them in battle." The fourth group contended, "Let us pray for their downfall."
>
> To those who exclaimed, "Let us fall into the sea," Moshe responded: "*Stand fast and witness the redemption of God.*" To those who argued, "We must return to Egypt," Moshe responded, "*For as you have seen Egypt today you shall never see them again!*" To those who maintained, "We should engage them in battle," Moshe responded, "*God will fight for you.*" Finally, to those who contended, "Let us pray for their downfall," Moshe countered, "*And you shall be silent.*"[14]

At this moment of unimaginable crisis, according to Midrashic thought, the Israelites respond with paralyzing internal division and strife.

What, however, gives rise to this picture in the rabbis' minds? There is no outright textual evidence that the nation is divided at this point.

Perhaps we can surmise that driving the rabbinic observations are not only hints from the text, but the testimony of history as well as the rabbis' own experiences with the Jewish community. Too often, we prove to be our own worst enemies, unable to unite in common idea and cause. The

---

12. Sforno, Shmot 14:7–8, 10; Malbim, Shmot 14:9–10.
13. Shmot 14:13–14.
14. Talmud Yerushalmi Ta'anit 2:5.

rabbis, therefore, use textual references from this dramatic moment to paint a picture that they consider to be, unfortunately, true to form.

— D ——————————————————

"[And Moshe said:] 'God will fight for you, and you shall be silent.' And God said to Moshe: 'Why do you cry out to me? Speak to the children of Israel and have them journey forth!'"[15]

The Talmud elaborates on the interchange between God and Moshe:

> At this point Moshe was engaging in lengthy prayer. God said to him, "My dear ones are about to drown in the sea and you are engaging in prayer?" "What then should I do?" asked Moshe. God responded, "Speak to the children of Israel and have them journey forth!"[16]

In this case, the rabbis are clearly building upon the *pshat*, a startling textual flow in which God implicitly chastises Moshe: *Moshe, "why do you cry out to Me?" There is a time and a place for everything. Do not counsel the people to stand silently and wait for My intervention. You can no longer rely on Me to save you without your own initiative. "Speak to the children of Israel and have them journey forth!" Tell the people to arm themselves with faith and move forward into the sea.*

Even Moshe must discover that the journey towards nationhood requires personal initiative, as well as reliance on God. The learning curve of independence encompasses not only the nation, but also its leader.

— E ——————————————————

"And the children of Israel went on dry land in the midst of the sea; and *the water was a wall for them, on their right and on their left.*"[17]

From this sentence, the rabbis in the Talmud paint a picture of the parting of the sea vastly different from the dramatic version portrayed in art forms ranging from classical paintings to modern cinema. The text indicates that the passage into the sea was not a broad highway but a narrow

---

15. Shmot 14:14–15.
16. Talmud Bavli Sota 37a.
17. Shmot 14:29.

pathway, just wide enough to create for each Israelite "a wall on the right and a wall on the left."[18]

The Torah Temima suggests that the miracle took this form to highlight its divine origin. Under these circumstances no one could claim that the sea simply happened to dry up.[19]

Perhaps this scene, as envisioned by the rabbis, underscores yet another point: *Pivotal life events are often experienced individually. Aloneness can be felt even in the midst of a multitude.*

Although surrounded by hundreds of thousands of others, each Israelite enters the sea alone. The courage required to move forward to the unknown is individual, the trepidation not alleviated by the presence of others. While the passage through the sea is a shared event, a step in the birth of a new people, it is also a personal birthing experience for each Israelite alone.

— **F** —

"And Israel saw the great hand that God inflicted upon Egypt, and the nation feared God, *and they believed in God and in Moshe His servant.*"[20]

A striking inclusion and a possible omission can be found in this passage.

1. *The inclusion:* "And they believed in God *and in Moshe His servant.*" Belief, not only in God but also in Moshe, is clearly a critical component in the events surrounding the birth of the Jewish nation.

On the eve of the revelation at Sinai, God says to Moshe, "And also in you will they believe forever."[21]

Centuries later, the Rambam will assert, as one of his Thirteen Principles of Faith: "I believe with complete faith that the prophecy of Moshe our teacher, peace upon him, was true and that he was the father of the prophets, both those who preceded him and those who followed him."[22]

There is, however, another dimension to "belief in Moshe." Moshe is not only a towering historical figure, not only the greatest prophet that we have ever known – he is Moshe Rabbeinu, Moshe our teacher, the progenitor

---

18. Talmud Bavli Yoma 4b.
19. Torah Temima, Shmot 15:29.
20. Shmot 14:31.
21. Shmot 19:9.
22. Rambam, Mishna Sanhedrin 10:1.

of rabbinic authority. Such authority is critical to halachic process, part of the glue that will unite and preserve our eternal nation.

2. *The possible omission*: the Torah emphasizes that the Israelites believed in "God and in Moshe His servant." *The text, notably, does not state that they believed in themselves.* This omission is, perhaps, a foreshadowing of this generation's eventual fate.

Self-doubt will lead to failure on the brink of entry into the land of Canaan. There, on the very border of the Promised Land, the Israelites' reaction to a pessimistic report offered by advance spies will reveal their inability to make the transition to freedom and conquest. This generation will, therefore, perish in the desert; only their children will inherit the Land.[23]

— **G** ——————————————————————————

At the banks of the Reed Sea, dramatic events forge the next stage in our nation's birth. Eventually, however, the drama and power of these events will fade. What will remain are the lessons that these events are meant to transmit. The Israelites' ability to carry those lessons forward will determine their ultimate success.

---

23. Bamidbar 13, 14.

3 Miriam's Song

Context

After recording the triumphant song offered by "Moshe and the children of Israel" on the banks of the Sea of Reeds, the Torah states: "And Miriam the Prophetess, the sister of Aharon, took the drum in her hand; and all the women went out after her with drums and with dances. And Miriam sang unto them: 'Sing to the Lord, for He is highly exalted; the horse and its rider He has thrown into the sea.'"[1]

Questions

Although Miriam has appeared in the text before, this marks the first time that she is mentioned by name. She must, therefore, be clearly identified.

Why, however, is she referred to specifically as "the prophetess, the sister of Aharon"? According to rabbinic tradition, Sara was also a prophetess;[2] yet, the text never identifies her as such. Also, why isn't Miriam described as the sister of Moshe as well as the sister of Aharon?

What is the nature of the song offered by Miriam and by the women on the banks of the Reed Sea? Is this a separate paean, different from the one chanted by "Moshe and the children of Israel"? If not, why does the Torah mention it?

If Miriam's song is unique, what is its message?

Approaches

—A—

Concerning the designation of Miriam as "the prophetess, *the sister of Aharon*," a number of explanations are offered by the commentaries.

---

1. Shmot 15:20–21.
2. Talmud Bavli Megilla 14a.

Rashi, quoting the Talmud, maintains that Miriam's prophetic ability was evidenced before Moshe was born, when she was only "Aharon's sister." At that time, she predicted, "My mother is destined to give birth to a son who will be the redeemer of Israel."[3]

Alternatively, continues Rashi, Miriam is identified as Aharon's sister because Aharon is destined, at a later time, to struggle on her behalf.[4] When Miriam is punished with leprosy for speaking ill of Moshe, Aharon pleads with Moshe to intercede for her welfare.[5]

The Rashbam, as is his wont, adopts the path of *pshat* and maintains that Miriam is referred to as the sister of Aharon simply because Aharon is the firstborn.[6]

The Ramban entertains the same approach as the Rashbam but prefers a different explanation: the text wants to ensure that all three siblings – Aharon, Miriam and Moshe – are mentioned in conjunction with the song at the Reed Sea. Miriam is therefore specifically referred to as the sister of Aharon, who would otherwise not be cited.[7]

Finally, Rabbi Shimshon Raphael Hirsch argues that Miriam occupied the same position among the women that Aharon occupied among the men. They both acted as Moshe's emissaries, carrying his messages to the people. Miriam is, therefore, referred to as the sister of her counterpart, Aharon.[8]

— **B** —

While the above commentators discuss why Miriam is referred to as Aharon's sister, they fail to explain why she is specifically identified as a "prophetess" in this context.

Rabbi Zalman Sorotzkin suggests that Miriam's prophetic vision centered on the redemption of the Israelites from Egypt. The Torah therefore refers to Miriam's prophetic ability only now, after that redemption is complete.[9]

---

3. Rashi, Shmot 15:20; Talmud Bavli Sota 12b–13a.
4. Rashi, Shmot 15:20; Mechilta, ibid.
5. Bamidbar 12:11.
6. Rashbam, Shmot 15:20.
7. Ramban, ibid.
8. Rabbi Shimshon Raphael Hirsch, ibid.
9. Oznaim LaTorah, ibid.

— **C** —

Perhaps the key to Miriam's identification as a prophetess lies in the nature and significance of her "song."

Does Miriam's song add a new, *prophetic* dimension to the events at the Sea of Reeds?

A review of the traditional sources would seem to indicate that the answer is no. Most scholars do not envision a substantial difference between the song of Moshe and the song of Miriam.

Some commentaries, for example, such as the Chizkuni, reflect an earlier Midrashic tradition[10] that Miriam led the women in a repetition of the entire text of Moshe's song after the men had finished.[11]

Other scholars, including the Ramban, maintain that Miriam and the women did not sing a separate song, at all. Miriam instructed the women to echo the words as they were chanted by Moshe and the men.[12]

— **D** —

A careful reading of the following hints in the text, however, reveals another possible approach.

1. Only one sentence is recorded in the Torah as the text of Miriam's song; it is a subtle variation on the first sentence of Moshe's song:

Moshe: "*I will sing to the Lord*, for He is highly exalted; the horse and its rider He has thrown into the sea."[13]

Miriam: "*Sing to the Lord*, for He is highly exalted; the horse and its rider He has thrown into the sea."[14]

2. As soon as Miriam concludes her song, the text states, *Vayasa Moshe et Yisrael mi'Yam Suf*, "And Moshe caused Israel to journey from the Sea of Reeds."[15]

As a rule, when the Torah speaks of the nation's journeys in the desert, the text simply states, *Vayisu B'nai Yisrael*, "And the children of Israel journeyed." Why does the Torah specifically state at this point that Moshe "caused Israel to journey"?

---

10. Midrash Mishlei 14.
11. Chizkuni, Shmot 15:21.
12. Ramban, Shmot 15:20.
13. Shmot 15:1.
14. Ibid., 15:20.
15. Ibid., 15:22.

— **E** —

Perhaps Miriam "the prophetess," the individual who, according to rabbinic tradition, was instrumental in convincing her father to move forward in the face of Pharaoh's decrees (see Shmot 2),[16] now plays a pivotal role in urging the Israelites to move forward from the site of their full redemption from Egypt?

Miriam's admonition could be imagined as follows: "*Sing to the Lord, for He is highly exalted; the horse and its rider He has thrown into the sea.*"[17] *Moshe, you and the men sing eloquently of future dreams:*

> I will sing to the Lord, for He is highly exalted…;[18] Peoples heard and they were agitated, terror gripped the dwellers of Philistia. Then the chieftains of Edom were astounded, trembling gripped the powers of Moav, all the inhabitants of Canaan melted away. May fear and terror fall upon them…until Your people passes through, Lord, until this people that You have acquired passes through. Bring them and plant them on the Mount of Your Sanctuary, the foundation of Your holy place that You, Lord, have made – the holy place, Lord, that Your hands established. The Lord shall reign for all eternity![19]

These dreams will only be realized, however, if we stop singing and move on. After all, all that has happened so far is, "the horse and its rider He has thrown into the sea."

Have we achieved our heritage? Has God given us the Torah? Have we entered our land? All of these challenges yet lie before us; and they will only be met if we move forward from the banks of this Sea.

So sing, yes, but with open eyes: "the horse and its rider He has thrown into the sea." Then, let the song end and let us move on.

In response to Miriam's song, the text relates: "And Moshe caused Israel to journey from the Sea of Reeds."[20] Understanding and acknowledging his sister's message, Moshe forces a reluctant nation to end their celebration and move forward from the sea.

---

16. Talmud Bavli Sota 12a.
17. Shmot 15:21.
18. Ibid., 15:1.
19. Ibid., 15:14–18.
20. Ibid., 15:22.

Had it not been for Miriam and her song, perhaps we would still be dancing and singing at the banks of the Sea of Reeds.

Points to Ponder

As the initial phases of our nation's journey continue to unfold, eternal lessons are transmitted with each step.

The ability to move on, to celebrate but not be paralyzed by achievement, will prove to be a critical skill, essential to our success across the ages.

For example, in our time, the creation of the State of Israel, after centuries of diaspora existence and in the shadow of the Holocaust, was nothing less than a monumental, miraculous achievement. Acknowledgement and celebration are certainly warranted. Sometimes, however, you can celebrate too long…

A number of years ago, however, during a discussion on Israel-diaspora relations, an official of the Israeli government complained to me: "Too many American Jews think that we are still dancing the hora and draining the swamps. They are blind to the changes taking place within the Zionist enterprise and to the complex internal and external challenges that we currently face."

No matter how great the achievement, celebration must invariably yield to challenge. If we "celebrate" too long, if we remain rooted in the glow of past accomplishments, we endanger those very accomplishments.

Only by moving forward, only by discerning and meeting new challenges that develop by the day, can we preserve the past even as we secure the future.

4 A Culinary Crucible?

Context

Responding to the complaints of the Israelites concerning lack of food, God introduces the miraculous fare that will sustain the nation during their travels: "Behold! I will rain down for you food from heaven; and the people will go out and collect each day's portion on its day, *that I may test them – will they follow My teaching or not?*"[1]

This refrain is repeated twice in the book of Devarim as Moshe, recalling the people's journey in the wilderness, states:

> And you shall remember the entire road upon which the Lord your God led you these forty years in the wilderness, *in order to afflict you, to test you*, to know what is in your heart – will you obey His commandments or not? And He afflicted you and let you hunger and He fed you the manna…in order to make you know that not by bread alone does man live, rather by everything that emanates from the mouth of God does man live…. [2] [The God] Who fed you manna in the wilderness…*in order to afflict you and in order to test you*, to do good for you in the end.[3]

Questions

Why does God associate the miracle of the manna with testing and affliction?

As the Abravanel asks, "What was the nature of the test administered by God through the bestowal of daily sustenance? …This was a kindness, not a test!"[4]

---

1. Shmot 16:4.
2. Devarim 8:2–3.
3. Ibid., 8:16.
4. Abravanel, Shmot 16:4.

Approaches

—**A**—

Rashi, apparently unable to discern a test within the manna itself, contends that the trial actually emerges from an ancillary source. God grants miraculous sustenance to the Israelites and simultaneously tests them by determining "whether they will observe the commandments associated [with that sustenance]."[5]

These commandments included the instruction to collect each day only the amount of manna necessary for that day, the prohibition of collection on the Shabbat, and the directive to collect a double portion on Friday in order to properly prepare for Shabbat.

—**B**—

Many other scholars, however, are unwilling to accept what they consider to be a somewhat facile solution to the mysterious "test" of the manna. The Ramban, for example, emphatically declares, "But this [Rashi's explanation] is not correct…. [The manna itself] was a trial to them."[6]

While the text supports the position that the manna itself was a trial, the question remains: exactly what was the test embodied in this miraculous food?

—**C**—

The scholars offer, with subtle variations, three global approaches. Each of these approaches carries overarching lessons that move well beyond the specific phenomenon of the manna.

1. God tested and developed the faith of the Israelites by depriving them of the usual forms of sustenance and survival.

The Ramban, among others, champions this position both in Parshat Beshalach and in the book of Devarim:

---

5. Rashi, ibid.
6. Ramban, ibid.

[God] could easily have led them through the surrounding cities. He led them, instead, through a wilderness of snakes, fiery serpents and scorpions, where the only bread fell from the heaven each day.[7]

And:

This was a serious trial for them: to have no other option, to enter a great wilderness…to have no sustenance other than the manna which fell on a daily basis and which melted when the sun waxed hot…. Nevertheless, they did all this in obedience to God's command…. From this [God] would know that they would obey His commandments forever."[8]

With this approach, the Ramban remains true to his general position concerning divine tests: *God tests man to actualize man's inherent potential.*[9] (See *Bereishit*: Vayeira 4, *Context.*)

Through the trial of the manna, by severely rationing and circumscribing the sustenance of the Israelites, God actualizes their internal potential for faith. This faith, once realized, will sustain them not only in the wilderness but through their turbulent journey across the face of history.

2. By providing the Israelites with the manna, God confronts the fledgling nation with the plethora of challenges that emerge with a life of ease. Far from a test of deprivation, the manna actually constitutes a *nissayon ha'osher*, a trial of wealth and plenty.

The Ohr Hachaim notes, for example, that the manna provides the Israelites with the unfamiliar phenomenon of leisure time. God, therefore, asks: "Will they walk in My ways?" *Will they use their suddenly available time productively in the pursuit of Torah study and observance?*[10]

The Sforno, for his part, suggests that God wants to determine whether the Israelites will follow His dictates when "they are sustained without any pain."[11] Man often turns to God in times of need but ignores Him in times of comfort. Through the manna, God challenges the Israelites: *Will you turn to Me when your sustenance is attained with ease?*

---

7. Ibid.
8. Ramban, Devarim 8:2.
9. Ramban, Bereishit 22:1.
10. Ohr Hachaim, Shmot 16:4.
11. Sforno, ibid.

3. As the Israelites journey towards national independence, the manna sensitizes them to their dependence upon God.

This message, arguably the most basic "test" incorporated in the miracle of the manna, is reflected in the following Talmudic conversation:

> The students of Rabbi Shimon bar Yochai asked: "Why did the manna not descend for Israel once annually?"
>
> [Rabbi Shimon bar Yochai] answered: "[In order that each Israelite] would worry – perhaps no manna will descend tomorrow…. Thus they all turned their hearts to their Father in Heaven."[12]

Centuries later, the Rashbam, mirroring the position of numerous other commentaries, elaborates upon the statement of Rabbi Shimon bar Yochai: "Since each and every day their eyes will turn to Me for their sustenance, they will come to believe in Me and walk in the ways of My Torah."[13]

The miracle of the manna thus emerges, with the first footfalls of our history, as a formative crucible conveying a lesson that, to this day, we forget at our own peril: *Whether we are wandering in the wilderness or living in a highly urbanized society, we are dependent upon God for our sustenance each and every day.*

— **D** —————————————————————————

How far, however, should our dependence upon God extend? Where does faith in Divine Providence end and the need for our enterprise begin?

In the parameters of the manna miracle, the rabbis perceive fascinating possible solutions to this perplexing, age-old quandary. So seminal is the wilderness experience of the Israelites in their eyes, it forms the paradigm from which we can derive the ongoing balance between faith and human endeavor.

The conclusions they reach, however, could scarcely be more disparate.

Three divergent viewpoints, each based upon a different interpretation of the miracle of the manna, are quoted in the Mechilta.

---

12. Talmud Bavli Yoma 76a.
13. Rashbam, Shmot 16:4.

1. Rabbi Eliezer Hamoda'i maintains that the phrase "each day's portion on its day," stated in connection with the manna, clearly indicates that an individual should only be concerned about his present sustenance. As long as today is provided for, he should have faith in God's Providence for the future. Therefore, proclaims Rabbi Eliezer, "Any individual who has provisions for today but questions, 'What will I eat tomorrow?' is among those who lack faith."

2. In stark contrast, Rabbi Yehoshua, basing his position upon the same phrase used by Rabbi Eliezer Hamoda'i, maintains that total reliance upon God's Providence is unacceptable even for future needs. The directive "each day's portion on its day," he argues, includes the obligation to prepare in advance by collecting enough manna on Friday for both Friday and Shabbat. "An individual," declares Rabbi Yehoshua, "who learns two *halachot* (Jewish laws) in the morning and evening and works all day is considered to have observed the Torah in its entirety." The study of Torah, in Rabbi Yehoshua's worldview, can and should be combined with the goal of personal self-sufficiency.

3. Finally, the most restrictive position is postulated by Rabbi Shimon bar Yochai: "The Torah was only given to the eaters of manna – [to an individual who] sits and learns and does not know from where he will obtain food and drink, from where he will obtain clothing and cover himself." Total dedication to Torah study accompanied by a complete faith in God's Providence is the life philosophy recommended by Rabbi Shimon[14] – a position that acquires greater poignancy in light of his own reputation for asceticism and mystical knowledge.

To the rabbinic mind, the manna is clearly much more than a miracle in the wilderness. This heavenly food represents the first sustaining interaction between God and His developing chosen people. How that interaction unfolds in those early years, they claim, creates the model for the interface between Divine Providence and human effort across the ages. The conclusions they reach continue to be debated to this very day.

Points to Ponder

The debate between Rabbi Eliezer Hamoda'i, Rabbi Yehoshua and Rabbi Shimon bar Yochai underscores that widely divergent viewpoints on

---

14. Mechilta, ibid.

critical life issues can exist side-by-side within the normative flow of Jewish thought.

In the centuries that follow, these positions generate continued controversy as the codifiers of Jewish law struggle to define the appropriate balance between Torah study and financial pursuits.

A small sampling of their observations serves to underscore the complexity of the issue. The Rambam, for example, maintains that any individual who decides to separate himself from earthly pursuits in order to "serve, worship and seek God" is considered to have reached the status of "the Holiest of Holies." This individual will receive, through Divine Providence, "provisions sufficient for his needs."[15]

Yet the Rambam elsewhere asserts that an individual who supports himself through charity in order to study Torah "desecrates God's name, demeans the Torah, extinguishes the light of Jewish thought, brings evil to himself and is excluded from the world to come, for one is forbidden to draw material benefit from Torah study in this world."[16]

This latter assertion brings protest from numerous sources including Rabbi Yosef Caro (the editor of the *Shulchan Aruch*), who writes a lengthy rejoinder in his commentary on the Rambam, the *Kesef Mishneh*.[17]

In his gloss upon the *Shulchan Aruch*, the Ashkenazic authority Rabbi Moshe Isserles comments in unusually expansive fashion on the issue. His words clearly reflect the conflicting issues which he attempts to resolve:

> An individual should make his Torah study primary and his livelihood secondary.... He should work as much as necessary each day to provide for his basic needs...and the remainder of the day and night should be occupied with the study of Torah.
>
> It is considered a great attribute for a person to sustain himself through the work of his hands...and anyone who decides to occupy himself in Torah study, not to work and to sustain himself through charitable funds desecrates God's name and demeans the Torah. Any Torah study which is not accompanied by work leads to sin and is certain to result in theft from the community.

---

15. Rambam, *Mishneh Torah*, Hilchot Shmita V'Yovel 13:13.
16. Ibid., Hilchot Talmud Torah 3:10.
17. Kesef Mishneh, Hilchot Talmud Torah 3:10.

Some authorities, however, permit a sage and his students to receive sustenance from donors in order to strengthen the hands of those who study Torah…. Not every individual is capable of immersing himself in Torah study and supporting himself [and therefore it is permissible] to receive a regular stipend.[18]

In our day, these already difficult issues acquire overlays of even greater complexity. Throughout the Jewish world, the phenomenon of increasing numbers of young Orthodox men opting to dedicate their lives solely to the study of Torah is hotly debated. Questions abound concerning the sustainability and even the desirability of this trend on a wholesale level. We have already noted some of the specific issues surrounding this phenomenon (see *Bereishit*: Toldot 3, *Points to Ponder*).

What should be clear, however, from the rabbinic approaches to the miracle of the manna, is that discussion on the interface between Divine Providence and man's efforts is not only appropriate, but necessary. The issues are not black and white. Today, the intrinsically laudable trend of increased Torah study must be assessed against the backdrop of limited communal resources, family dynamics, the benefits of self-sufficiency, relationships between different segments of the Jewish community, and more.

Too often, when it comes to this and similar issues, positions are staked out without periodic reassessment and without any credence given to the possibility of valid opposing viewpoints. The openness shown by the rabbis as they debate the lessons of the manna would serve us well today.

---

18. Shulchan Aruch, Yoreh Deah, Hagaot HaRema 246:21.

Yitro

CHAPTER 18:1–20:23

יתרו

פרק יח:א-כ:כג

Parsha Summary

God's law revealed; a nation born...

 Upon hearing of the divinely orchestrated Exodus from Egypt, Yitro, Moshe's father-in-law, gathers Moshe's wife (Tzippora) and children (Gershon and Eliezer) and journeys with them to the Israelite encampment near Mount Sinai. Moshe greets his father-in-law warmly and regales him with the details of God's miraculous intervention on behalf of the Israelites. Yitro rejoices and joins Moshe in a celebratory meal together with Aharon and the elders.

 When Yitro witnesses the overwhelming burdens of leadership that have been thrust upon Moshe, he encourages his son-in-law to delegate elements of governance to others, in an ordered, hierarchical fashion. Moshe agrees and Yitro (apparently) returns to his home in Midian.

 On the first day of the third month after the Exodus, the Israelites arrive at the Wilderness of Sinai and encamp at the foot of Mount Sinai. Moshe ascends the mountain where God speaks to him concerning the selection of the Israelites as God's chosen people. Moshe descends and shares God's message with the nation, whereupon they exclaim: "All that the Lord has spoken, we will do!"

 God delivers a series of instructions to Moshe preparatory to Revelation, including the commandment of hagbala *(to set a boundary around the mountain, preventing the Israelites from ascending during the onset of Revelation).*

 With thunder, lightning and the sounding of the shofar, the Revelation at Sinai begins, as God conveys the Ten Declarations[1] to the Israelites. Frightened by the powerful scene unfolding before them, the nation retreats and

---

1. Although these principles are popularly known as the "Ten Commandments," the Torah does not refer to them as *mitzvot* (commandments), but as *devarim* (declarations or utterances). Shmot 20:1.

asks Moshe to serve as God's representative in the giving of the law. Moshe reassures the people that God only means to inspire in them an appropriate sense of awe.

The parsha closes as God transmits additional edicts to Moshe.

1 The Mystery of Moshe's Father-in-Law

Context

Upon hearing of the Israelites' successful Exodus from Egypt, Moshe's father-in-law, Yitro, gathers Moshe's wife and children and journeys to the Israelite encampment near Mount Sinai. After a mutually respectful reunion with his son-in-law and a celebratory meal including Aharon and the elders, Yitro counsels Moshe concerning the governance of the people. Moshe accepts his father-in-law's suggestions and the Torah then records: "And Moshe released his father-in-law and he [Yitro] returned to his land [Midian]."[1]

Yitro, thus, apparently departs before *Matan Torah* (the Revelation at Sinai) even begins.

Many chapters later in the text, however, Yitro suddenly reappears in the Israelite camp. In the book of Bamidbar (Parshat Beha'alotcha), after Revelation, as the nation begins its momentous journey away from Mount Sinai, the Torah abruptly interrupts the narrative to record the following conversation between Moshe and his father-in-law:

Moshe: "We are journeying to the place in which God has said 'I will give it to you.' Go with us and we will treat you well, for the Lord has spoken of good for Israel."

Yitro: "I will not go, for only to my land and to my birthplace shall I go."

Moshe: "Please do not leave us, for you know our encampments in the wilderness and you shall be as eyes for us. And it shall be if you come with us, and the good that God will bestow upon us, we will bestow upon you."[2]

There, the conversation ends. Yitro does not openly appear again in the Torah text.

---

1. Shmot 18:1–27.
2. Bamidbar 10:29–32.

Questions

Did Yitro end his first visit to the Israelites by returning to Midian before Revelation? If so, why does the text inexplicably record his presence, chapters later, as the Israelites prepare to depart from Sinai? If he never left in the first place, why does the Torah state in Parshat Yitro, "And Moshe released his father-in-law and he returned to his land"?

What was the final outcome of the conversation between Moshe and Yitro in the book of Bamidbar? The Torah records no conclusion. Does Yitro ultimately return to Midian or does he join his son-in-law's people in their historic journey from Sinai after Revelation?

On an even more basic level, why does the Torah bother to record the visit(s) of Yitro to the Israelite encampment at all, particularly as bookends to Revelation, the formative event of Jewish history? Of what lasting importance is Yitro's ultimate decision? Why should we care whether or not one additional individual joins the Israelites in their journey? And if Yitro's fate is so important, why isn't the text clear concerning his final decision?

Approaches

—**A**—————————————————————————

Faced with the puzzling textual information concerning Yitro's appearance(s) at Sinai, the early scholars take a step back and raise a related, yet even more basic, issue: Why did Yitro journey to the Israelite encampment in the first place?

Among the suggestions they offer are two possibilities recorded in the Talmud, based on the verse "And Yitro, the priest of Midian, the father-in-law of Moshe, *heard all that God had done for Moshe and Israel his nation…*"[3]

What did Yitro hear? "Rabbi Yehoshua maintains that he heard the news of the battle with Amalek…. Rabbi Eliezer Hamoda'i argues that he heard the news of Revelation."[4]

The Talmud goes on to explain that the debate between Rabbi Yehoshua and Rabbi Eliezer concerning Yitro's motivations hinges upon a fundamental disagreement over the timing of his visit to the Israelite encamp-

———————————

3. Shmot 18:1.
4. Talmud Bavli Zevachim 116a.

ment. Rabbi Yehoshua, in consonance with the flow of the text before us, maintains that Moshe's father-in-law arrives prior to Revelation. Rabbi Eliezer, on the other hand, evidence of the text notwithstanding, claims that Yitro does not arrive until after the Torah is given. Only upon hearing of that momentous event, argues Rabbi Eliezer, does Yitro journey to his son-in-law's people.[5]

Central to Rabbi Eliezer's position is a well-known yet often misunderstood rule of traditional Torah study: *Ein mukdam u'me'uchar ba'Torah* – the text does not necessarily follow chronological order. Thus, even though the Torah records Yitro's appearance as occurring before *Matan Torah*, he does not actually arrive until after Revelation is complete.

This rule is invoked sparingly by the scholars only when they feel that the events in the text cannot be understood in the sequence in which they unfold. *Everyone agrees that, on the whole, the Torah does follow chronological order in its description of events.*

— **B** —

Centuries later, in their struggle to explain Yitro's sudden reappearance in the book of Bamidbar, the commentaries base their approaches upon the dispute between Rabbi Yehoshua and Rabbi Eliezer.

The Ibn Ezra, for example, maintains that Rabbi Eliezer is correct: Yitro does not arrive until after Revelation. The record of Yitro's visit prior to Revelation is temporally out of place. Furthermore, although the Torah records two conversations concerning Yitro's future plans (one before Revelation and one after), *only one conversation actually takes place.* The Torah simply refers to that conversation twice.

After listing a series of proofs to bolster his position, the Ibn Ezra addresses the obvious question: if Yitro arrives only after Revelation, why does the Torah chronicle his visit in detail in Parshat Yitro before *Matan Torah* even begins? The Ibn Ezra postulates that the Torah wants to create a distinction between Yitro's visit and the attack of the nation of Amalek, recorded at the end of the previous parsha, Beshalach. Yitro's commendable behavior towards the Israelites is to be seen in stark contrast to the unprovoked hostility of the Amalekites.[6]

---

5. Ibid.
6. Ibn Ezra, Shmot 18:1.

In this way, at the dawn of Jewish history, the Torah demonstrates that the approach of normative Judaism to the non-Jewish world is far from monolithic. While those, like Amalek, who perpetuate evil are to be resisted in implacable fashion, "Righteous Gentiles" such as Yitro are to be treated with respect and honor.

Centuries later, this distinction between Yitro and Amalek is again clearly drawn as the fate of their progeny is determined. When Shaul, the first king of Israel, prepares to wage war against the Amalekites, he warns the descendents of Yitro to evacuate Amalekite territory and escape the looming conflagration.[7]

— **C** —

After lengthy discussion, the Ramban ultimately disagrees with the two basic arguments of the Ibn Ezra and arrives at a conclusion that preserves the flow of the Torah text from Parshat Yitro to Parshat Beha'alotcha.

Yitro, he argues, arrives at the wilderness of Sinai before Revelation, as indicated in the text and as maintained by Rabbi Yehoshua. The two conversations between Moshe and Yitro recorded in the text, he continues, both occur. Yitro discusses his plans with Moshe before Revelation, returns to Midian, subsequently rejoins Moshe at Sinai after Revelation and the second conversation takes place.[8]

— **D** —

Finally, the Abravanel presents a third option, agreeing with the Ramban on one point and with the Ibn Ezra on the other. Like the Ramban, the Abravanel maintains that Yitro arrives before Revelation. He claims, however, that Moshe's father-in-law then remains with the Israelites for two years, sharing in the experience of *Matan Torah*. Only one conversation takes place between Moshe and Yitro concerning Yitro's future plans. Agreeing with the Ibn Ezra, the Abravanel believes that this dialogue occurs after Revelation but is also briefly referenced in Parshat Yitro, two years before it occurs.[9]

---

7. Shmuel I 15:6.
8. Ramban, Shmot 18:1.
9. Abravanel, ibid.

— **E** —————————————————————————————

If the authorities disagree concerning Yitro's arrival at Sinai, even greater debate surrounds the mystery of his ultimate fate.

Some scholars maintain that Moshe's father-in-law returns to his homeland for practical reasons. The Sforno, for example, suggests that Yitro believed that he could not, at his advanced age, tolerate the environment of a new land. Moshe was successful, however, in convincing his father-in-law's descendents to join the Israelites' historic journey.[10]

The Sifrei quotes Yitro as offering arguments which in the centuries to follow will often be raised by those choosing to live in the diaspora: *I will not join you because of my familial obligations and because of my material success outside the land.*[11]

— **F** —————————————————————————————

Other sages, while agreeing that Yitro returns to Midian, attribute higher motives to his decision.

An early source, none other than Rabbi Eliezer Hamoda'i, the Tannaitic scholar who weighed in concerning Yitro's arrival (see above), maintains that Moshe's father-in-law offers the following rationale: *What good can I possibly do, Moshe, if I join you on this journey? A candle only makes a difference where it is dark. You, Moshe, are like the sun while Aharon is like the moon. In the face of your illumination, I, a mere candle, will have no effect at all. I will therefore return home, to Midian, where I will convert the members of my family, bringing them under the cover of the wings of the Almighty.*[12]

— **G** —————————————————————————————

Virtually alone among classical commentaries, the Ramban demurs and maintains that *Yitro actually decides to join the Israelites upon their departure from Sinai.* As indicated above, the Ramban adheres to the *pshat* of the text in maintaining that Yitro actually visited Sinai on two occasions, once before and once after Revelation. After the first of these visits Moshe's father-in-law returned to Midian. After the second visit, however, Moshe

———————————

10. Sforno, Bamidbar 10:30.
11. Sifrei, ibid.
12. Mechilta, Shmot 18:27.

successfully convinces Yitro to remain and to throw his lot in with the fledgling Jewish nation.[13]

— **H** —

Regardless of the positions we adopt concerning Yitro's visits, motives and final decision, the fundamental questions remain: Why does the Torah bother to record these events at all, particularly as bookends to *Matan Torah*, the formative event of Jewish history? Of what significance is the possible decision of one more individual to join the Israelites' journey? And, if Yitro's fate is so important, why isn't the Torah clear concerning his final decision?

Answers to these questions may well lie in two basic truths concerning Revelation which will be discussed in greater depth elsewhere (see Ki Tissa 5, *Approaches* A2).

1. Revelation is not a one-time event but an ongoing phenomenon. The Torah is received anew in each generation through study, observance and halachic application.

2. Revelation unfolds not only in communal but in individual, personal terms. At the foot of Mount Sinai, each individual struggled with his own commitment to God's newly given law. Similarly, in each generation, as the Jewish nation renews its commitment to Torah, every individual struggles to determine his or her relationship with that law.

Suddenly, the Torah's intent becomes clear.

The text chooses Yitro, the one individual present at Sinai whose relationship to Revelation most clearly mirrors our own across the ages – an "outsider" who did not personally witness the miracles of the Exodus, the parting of the Reed Sea, the defeat of Amalek; a "latecomer" whose information concerning God's Revelation is (at least according to most authorities) heard rather than seen.

The text then brackets the narrative of national Revelation with the account of Yitro's individual, internal struggle as he decides whether to accept or to reject the laws given at Sinai, to affiliate with the Israelites as they begin their journey or to return to the known comforts of home.

Through this focus on Yitro, the Torah foreshadows the personal struggle of each Jew in every generation.

---

13. Ramban, Shmot 18:1.

Distant from Sinai, we, too, must decide whether or not to heed Matan Torah's *eternal call; we must determine to what extent we will truly be part of our people's ongoing journey from Revelation to the end of days.*

Yitro's choice remains open in the text to indicate that for each of us, regardless of our background, our place in our people's saga is not a foregone conclusion. There are no assurances, no inherited certainties. Like Yitro, we face overwhelming choices as we map out our spiritual paths. Concerning our place in the journey of our people, the jury is out until we decide; and the process of deciding courses through our entire lives.

Points to Ponder

If the story of Moshe's father-in-law reflects the universal struggle of all Jews for philosophical self-definition, it also validates the spiritual journey of one specific subset within our community: converts to Judaism.

Great misunderstanding abounds concerning the attitude of Judaism towards conversion. The traditional Jewish community's apparent reluctance to accept potential converts is often interpreted as negativity towards conversion and converts themselves. Nothing could be further from the truth. Our approach towards potential converts actually mirrors our fundamental belief in the inherent potential value of all human beings, Jew and non-Jew alike (see *Bereishit*: Noach 4). *We hesitate to convert others to Judaism simply because we believe that those outside of our faith tradition are under no obligation to be like us.* We do not maintain that an individual must worship as we do, nor do we contend that only our path will afford "redemption."

We therefore work mightily to ascertain that an individual wishing to convert:

1. Fully understands why he is doing so

2. Recognizes that, from our perspective, he is not required to convert

3. Spends time in serious study and comes to realize exactly what his decision to convert will entail

In short, we insist that a potential convert reflect knowledge and commitment.

If over time and through a serious course of study, an individual demonstrates a true desire to convert and a commitment to Jewish law and practice, we are obligated to accept him fully.

Numerous sources within our tradition reflect the high regard in which righteous converts are held.

For example:

1. A specific mitzva is found in the Torah instructing us to "love the convert."[14] This commandment exists over and above the general edict "Love for your friend as for yourself,"[15] which also applies to converts.[16]

2. God Himself is described in the Torah as One Who "loves the convert, providing him with bread and garment."[17]

3. Conversion features prominently at pivotal moments in our nation's history through the contributions of important figures such as Yitro and Ruth.

4. We beseech God in our daily prayers to judge us favorably in the merit of our nation's righteous individuals, including the *geirei tzedek* (righteous converts).[18]

5. Most significantly, as noted before (see *Bereishit*: Vayeishev 4, *Approaches* B), the laws of conversion themselves are derived by the steps taken by the Israelites and those who stand with them at Sinai, before and during Revelation.[19] We are, in a real sense, a nation of converts, our Jewish identity determined by our ancestors' acceptance of Torah law at Sinai or thereafter.

Does Yitro eventually convert to Judaism? The answer remains unclear, as well it should. After all, conversion is a difficult process and not all can or should see it through.

If Yitro did convert, however, we can be certain that he was welcomed with open arms by Moshe and the Israelites.

---

14. Devarim 10:19.
15. Vayikra 19:18.
16. Rambam, *Mishneh Torah*, Hilchot Deiot 6:4.
17. Devarim 10:18.
18. Daily *siddur*.
19. The Jews at Sinai underwent circumcision, immersed themselves in pure waters in preparation, and then accepted the "yoke of the mitzvot." Talmud Bavli Kritot 9a.

2 A Healthy Distance

Context

The physical posture of the Israelites during the Revelation at Sinai is clearly delineated in advance when, preparatory to *Matan Torah*, God instructs Moshe: "Set a boundary for the people roundabout saying, 'Beware of ascending the mountain or touching its edge; whoever touches the mountain shall certainly die…'"[1]

This commandment of *hagbala* (setting a boundary), however, will not be divinely enforced. Instead, God commands the Israelites to execute anyone who crosses the mandated perimeter.[2]

Questions

Even the most familiar scenes of our history warrant critical assessment.

Why is the moment of closest contact between man and God marked by divinely mandated distance, on pain of death? Why must the Israelites remain at the foot of Mount Sinai during Revelation?

Furthermore, in a setting marked by monumental supernatural miracles, why does God leave the enforcement of the boundary around Mount Sinai to man? God can certainly protect the perimeter surrounding the mountain through any number of divinely ordained means.

What are the lessons to be learned from this God-orchestrated scene at Sinai?

Approaches

— **A** —

A fascinating rationale for the phenomenon of *hagbala* is offered by Rabbi

---

1. Shmot 19:12.
2. Ibid., 19:13.

Shimshon Raphael Hirsch. The physical setting at Sinai, says Hirsch, is designed to prove that the word of God came "to the people" rather than "out of the people." By insisting that the Israelites remain at the foot of Sinai to receive divine law, God clearly demonstrates for all to see that the people themselves are not the authors of that law.

The foundations of Jewish law are objective, eternal and not subject to changes wrought by time and circumstance. The Torah is not the product of a nation contemporary with the time of Revelation, but a divinely ordained document speaking to all times and places.[3] (For a fuller discussion of the tension between contextual and eternal aspects of the Torah, see Mishpatim 1, *Context*.)

— B —

Moving beyond Hirsch's suggestion, the decree of *hagbala* also reflects a fundamental dialectic lying at the core of man's connection to God. At the moment of Revelation, as God launches His eternal relationship with His chosen people, He uses the scene at Sinai to define the very parameters of that relationship.

The God-man relationship will be forged out of a tension between distance and familiarity.

On the one hand, God is certainly remote, existing in a realm beyond our comprehension and often acting in ways we simply do not understand. On the other hand, as the psalmist maintains: "God is near to all who call Him, to all who call Him in earnest."[4] We are meant to see God as accessible, interested and involved in our daily lives, near enough to be "found" if we only seek Him out.

This balance between distance and familiarity in our relationship to God is reflected in many ways within our tradition. Three of them follow.

1. Each day, at climactic moments of our prayer service, we recite the Kedusha, a proclamation of God's holiness. Central to this proclamation is the vision of the prophet Yeshayahu, who witnesses the heavenly hosts exclaiming, "Holy, holy, holy, is the Lord of Hosts; the whole world is filled with His glory."[5]

---

3. Rabbi Shimshon Raphael Hirsch, Shmot 19:12.
4. Tehillim 145:18.
5. Yeshayahu 6:3.

To be holy within Jewish thought means to be separate, removed. Three times, in the prophet's vision, the heavenly beings declare God's separateness. In Jewish law, the repetition of an event or phenomenon three times creates a reality. God's absolute remoteness is thus mirrored in the threefold proclamation of the angels.

In the very next breath, however, these very same celestial beings declare, "The whole world is filled with His glory." God, the angels say, is apparent and easily reached in every aspect of our physical surroundings. We need only look around us to find Him.

The Kedusha thus reflects the dichotomy created by a God who is beyond our ken and who, at the same time, fills the world with His splendor.

2. Two seemingly conflicting elements are essential to the formation of a personal relationship with God: *yira* and *ahava* (fear and love): "And now, Israel, what does the Lord your God ask of you but to fear the Lord your God, to walk in all His paths, and to love Him, and to serve the Lord your God with all your heart and with all your soul."[6]

You can only love and fear the same being when you embrace the complexity inherent in the bond between you.

This truth is perhaps best demonstrated by focusing on the human associations which, in their own small way, most closely mirror our relationship with God. Consider, for example, the contradictory currents that course through a healthy parent-child relationship or a strong teacher-student bond. These relationships are not one-dimensional. A parent who tries to become his child's friend (a phenomenon which is unfortunately much too common in our own day) will simply not be an effective parent. A rabbi or teacher who forgoes the respect and authority due his position loses some of his ability to successfully educate. Yet, while maintaining the space demanded by the relationship, both the parent and the teacher must still remain – each to different degrees – accessible, warm and caring.

The complexity of the parent-child bond is, in fact, codified in halacha through two distinct sets of laws that are designed to mold and govern the attitude of a child to his parent.

---

6. Devarim 10:12.

The laws of *kavod* (honor) speak to the personal care that must be shown to parents during times of need, such as infirmity and old age.[7]

The laws of *yira* outline the respect that must be shown to parents at all times. Included are the prohibitions of calling a parent by his first name, sitting in a parent's seat, contradicting a parent in public, etc.[8]

Through the laws of *kavod* and *yira*, the halacha reflects the balance meant to be struck between the warmth a child should feel towards his parent and the awe in which that parent must be held.

In a different realm but somewhat parallel fashion, our relationship with God must be forged out of a similar tension.

God, therefore, mandates distance at the moment of His closest contact with man, striking the balance upon which their eternal shared relationship will be built.

3. The Kohanim (priests) are fixtures within the Temple service, representing the nation through the performance of sanctified rites and rituals before God. Even the Kohen Gadol (High Priest), however, is prohibited from entering the *Kodesh Kadashim* (Holy of Holies), the centerpiece of the Temple, except on the most sacred day of the year, Yom Kippur.[9]

Why shouldn't the highest Temple functionary be allowed free access to every part of the Temple at all times? Why limit his entry to the holiest site in the world?

Once again, the answer would seem to lie in the balance at the core of our relationship with God. Even the Kohen Gadol might become too familiar in his attitude towards the Holy of Holies and fail to treat this site with the reverence it so richly deserves. By severely limiting the High Priest's entry into the *Kodesh Kadashim*, the Torah ensures that he, and by definition the entire nation, will never lose sight of the Temple's sanctity.

Through these sources and others, our tradition reminds us that we must continually struggle to maintain the balance – rooted at Sinai – between distance and familiarity, so critical to our relationship with God.

If we lose the sense of awe meant to be present in our approach to the divine, our worship becomes pedestrian, rote and uninspired. If, on the

7. Talmud Bavli Kiddushin 31b.
8. Ibid.
9. Vayikra 16:2–3.

other hand, we view God as unreachable and inaccessible, we will never succeed in truly experiencing His personal presence in our lives.

—— C ——

Finally, the commandment of *hagbala* at Sinai reiterates a message conveyed by God to Moshe earlier on this very same spot (see Shmot 3, *Approaches* E). During the vision of the burning bush, God ushered Moshe into leadership with the charge: "Do not come nearer to here. Take off your shoes from your feet, for the place upon which you stand is holy ground."[10] *Do not look for Me, Moshe, in esoteric visions of a burning bush. Stand where you are, rooted to the ground. There, sanctity will be created, wherever you stand, as you work My will within your world.*

By commanding the Israelites to remain at the foot of Mount Sinai during the onset of Revelation, God now transmits the same message on a national scale: *As our shared journey begins, understand full well where and how My Divine Presence will be found. Do not search for Me in the mist-enveloped summits of Sinai. Do not seek Me in lofty, mysterious realms removed from the reality of your lives.*

Stay at the base of the mountain, rooted with your neighbors in your world, and there receive My Torah. Remember always that I will enter your lives as you obey the Torah's laws and pursue its goals. Partner with Me in the creation of sanctity in your world, and through that partnership you will discover and discern My Divine Presence.

—— D ——

We can now also understand why God hands the enforcement of the edict of *hagbala* to the Israelites, rather than maintaining the designated perimeter Himself, through divine intervention.

The partnership established at Sinai invests the Israelites with immediate personal and societal responsibilities.

As God transmits the law during Revelation, He also launches the process of legal jurisprudence. Included will be the people's obligation to judge and to punish transgressors, to the best of their ability, as mandated by divine decree.

---

10. Shmot 3:5.

This responsibility begins immediately. God, therefore, does not enforce His own ruling of *hagbala*. He instead relegates that task to His new partners, the people themselves.

3 A Healthy Distance, Revisited

Context

As the dramatic moment of Revelation approaches, thunder and lightning break forth, a thick cloud envelops Mount Sinai, and a powerful, rising shofar blast is heard.

Against this backdrop, God summons Moshe to the summit of Mount Sinai, where the following dialogue takes place:

God: "Descend, warn the people, lest they break through to God to see, and many of them will fall…"

Moshe: "The people cannot ascend Mount Sinai, for You have testified to us, 'Create a boundary around the mountain and sanctify it.'"

God: "Go, descend! And then you shall ascend – you and Aharon with you. But the priests and the people shall not break through to ascend to God, lest He burst forth against them."

No sooner does Moshe descend the mountain and deliver God's message, than Revelation begins.[1]

Questions

How are we to understand the puzzling dialogue that unfolds between Moshe and God, on the summit of Mount Sinai, in the direct shadow of *Matan Torah*?

Why does God summon Moshe to the summit of Mount Sinai, only to immediately command him to again go down and issue to the Israelites a warning which they have already received? (See Yitro 2.)

Why is the reiteration of this warning of *hagbala* necessary in the first place? If it is necessary, why doesn't God direct Moshe to transmit it to

---

1. Shmot 19:16–20:1.

the people without – seemingly needlessly – ascending and descending the mountain?

When Moshe objects that the people have already been warned, why doesn't God answer substantively? He simply seems to offer the frustrating response (which children so often hear with chagrin from their parents): *Do it because I told you so!*

God promises that Moshe will ascend the mountain again, together with Aharon, apparently to experience Revelation. Yet, no sooner does Moshe go down and deliver God's message to the nation, than God, seemingly without warning, launches into the Ten Declarations and begins the process of Revelation. In our mind's eye, we can almost picture Moshe running towards the mountain, frantically waving and shouting: *Wait! Don't start without me! I'm supposed to be up there!*

Some authorities maintain, in spite of the textual evidence to the contrary, that Moshe does ascend Mount Sinai again before Revelation commences.[2] Other scholars, however, accept the *pshat* of the text placing this great leader at the foot of the mountain as God begins to speak to the people.[3] For these commentaries, the question remains: why does God orchestrate Moshe's movements preparatory to Revelation in such a strange way?

Approaches

—**A**———————————————————

A number of interesting interpretive twists are proposed by the commentaries as they struggle to explain the interchange between God and Moshe on the summit of Mount Sinai.

The Ohr Hachaim, for example, suggests that God reiterates the warning of *hagbala* because He is concerned over the nation's potential for religious zeal. Perhaps the people will arrive at the erroneous conclusion that the heightened religious experience of a close encounter with the divine is worth the cost of their lives. They will, therefore, deliberately cross the forbidden perimeter around Sinai in search of spiritual ecstasy. To forestall this possibility, God instructs Moshe to clearly inform the Israelites

2. Ibn Ezra, Shmot 19:25; Ramban, Shmot 20:15.
3. Sforno, Shmot 19:24; Rabbi Shimshon Raphael Hirsch, 19:20–25.

that such "religious escapism" is not what God wants. The people's role is, instead, to live in and sanctify the physical world.[4]

The Rashbam, wrestling as always with the *pshat* of the text, suggests that Moshe does not object when God commands him to reiterate the warning to the people. It is, after all, natural to issue multiple warnings as a critical moment approaches.

Moshe, instead, questions whether the rules have now changed: *Originally, Lord, You commanded the people not to ascend the mountain.*[5] *Now, however, You instruct me to tell the nation not to "break through and see."*[6] *Am I to tell them that even viewing from afar is forbidden?*

God assures Moshe that the rules have not changed. The people are only prohibited from "ascending to God."[7]

While the Ibn Ezra agrees with the approach of the Rashbam, he also records a fascinating quote in the name of Rav Saadia Gaon. The Gaon maintains that for years he pondered and yet never understood Moshe's rejoinder to God: "The people cannot ascend Mount Sinai, for You have testified to us…." Is Moshe, wondered the Gaon, really objecting to a direct order from God?

Then, however, the Gaon happened upon an edict recorded in the book of traditions of the Persian kings. This rule states that a king's messenger is not permitted to say "I have done your bidding" to the king, until the messenger is commanded to another task. Now that God has told Moshe to speak again to the people, Moshe can safely respond: *Lord, I obeyed Your first instructions and the people have been properly warned, as You commanded.*

Moshe's rejoinder to God is, thus, not an objection but a report.

How telling that Saadia Gaon considers Persian etiquette an acceptable source for the illumination of a biblical passage![8]

— **B** —————————————————————

None of the above approaches, however, addresses why God would command Moshe to ascend and descend the mountain, seemingly without

---

4. Ohr Hachaim, Shmot 19:21.
5. Shmot 19:12–13.
6. Ibid., 19:21.
7. Ibid., 19:24; Rashbam, Shmot 19:23.
8. Ibn Ezra, ibid.

reason. Nor do these scholars explain why God suddenly commences Revelation once Moshe has come down the mountain, without allowing him the opportunity to ascend Mount Sinai again.

A surprising answer to these questions is offered in the Midrash Rabba.

With striking candor, the Midrash entertains the notion that God's instructions to Moshe at this critical juncture might actually be "busy work" motivated by an external concern. God is concerned that if Moshe is present at the summit of Mount Sinai at the time of the transmission of the Ten Declarations, the Israelites will be uncertain as to whether the law actually emanates from God or from Moshe, from a divine or a human source. God therefore directs Moshe to descend Mount Sinai and once again warn the people, even though (as this great leader himself maintains) that warning is unnecessary. In this way, God ensures that Moshe is at the foot of the mountain as Revelation commences, and that the divine origin of the law is clear.[9]

— C ———————————————————————

A final, entirely different approach can be suggested to the strange sequence of events before us.

God wants Moshe himself to learn a critical lesson that will speak to the underpinnings of leadership throughout Jewish history: *At the onset of revelation, Moshe, your place is with the people at the base of Mount Sinai. There will be a time when you will again ascend the mountain, a time when your leadership role will raise you above the nation. Now, however, your place is with them, learning the very lessons of* hagbala *that they are learning* (see Yitro 2).

Remember always that true leadership is marked by connection to the people. You must rise to leadership from their midst.

As with other important lessons in Moshe's life, however, God does not convey the message directly; He wants Moshe to learn the lesson on his own (see Shmot 6, *Approaches* D).

God's methods thus become clear in retrospect: *When I told you to go down the mountain, Moshe; when I commanded you to reiterate the warning to remain at the mountain base; when I refused to explain Myself; when*

---

9. Midrash Rabba Shmot 28:3.

I manipulated your presence at the base of Mount Sinai during the onset of Revelation – it was because this time, Moshe, I was speaking to you!

I wanted you to come to realize on your own that, at the most critical moment of your nation's history, your place is with your people; that the rules which apply to them apply to you; that you must always be connected to those who are entrusted to your care.

Learn these lessons well, Moshe, and your leadership will endure.

4 The Top Ten?

Context

Finally God commences the process of Revelation with the transmission of the Ten Declarations to the Israelites: "I am the Lord your God...; You shall have no other gods before Me...; Do not take the name of the Lord your God in vain...; Remember the Sabbath day to keep it holy...; Honor your father and your mother...; Do not murder; Do not commit adultery; Do not steal; Do not bear false witness against your friend; Do not covet...."[1]

While the Ten Declarations are clearly singled out as the dramatic opening communication of Revelation, the rabbis in the Talmud debate as to how they were actually communicated. Rabbi Yehoshua ben Levi[2] and Rabbi Yishmael maintain that the first two declarations ("I am the Lord..." and "You shall have no other gods before Me...") were spoken by God directly to the nation, while the eight other principles were transmitted through Moshe. Their colleagues disagree, arguing that all ten principles were communicated directly by God to the people.[3]

Questions

Whatever position we accept concerning their transmission, the very existence of these Ten Declarations as a unit creates a serious philosophical problem.

In total, God transmits to the Israelites six hundred thirteen commandments over the course of Moshe's career. While some of these commandments might seem to us more important than others, in reality we have

---

1. Shmot 20:1–14.
2. Pesikta Rabbati 22.
3. Talmud Bavli Makkot 24a.

no way of judging the significance of specific mitzvot. Obedience to God demands that we treat all of the commandments with equal seriousness.[4]

Why, then, does God single out ten mitzvot from among the six hundred thirteen for specific emphasis? Does He not, by doing so, create a hierarchical structure within the commandments as a whole? Why, in addition, does the Torah refer to these ten commandments in this context as *dibrot* (declarations)? Why not use the usual terms *mitzvot* (commandments), *chukim* (edicts), or *mishpatim* (statutes)?

The danger created by the singling out of these ten principles actually becomes evident later in Jewish history. While the Mishna states that the Ten Declarations were recited as part of the daily service in the Temple,[5] the Talmud testifies that their recitation was later abrogated by the rabbis because of the attacks of heretics who claimed that only these ten principles, and not six hundred thirteen, were actually commanded by God.[6]

Once again, therefore, we are forced to ask: why does God single out these principles for emphasis if all the Torah's laws are divinely ordained?

Approaches

The amount of literature written concerning the Ten Declarations is vast, and a full analysis is certainly well beyond the scope of our study. We will, instead, choose a few general thoughts from among the myriad of ideas suggested by the rabbis as to why these ten principles are singled out for emphasis.

—**A**———————————————

While the Ten Declarations are mitzvot themselves, they can also be seen as chapter headings for the other six hundred three commandments. Numerous scholars maintain that, properly categorized, all six hundred thirteen commandments of the Torah can be subsumed under the rubric of the Ten Declarations.

This idea may well be reflected in the well-known debate between Rabbi Yishmael and Rabbi Akiva concerning the manner in which the six hundred thirteen mitzvot of the Torah were transmitted. Rabbi Yishmael

---

4. Pirkei Avot 2:1.
5. Mishna Tamid 5:1.
6. Talmud Bavli Brachot 12a.

maintains that the general principles of the law were transmitted at Sinai while the specifics were only given later to Moshe in the Sanctuary. Rabbi Akiva disagrees, arguing that both generalities and particulars were transmitted to Moshe at Sinai.[7]

Both of these scholars, however, agree that the mitzvot were conveyed with distinctions between general principle and specific detail. The Ten Declarations can therefore be understood as an introductory overview to Jewish law which is then followed by detailed analysis.

With deliberate planning, God unveils the Torah step by step, so as to highlight both purpose and procedure. From this point on, His chosen nation will be challenged to blend detailed observance with overarching vision, to make lofty ideals concrete through painstaking ritual practice.

Before revealing the myriad details that will comprise the obligations upon the Israelites, therefore, God grants His people a glimpse of the law's ultimate objectives. The purpose of the six hundred thirteen mitzvot will be to create a society that truly lives by the fundamental principles outlined in the Ten Declarations. With the vision of these principles before them always, the Israelites will never lose sight of the goals towards which their religious practice must lead.

At the same time, however, God embeds the entirety of the law within the Ten Declarations. The only way to really live by these overarching principles is to *bring them to life* through concrete, detailed daily observance.

The Midrash goes a step further by suggesting that the inclusion of all six hundred thirteen mitzvot in the Ten Declarations is symbolically referenced in the text itself.

The number of letters in the passage containing these principles equals six hundred thirteen plus seven – representing, says the Midrash, the total number of commandments plus the seven days of creation. Through the text of the Ten Declarations, God hints to the fact that the purpose of creation is now revealed in the unfolding commandments of the Torah.[8]

—— **B** ——————————————————————————

The structure of the Ten Declarations carries significant lessons as well.

---

7. Ibid., Sota 37b.
8. Bamidbar Rabba 13:15–16.

According to most authorities, these laws were transmitted by God in two columns of five principles each,[9] as follows:

1. I am the Lord your God...	6. Do not murder
2. You shall have no other gods before Me...	7. Do not commit adultery
3. Do not take the name of the Lord your God in vain...	8. Do not steal
4. Remember the Sabbath day to keep it holy...	9. Do not bear false witness against your friend
5. Honor your father and your mother...	10. Do not covet...

Careful study of these columns reveals striking patterns:

1. The principles found in the first column are *mitzvot bein adam la'Makom* (laws between man and God), while the declarations in the second column are *mitzvot bein adam l'chaveiro* (laws between man and his fellow man).

This distinction between laws governing our relationship with God and laws governing our relationship with man establishes, from the moment of Revelation, the majestic scope of Jewish law. Halacha governs every aspect of human activity and shapes each of the manifold relationships that we establish throughout our lives. The complete Jew is one who, in the words of King Shlomo, finds "favor and good understanding in the eyes of God and of man."[10]

One principle, however, seems out of place. Why is "Honor your father and your mother" included in the series of laws governing our relationship with God? Shouldn't this principle be categorized among the edicts shaping our behavior towards those around us?

By including "Honor your father and mother" in the first set of declarations, the Torah underscores the unique nature of the parent-child bond

---

9. Ibid., 14:10.
10. Mishlei 3:4.

within the panoply of human relationships. *In many ways, our parents are God's representatives within our world.* They partner with God in our physical creation and they are the bearers of the divinely inspired traditions, values and practices that are meant to shape our lives.

When we honor our father and mother, we honor the God with Whom they partner and Whose traditions they bear.

2. The first five commandments are *specific to the Israelites* while the second set is *universal in scope.*[11]

As His chosen nation is forged at Sinai, God underscores a familiar defining balance first struck centuries earlier. At the dawn of Jewish history, the patriarch Avraham turned to his neighbors and declared: *Ger v'toshav anochi imachem,* "I am a stranger and a citizen together with you."[12] With these words the first patriarch delineated the tension essential to his descendents' self-definition across the ages – a tension which, as we have seen, is reiterated over and over again as Jewish history unfolds (see *Bereishit:* Chayei Sara 1, *Approaches* E, F; Bo 3, *Approaches* H).

The Jew is, at once, "apart from" and "a part of" the society around him.

Echoing across the generations from the dawn of the patriarchal era to the dawn of the national era, this pivotal balance is reflected in the very structure of the Ten Declarations. God's chosen people will only fulfill their ongoing role as a "light unto the nations" through constant, careful calibration between the exclusive and universal components of their own identity. Throughout their history, they will be challenged to map out a path allowing them to maintain their individuality even as they contribute to the world.

Once again, however, the commandment of "Honor your father and your mother" seems to be in the wrong column. Isn't respecting one's parents a universal obligation?

By placing this mitzva among the obligations specific to the Israelites, God underscores the overwhelming importance of the parent-child relationship within Jewish experience. This bond is the singular foundation upon which Jewish continuity rests. Central to the revolution wrought by

11. Pesikta Rabbati 21.
12. Bereishit 23:4.

the patriarchs and matriarchs was the determination that the home, rather than outside society, would raise their progeny. From that time on, the family has been the single most important educational unit in the survival of the Jewish people and the perpetuation of their heritage (see *Bereishit*: Vayechi 4, *Approaches* B).

As the Jewish nation is forged through God's Revelation, the centrality of the home is underscored once again.

3. The Declarations are deliberately arranged into parallel columns of five so as to create pairs, each pair consisting of one mitzva from column A and one from column B. The mitzvot of each pair are thematically connected, each mitzva informing and elaborating upon its mate.

The Midrash offers this analysis:

"I am the Lord your God..." is paired with "Do not murder." Each man, created in the image of God, is of inestimable value. If one individual murders another, he diminishes God's presence in the world.

"You shall have no other gods before me..." is paired with "Do not commit adultery." An individual guilty of idolatry betrays his relationship with God.

"Do not take the name of the Lord your God in vain..." is paired with "Do not steal." Theft is the first step on a path that inevitably leads to denial and false vows.

"Remember the Sabbath day to keep it holy..." is paired with "Do not bear false witness against your friend." By desecrating the Shabbat, an individual renders false testimony. His actions implicitly declare that God neither created the world nor rested on the seventh day.

"Honor your father and your mother..." is paired with "Do not covet..." A child reared in an environment of jealousy and bitterness will eventually denigrate his own parents and covet the parents of others.[13]

Other suggestions concerning the significance of the paired declarations are offered by scholars across the generations.

— C —

In summary: the Ten Declarations are, in fact, ten mitzvot out of six hundred thirteen.

---

13. Mechilta, Yitro 8:13.

In their dramatic context at the moment of Revelation, however, these commandments are invested with heightened significance. They are transformed into "Declarations," introducing the Israelites to the detailed laws that will follow and establishing fundamental principles that will course through those laws.

5 Unwritten Law

In this study we will depart from the usual format in order to cover material essential to our understanding of the Revelation of Jewish law. This study specifically deals with what is *not* included in the text: Torah She'b'al Peh (Oral Law).

I studied in yeshiva all my life and learned Talmud for years. But not until a friend and I embarked upon a review of the Rambam's introduction to his commentary on the Mishna did I truly begin to understand the nature and process of Oral Law. I believe the Rambam's perspective to be of such pivotal importance that I now include a review of this material, together with additional commentary, in every university class I teach (no matter the subject).

A brief outline of that lesson is contained below.

Context

Simultaneously with the Revelation of Written Law at Sinai, God launches an oral process of law. This Oral Law is transmitted over the generations until it is first officially codified in writing, for fear of its being lost, by Rabbi Yehuda Hanasi in the Mishna (circa 200 CE). The oral process continues beyond the Mishna, resulting in the redaction of the Talmud Yerushalmi in Israel (circa 350 CE) and the Talmud Bavli in Babylon (circa 500 CE). The development of the Oral Law continues beyond the editing of the Talmud, to this day.

Concerning the authority of the oral tradition the Talmud testifies, "Rabbi Chiya bar Abba stated in the name of Rabbi Yochanan: God revealed to Moshe the details of the Torah, the details of rabbinic thought and all that the scholars are destined to innovate."[1]

The Midrash adds, "Even that which a diligent student is destined to state before his teacher was already given to Moshe at Sinai."[2]

---

1. Talmud Bavli Megilla 19b.
2. Midrash Rabba Vayikra 22:1.

153

Questions

What is the nature and origin of Oral Law and how does it differ from Written Law?

If the entire body of Oral Law was transmitted at Sinai, how can we explain the many rabbinic disputes recorded in the Talmud and elsewhere? Were the rabbis unaware of, or did they forget, specific laws?

Why was this body of law transmitted orally? Why was it not included in the written text?

Approaches

Some scholars certainly do take a literal approach to the Talmudic and Midrashic statements concerning Oral Law, maintaining that God revealed every element of halacha to Moshe in prophetic vision, prior to the law's unfolding. The Ran, for example, claims that all rabbinic opinions destined to be offered across the face of history, even disputing opinions, were fully shown to Moshe in advance at Sinai.[3]

The Rambam, on the other hand, views the development of halacha very differently. His position, clearly outlined in his introduction to his commentary on the Mishna, accepts the notion of *a law that develops over time, based upon a process which is rooted at Sinai.*

Central to the Rambam's approach is recognition of five distinct, separate component parts of Oral Law. Each of these sections possesses unique attributes and each is essential to the functioning of the law. Together, they form an ingenious legal system that is rooted at Sinai yet remains totally relevant and applicable to this day.

—— **A** ——

Peirushim hamekubalim mi'pi Moshe (commentaries received directly from Moshe) and *halacha l'Moshe mi'Sinai* (law given to Moshe at Sinai).

These first two sections of Oral Law share one distinct feature: both are received, directly and unchanged, across the ages from Moshe.

The first segment consists of commentary on the text, which Moshe transmits directly to the nation.

The second segment contains a group of additional unwritten laws conveyed by God to Moshe at Sinai simultaneously with the written text.

3. Drashot HaRan, drash 7.

These laws are subsequently handed down by Moshe to the people. For example:

1. The Torah states, "And you shall bind them as a sign upon your arm and they shall be as ornaments between your eyes." The text, however, does not define exactly what we were supposed to place upon our arms and heads. The detailed laws that define tefillin fall into the category of *halacha l'Moshe mi'Sinai*.

2. Much of Jewish law is dependent upon measurement. According to many authorities, the exact values of these measurement standards are specified in *halacha l'Moshe mi'Sinai*.

Peirushim hamekubalim mi'pi Moshe and *halacha l'Moshe mi'Sinai* are exceptions to the general rules of Torah She'b'al Peh, in that these sections of Oral Law, according to most authorities, reflect characteristics usually reserved for the Written Law: *the laws within these sections are immutable and non-debatable*. Once a specific law is acknowledged as a *peirush hamekubal mi'pi Moshe* or a *halacha l'Moshe mi'Sinai*, that law is no longer subject to critical discussion and must be observed as stated.

This raises a serious question: if these laws are similar to Written Law, why weren't they included in the Torah text?

As will become clear in our analysis, the bodies of Written Law and Oral Law each reflect different strengths and weaknesses. The strength of Written Law lies in its permanence and in the ease of its reliable transmission, while the weakness of Written Law is found in its inflexibility and in its inability to adapt to changing times and circumstances. The opposite is true of Oral Law. Oral Law's strength is found in its flexibility and its adaptability, while its weakness lies in its fragility and its potential for faulty transmission.

Why, then, create two units of law that evidence the weaknesses of both Oral and Written Law and none of their strengths? Why create sections of Oral Law that are neither adaptable nor flexible? If these laws are immutable, why not simply write them down?

The answer may well lie in the messages conveyed by the very existence of these units of law.

By insisting that Moshe descend from the summit of Sinai armed not only with the Written Law but with information that only he possesses, God establishes at least three important principles, which will become critical to the unfolding of the entire Oral Law.

1. *Not everything is written down*. The Torah text is incomplete and cannot be understood as a freestanding document. By establishing immediately, from the moment of *Matan Torah*, that oral elaboration is necessary for the understanding of the text, the Torah creates the mindset necessary for the acceptance of an oral tradition. In this way, the first two sections of Oral Law "prime the pump" of halachic process.

2. *Rabbinic authority is essential to the halachic process*: When Moshe Rabbeinu, the first "Rabbi," descends Mount Sinai he is privy to information that only he possesses. His essential role in the unfolding of the law is thus firmly established.

This central role will become even more pronounced as Moshe moves from simply transmitting the law to interpreting and even creating law (see below). Moshe thus emerges as the progenitor of rabbinic authority across the ages.

3. *Human involvement is essential to the development and transmission of law*. The law received at Sinai and beyond cannot be transmitted simply through the handing over of an existing text. Personal involvement in explaining, interpreting and eventually creating law is essential.

The relationship between teacher and student, parent and child is thus interwoven into the very fabric of the halachic process. Across the ages, our tradition will be formed not only through the cut and dried legal text but through personal wisdom, insight and example.

The sum total of all laws and interpretations contained within the *peirushim hamekubalim mi'pi Moshe* and *halacha l'Moshe mi'Sinai* is small when seen against the totality of Jewish law. These two sections are foundational, however, in setting the stage for all that is to follow.

— B —

Hadinim shehotziu al darchei hasvara (laws that are determined through the application of hermeneutical principles and logical method).

This third section of Oral Law is, in many ways, the most pivotal and the most revolutionary. As the Jewish nation moves away from Sinai, they will confront issues not clearly addressed in either the Written Law or in the first two God-given sections of Oral Law. Faced with these new concerns, halachic thought could well have accepted that some areas of life are simply outside the purview of Jewish law.

That approach is emphatically rejected.

Every aspect of our lives, in every generation, ties into our Jewishness and our observance of Jewish law.

Are we then supposed to wait for additional information from God in order to determine our course? Are subsequent mini-revelations meant to take place as our path is illuminated through prophetic pronouncements?

Once again, normative Judaism clearly rejects that path.

Instead, God takes the dramatic, revolutionary step of handing divine law over to man for interpretation and application. Using rules of study transmitted together with the Oral Law at Sinai, the rabbis are charged with analysis of the text and with the application of its laws to ever changing times and circumstances.

God, Himself, agrees to accept their conclusions as law.

This step is much more astounding than it first sounds, with ramifications that shape the very nature of Jewish law. *In short, as God retreats from active involvement in decision making, He relinquishes His infallible control over the course of the law.* Limited man, prone to error, is now to determine halacha's path. Disputes become inevitable, as scholars of different outlooks, perspectives and abilities examine the facts before them and struggle to apply these facts to the circumstances of their day.

As far as truth goes, the rabbis make an astounding claim. When faced with conflicting halachic positions they state, *Eilu va'eilu divrei Elokim chaim,* "These and these are the words of the living God." *Both positions are true.*[4]

How is this possible? How can contradictory positions both be correct? If one scholar decides that a piece of meat is kosher, while another scholar claims it is not – are they both right?

Strangely enough, Jewish law answers emphatically: Yes!

The definition of truth within the halachic process has changed. Truth is no longer defined by objective fact but, rather, by loyalty to the process.

If two contradictory positions are presented by experts in the law, both having been arrived at through appropriate study of the text and loyal application of the rules, both positions are true.

For the sake of unified observance, however, decisions must of course be made, and the law itself dictates how that is to be done. The rule is simply

---

4. Talmud Bavli Eruvin 13b.

stated: *majority rules*. When possible (as in the days of the Sanhedrin), votes are taken and the majority opinion becomes law.

These majority decisions, however, do not determine truth and falsehood. They only point the way to practical observance, determined by man and agreed upon, after the fact, by God.

A famous halachic-aggadic story in the Talmud dramatically reflects the ramifications of this theological path.

Rabbi Eliezer ben Hyrcanus debated a specific law with his contemporaries in the *beit midrash* (house of study). Alone against the majority position, Rabbi Eliezer remained steadfast and attempted to bolster his arguments by invoking a series of supernatural miracles designed to prove that God agreed with his view. At Rabbi Eliezer's request God caused a carob tree to move, a water canal to flow upstream and the walls of the *beit midrash* to move in. When all of these "proofs" were rejected by his colleagues, Rabbi Eliezer turned heavenward and exclaimed, "If the halacha accords with me, from the heavens let it be proven!" Immediately, a heavenly voice proclaimed, "What is your argument with Rabbi Eliezer, with whom the law accords in all places?"

At that point, Rabbi Yehoshua rose to his feet and declared, "The matter is not in heaven!"

The law was decided against the position of Rabbi Eliezer.

The Talmud goes on to relate that, after this event, Rabbi Natan asked Eliyahu Hanavi (Elijah the Prophet): "What was the Holy One Blessed Be He doing at that moment [when Rabbi Yehoshua rejected the heavenly voice]?" The prophet responded: "He [God] was laughing and saying, *Nitzchuni banai, nitzchuni banai,* 'My children have prevailed over me.'"[5]

While this tale may or may not be understood literally, the overarching message conveyed is clear. *Once the halacha is given to man, God is no longer involved in the decision-making process. As long as loyalty to the process is shown, God will agree with the decisions reached by the rabbis in their best efforts to determine the truth.* Even if the law does not follow the path that God might have "intended," the rabbinic decisions remain intact, with God's blessing.

As Rabbi Moshe Feinstein declares in the introduction to his landmark responsa volumes, *Igrot Moshe:*

---

5. Talmud Bavli Bava Metzia 59b.

Once a scholar has properly researched the Talmud and halachic literature with all his ability, with seriousness and with a fear of the Holy One Blessed Be He…and arrives at a conclusion which he believes to be correct…then, that is "truth" in *psak* (halachic legislation); and the scholar is obligated to proclaim the law as he sees it…even though in the heavenly sphere his conclusion might not have been deemed correct.[6]

Carrying the thought one step further, some scholars suggest that the root word in God's response to Rabbi Yehoshua, "*Nitzchuni banai, nitzchuni banai*," is not *nitzachon* (victory) but *netzach* (eternity). According to this suggestion, God proclaims: *My children have made Me and My law "eternal." By accepting that the halacha is given to man for application, they have ensured that the law will be relevant in every situation and in every generation.*

While the authorities of other faith traditions, such as Catholicism's pope, claim to speak in the name of God, halachic authorities speak for themselves. They do not sit and wait for divine inspiration but, instead, turn to their books. Armed with the law and with the talent granted to them by God, they attempt to reach divine truth in any given situation. These scholars find reassurance, however, in the knowledge that if they have remained loyal to the process of study in a real attempt to find that truth, God will accept whatever conclusion they reach. In this way, Jewish law continues to address cutting-edge issues in our day – from genetic engineering to space travel to intellectual property – in a relevant, coherent manner consonant with the foundations of the law at Sinai.

Loyalty to the halachic process preserves the process itself and is more important than any one specific decision.

— **C** —————————————————————————

Gezeirot (rabbinic decrees) and *takanot* (rabbinic edicts).

The final two sections of Oral Law share a major feature: *gezeirot* and *takanot* are not the result of interpretation and application of previously derived law. They are, instead, *new laws created by the rabbis*. Each of these sections, however, responds to a different theological need.

---

6. Introduction, *Igrot Moshe* (Brooklyn: Moriah Offset Co., 1959).

1. *Gezeirot* are laws created by the rabbis for the purpose of protecting existing Torah law. Examples of *gezeirot* include *muktza* (items forbidden to be handled on the Shabbat and festivals), the requirement to wait between consumption of meat and milk, numerous Shabbat prohibitions, etc.

The authority of the rabbis to legislate *gezeirot* is derived from the biblical commandment "And you shall guard my charge."[7] This statement is interpreted by the Talmud to mean "Create a protection for my charge."[8]

Great care was shown by the rabbis in the creation of *gezeirot*, with the Talmud emphatically declaring, "One may not enact a *gezeira* upon another *gezeira*."[9] And even, "One may not enact a *gezeira* that most of the community will not be able to tolerate."[10]

The legislation of *gezeirot* is generally understood to have ended with the close of the Talmud (although some *gezeirot* were apparently enacted in the Geonic era).[11]

2. *Takanot*, on the other hand, are laws created by the rabbis to respond to changing circumstances and needs within the Jewish community. Wide-ranging, *takanot* deal with all aspects of Jewish life and can best be understood as "course corrections" built into the *halachic* system to safeguard the flow and ultimate goals of Jewish law across the ages. The very term *takana*, in fact, derives from the root *l'takein*, which means "to fix" or "to correct."

Unlike *gezeirot*, which are universal in application, *takanot* are often limited to specific Jewish communities and to particular times.

The historical study of *takanot* is, therefore, fascinating, as these laws provide windows into the various eras of Jewish history. Through the research of *takanot*, we gain a glimpse of the pressing issues concerning which the rabbis felt the need to legislate in their particular place and time.

Takanot can be dramatic.

One powerful early *takana* which resonates with sorrow across the ages, for example, concerns the laws of *pidyon shvuyim* (the redemption of captives). According to Torah law the redemption of Jewish captives from

---

7. Vayikra 18:30.
8. Talmud Bavli Yevamot 21a.
9. Talmud Bavli Beitza 3a.
10. Talmud Bavli Bava Kama 79b.
11. Rabbeinu Asher, Shabbat 2:15.

an enemy is an overarching obligation, with no upper limit placed upon the efforts which must be exerted.[12]

The Mishna, however, issues a startling ruling: "One may not redeem captives for more than they are worth."[13]

The Talmud explains this *takana* to mean that the community may not accede to exorbitant demands made by hostage-takers. Doing so, say the scholars, would bankrupt the community or ensure, God forbid, additional hostage taking.[14]

Although in a perfect world nothing should prevent us from redeeming those who are captured, by the Mishna's time the world is far from perfect. In order to prevent the law from being used against itself, therefore, the rabbis must limit our concessions to our enemies.

How little is changed, unfortunately, since the Mishna's time! Today, this rabbinic decree could well be summed up in the far too familiar adage "You don't negotiate with terrorists."

Takanot, on the other hand, can also be technical and routine.

Consider, for example, the edict of *basar chutz* (outside meat), mandated in a number of European communities and even in some American communities at the turn of the nineteenth century. In order to build up the communal infrastructure of fledgling communities, some rabbis forbade the import of kosher meat from other towns. In this way they ensured the patronage of local merchants and increased the chances for their success.

Other well-known, varied *takanot* include the observances of Chanuka and Purim, the prohibition on polygamy, the prohibition on reading someone else's mail, numerous observances meant to mark the memory of the Temple, and many more.

Two final comments must be made concerning *takanot* lest they be misunderstood.

1. *Takanot* are not afterthoughts, mandated because of the inability of the original law to respond to new circumstances. The opposite is true. *Takanot* are an integral part of the system from the outset, built-in safety valves to allow halacha to adapt.

Proof of the foundational nature of *takanot* can be found in the fact

---

12. Rambam, *Mishneh Torah*, Matanot La'evyonim 8:10.
13. Talmud Bavli Gittin 45a.
14. Ibid.

that, according to the Talmud, the first *metaken* (legislator of *takanot*) was none other than Moshe himself.[15] In spite of the fact that he receives the law directly from God, Moshe finds it necessary to exercise his right to correct the course of the law in his own time.

2. *Takanot* are not a reflection of God's inability to predict and mandate for changing need within the original Torah law. Instead, an essential two-step process unfolds which preserves both the law and its fundamental goals.

God first sets the standard to which the law aspires and then allows us to deal with practical concerns. Had God, for example, limited the obligation of *pidyon shvuyim* from the beginning, we would never have fully appreciated the overarching requirement to redeem captives against great odds. God therefore decrees the optimal law, but also allows the rabbis to adjust that law through the legislation of *takanot* when absolutely necessary.

Literally thousands of *takanot* have been legislated across the centuries and continue to be legislated today, adjusting the course of Jewish law to meet ever-evolving needs.

—— **D** ——————————————————————————

Together, the component sections of Oral Law create a magnificent legal tapestry which interweaves loyalty to the past with the ability to address all issues at all times.

The honesty with which the rabbis approached the journey of Jewish law across the ages is perhaps best reflected in this wonderful segment of a tale recorded in the Talmud.

When Moshe ascended Mount Sinai to receive the Torah, he found God sitting and tying crowns onto some of the letters in the text (certain letters in the Torah are adorned with *tagim*, crowns). Moshe inquired as to the necessity of these crowns and God informed him that, many generations in the future, a sage by the name of Rabbi Akiva ben Yosef would derive a multitude of laws from each of the textual adornments.

"Master of the Universe," exclaimed Moshe, "show him to me!"

God responded by miraculously transporting Moshe into the future, to the class of Rabbi Akiva. As he sat in the back of the *beit midrash*, however,

---

15. Talmud Bavli Brachot 48b, Megilla 32a.

listening to the dialogue between Rabbi Akiva and his students, Moshe became increasingly upset. He did not understand what they were saying at all! There seemed to be no connection between the legal discussion surrounding him and the Torah that he was receiving at Sinai.

Until, suddenly, the scholars arrived at a specific point in the discussion and a student inquired of Rabbi Akiva, "Rebbe, from where do you know this point?"

"That?" responded Rabbi Akiva. "Why, that is a law given to Moshe at Sinai!"

Tremendously relieved, Moshe is transported back to Mount Sinai to receive the Torah.[16]

Once again, the lesson taught by an aggadic tale seems clear.

Were Moshe to attend a class today dealing with the attitude of Jewish law towards, for example, genetic engineering, he would have no idea what the participants were talking about. Yet every aspect of the laws discussed in that class could somehow be traced back to sources in the Written Law, Oral Law and legal process received by Moshe at Sinai.

Therein lies the brilliance of halacha: a legal system rooted at Sinai which remains as timely, relevant and applicable as if it were revealed today. This system, more than anything else, has guided and preserved our people across the centuries, enabling us to reflect God's will in our daily lives.

Points to Ponder

Many years ago, I was involved in the construction of the community *eruv* (a legal concept represented by a boundary that allows members of a community to carry items outside their homes on Shabbat). In those days, such construction consisted principally of attaching stakes of wood to the bottom of utility poles in such a way that if the top of the stake were continued upwards in an imaginary straight line, the line would intersect with a specific horizontal wire near the top of the pole.

Sounds easy enough, but the problem is, however, that utility poles are rarely straight. The imaginary lines, therefore, often ended up in the middle of the pole (if the poles, themselves, were leaning outward) or in outer space (if the poles were leaning inward). Great care, therefore, had

---

16. Talmud Bavli Menachot 29b.

to be exercised concerning the proper adjustment and placement of those wooden stakes.

One day, as I worked "in the field" together with one of my congregants, we encountered a particularly problematic pole on which we focused for about an hour. Finally, after I felt satisfied with my efforts, my congregant turned to me and said: "Rabbi, I really didn't want to bother you while you were working, but…*do you really think that God cares* whether or not that piece of wood is an inch this way or an inch that way? Do you really think God cares to the point that you spent so much of your precious time on this specific pole?"

For a few moments, I was speechless. My congregant, after all, did have a point. What kind of God did I believe in – a God Who was concerned about the minute measurements of a wooden stake on a utility pole? Didn't God have more important things to be worried about?

After a moment, however, I answered with an automatic response that has since become a critical guidepost in the formation of my outlook on halacha.

"I don't believe that God cares," I replied. *"I believe that God cares that we care."*

God wants the process of halacha to be woven into the daily actions of our lives. He wants us to care about Jewish law as deeply as – no, more deeply than – we care about so many transient concerns that continually occupy our attention. Willing adherence to the detailed dictates of Torah and rabbinic law reflects a loyalty to God and to the process He launched at Sinai.

If after careful deliberation, the scholars determine that we must exactingly adjust and place a wooden stake at the bottom of a utility pole in order to create a kosher *eruv*, we should care enough about halachic process to spend whatever time is necessary to carry out that mandate.

Loyalty to the process, shown by allegiance to detail, demonstrates that we care; that we recognize the precious, essential nature of Jewish law; and that, whatever the necessary effort, we truly desire to make that law part of our lives.

Mishpatim   משפטים

CHAPTER 21:1–24:18   פרק כא:א–כד:יח

Parsha Summary

Detailed law, majestic vision…

    As the Israelites stand rooted at Sinai, God abruptly transitions from the drama to the details. Against the backdrop of Revelation, He transmits to the nation a litany of edicts, primarily interpersonal in nature, that will form the foundation of their newfound responsibilities.

    Included in this wide-ranging parsha are laws concerning the treatment of indentured servants, murder, manslaughter, personal injury, damage caused by one's property, theft, self-defense, custodial responsibilities, sensitivity to the poor and vulnerable, judicial integrity, Shabbat, Shmita (the sabbatical year), the holidays and other areas of personal obligation.

    Towards the end of the parsha, the Torah returns to the scene at Sinai as it outlines a series of actions taken by Moshe to concretize the covenant between God and the nation. Moshe then, at God's command, ascends partway up the mountain, together with Aharon, Aharon's sons (Nadav and Avihu) and seventy elders from among the people. There, they witness a majestic vision of God.

    Finally, the parsha ends as Moshe responds to God's further command and enters the cloud enveloping the summit of Mount Sinai.

1 Slavery Condoned?

Context

Parshat Mishpatim opens with laws concerning an *eved Ivri* and an *ama Ivria* (a male and a female Hebrew servant).[1] Later in the parsha, select laws concerning an *eved Cana'ani* (a Canaanite [non-Hebrew] slave) are also recorded.[2]

These topics are discussed elsewhere in the Torah text, as well.[3]

Questions

Like a jarring, wrong note in an otherwise perfect symphony, the opening text of Parshat Mishpatim hits us with powerful, unsettling force.

How can the Torah condone slavery of any kind? Doesn't God fundamentally desire freedom for all mankind?

Were the Israelites redeemed from Egyptian slavery only to become masters of slaves of their own? Over and over again, the Torah emphasizes that the slavery/Exodus experience is meant to create a nation sensitive to the vulnerability and pain of others. How can the Jew, then, possibly become an enslaver?

Even if we were to accept the existence of slavery, why does the Torah open Parshat Mishpatim specifically with a discussion of the laws of servitude? The significance of this textual juncture cannot be overstated. As Mishpatim begins, the Torah abruptly transitions from the powerful drama of Revelation to the concrete substance of halacha. Detailed, practical edicts are presented one after another, staccato, as the Israelites begin to learn the nature and extent of their new obligations. Surely the topic that opens this legal compendium must be chosen with great care. Given the broad range

---

1. Shmot 21:1–11.
2. Ibid., 21:20–22, 26–27.
3. Vayikra 25:10, 39–46.

of available possibilities, why does God specifically showcase the issue of slavery at this critical moment?

Approaches

We would certainly feel much more comfortable had God simply prohibited the institution of slavery in its entirety. Such is clearly not the case. We are, therefore, compelled to struggle with the information before us as we attempt to correlate the Torah's approach to slavery with its general attitude towards human rights.

As a first step, we must distinguish between the institutions of *eved Ivri*, the Hebrew servant, and *eved Cana'ani*, the Canaanite (non-Hebrew) slave.

I. *Eved Ivri* – The Hebrew Servant

—**A**—

An *eved Ivri* is not a slave, at least not in the classical sense of the word. His position is much closer to that of an indentured servant, an individual whose services are sold to someone else for a period of time. Following are some of the key laws which govern the status of an *eved Ivri*.[4]

1. An individual becomes an *eved Ivri* in only one of two ways. Either he becomes so destitute that he can no longer support himself or his family, or he is found guilty of the crime of theft and is unable to pay his obligations.

In the first of these cases, the individual sells himself into *avdut* (servitude) in order to accrue the provisions necessary for survival. In the latter instance, the court sells the thief into servitude. The funds accumulated through this sale are applied towards the payment of his debts.

2. An *eved Ivri* is not "owned" by his master. He has simply sold the rights to his labor for the tenure of his *avdut*.

3. An *eved Ivri* who is sold into servitude by the court may only be sold for a six-year tenure. After that time he is to be set free. An individual who sells himself into servitude, according to most authorities, may determine the length of his period of *avdut*.

---

4. Rambam, *Mishneh Torah*, Hilchot Avadim 1–4; Aruch Hashulchan, Yoreh Deah 267:136–177.

4. If the *Yovel* (Jubilee) year falls at any point during an *eved Ivri*'s period of servitude, the servant is immediately freed.

5. If an *eved Ivri* who has been sold by the court desires to remain in servitude after his six-year tenure, he must undergo a ritual in which his ear is pierced at the doorpost of his master's home. He then remains in his master's service until the advent of the Jubilee year.

6. Strict regulations circumscribe the treatment of an *eved Ivri* at the hands of his master. The *eved Ivri* cannot be assigned "backbreaking work," he may not be physically disciplined, he and his family must receive sustenance and care to such an extent that the rabbis proclaim in the Talmud, "*Anyone who purchases [the services of] an eved Ivri, it is as if he has purchased a master.*"[5]

7. If an *eved Ivri* acquires the funds necessary to pay off the balance of his tenure he may do so and thus attain immediate freedom. Changes in the market value of his labor are always computed in the servant's favor.

8. The master of a court-sold *eved Ivri* may designate a Canaanite maidservant as a concubine for the *eved*. The progeny of their union are to be considered Canaanite slaves in the master's employ.

9. The above laws of indentured servitude only apply to males. A female becomes an *ama Ivria* when, as an underage child, she is sold into indentured servitude by her impoverished father who is unable to provide for her.

10. Like an *eved Ivri*, an *ama Ivria* is freed either at the end of her six-year tenure, with the advent of the Jubilee year or upon payment of the value of her remaining years of service. An additional opportunity for personal advancement is, however, provided for the *ama Ivria*. If she reaches the age of maturity during her tenure as a servant, her master must either offer to betroth her in marriage to himself or to his son or grant her immediate freedom. This betrothal must be entered into of the *ama*'s own free will.

11. The institutions of *eved Ivri* and *ama Ivria* were suspended simultaneously with the suspension of the observance of the Jubilee year (at the onset of the exile of the ten tribes of Israel, circa 730 BCE).[6]

---

5. Talmud Bavli Kiddushin 20a.
6. Rambam, *Mishneh Torah*, Hilchot Shmita V'Yovel 10:8–9.

— **B** —

While many of the above laws certainly seem alien to our modern sensibilities, an objective review reveals a striking positive pattern. In direct contradistinction to classical slavery, the institutions of *eved Ivri and ama Ivria* are clearly designed to provide individuals in difficult straits with the opportunity for rehabilitation and personal advancement.

Consider the future prospects in ancient times for an individual who has fallen into a cycle of debilitating poverty. How will he provide for his family? Are he and the members of his household fated to continued reliance on the benevolence of others?

An alternative path is presented by Torah law.

By selling his services as an *eved Ivri*, the destitute individual receives immediate economic relief and embarks upon a complex path of financial and social correction. As he and his family enter into an extended period of personal security, he begins to relearn the value of his labor. He has once again found a way to provide for those dependent on him.

True, all that the *eved* physically produces will, for a time, belong to another. This limitation, however, will hopefully encourage him to strive for the moment when he will once again "own" the fruits of his own efforts. The servitude agreement is, after all, limited by time, and the possibility for early redemption is ever present.

In the meantime, the proceeds of the *eved's* sale can be set aside for future needs, as he and his family are supported by his master for the duration of his *avdut*.

— **C** —

Even more striking is the radical institution of *ama Ivria*, through which the Torah addresses the bleak future confronting the minor daughter of impoverished parents. Here the circumstances are even direr. This child, through an accident of birth, faces a lifetime of overwhelming poverty and hard labor with no real possibility of reprieve.

Once again, however, Jewish law steps in and dramatically alters the reality.

Such a child's labor, the halacha states, can be sold to the head of a household of greater means. While in that family's employ, the child is to be cared for and treated with the respect due to all indentured servants.

Even further, the law stipulates that, upon reaching adulthood, this young woman can be transformed in one fell swoop from pauper to "princess" through marriage to the master of her new household or his son. This marriage is, in fact, the desired objective of the entire *ama Ivria* process, as can be seen from the fact that the original purchase price of the *ama*'s services becomes the betrothal gift.

In the midst of a world marked by class and caste distinction, Torah law creates a society blind to such boundaries. Even the poorest child can realistically aspire to dramatic changes in the trajectory of her life, to breaking out of the overwhelming poverty into which she was born.

—— **D** ————————————————————————————————

Finally, one last piece of the puzzle falls into place when we consider the fate of a convicted thief. Here, as the court forcibly sells the convict into servitude to repay his debt, the concept of *eved Ivri* acquires additional overlays of significance. The thief's sentence of servitude is, at once:

1. *Compensatory*: The funds gained by the servant's sale are used to compensate the victim of the original theft for his loss.

2. *Punitive*: The thief is "robbed" of his independence as not only his physical labor but the very fruit of his loins (in certain cases; see above, A8) become the possessions of another. Hopefully, this forcible loss of freedom will move the indentured servant to remorse as he considers his past actions and their effect upon his own condition.

3. *Rehabilitative*: In place of incarceration, halacha mandates the assignment of the convict to a successfully functioning household. The thief thus spends the years of his servitude in an environment where he is surrounded not by other (potentially incorrigible) criminals, but by productive members of society. As he witnesses the positive choices made by those who populate his new world, he begins to learn of roads not taken in his own past and of the steps he can now take towards a brighter future.

How enlightened the Torah's approach now seems when compared to the penal system of our own day, a system which, more often than not, only turns criminals into bitter, better criminals!

By directly applying the value of the thief's labor towards the remediation of the effects of his own crime, by punishing him with an embarrassing loss of independence coupled with a growing sensitization to the value of his own labor, by placing the thief into a functioning household meant to model successful behavior, the Torah optimizes the chances for the thief's own rehabilitation.

The actual success of the *eved Ivri* endeavor will, of course, remain dependent upon the goodwill of the host family as well as upon the *eved's* own buy-in. Nonetheless, a real chance for true change has been offered.

—— **E** ——

We can now understand why the laws of *eved Ivri* and *ama Ivria* are recorded specifically at the beginning of Parshat Mishpatim.

The measure of a society can be determined by the care it shows towards its most unfortunate citizens. As the Torah transitions, therefore, from the lofty drama of Revelation to the concrete, practical obligations of Jewish law, the text opens with the laws of indentured servitude. These finely tuned edicts will shape the approach of the new Israelite nation to those within its borders who are most in need.

—— **F** ——

Our analysis also explains the seemingly strange treatment of the court-sold *eved Ivri* who wishes to remain in servitude after the conclusion of his six-year tenure. The Torah states: "And his master…shall bring him to the door or to the doorpost, and his master shall pierce his [the slave's] ear with the awl, and he shall serve him forever[7] [until the advent of the Jubilee year[8]]."

Numerous sources within rabbinic literature view this procedure as a deterrent: "Let the ear which heard at Mount Sinai 'They are My servants'[9] – and not servants to man – now be pierced, for this individual chooses to acquire a mortal master."[10]

At first glance, this rabbinic approach seems strange. If God does not want the *eved* to remain in servitude, why not simply prohibit this choice by mandating enforced freedom at the end of the *eved's* sentence?

If, however, as we have suggested, the institution of *eved Ivri* is at least partially rehabilitative in purpose, the Torah's intent becomes abundantly

---

7. Shmot 21:5–7.
8. Talmud Bavli Kiddushin 21b.
9. Vayikra 25:42.
10. Talmud Bavli Kiddushin 22b.

clear. Through his desire for continued servitude, the *eved* shows that he is not yet ready to reenter society as a free man. Were God to force him out the door of this household, he would soon end up as a servant to another household, or worse. The Torah, therefore, commands one last-ditch effort to change the *eved*'s perspective. If that attempt fails, he is to remain in his state of servitude until the Jubilee year.

The choice for freedom and independence cannot be mandated; it must be made freely.

II. *Eved Cana'ani* – The Canaanite (Non-Hebrew) Slave

—**A**—————————————————————————

While the issues surrounding the *eved Ivri* are complex, they pale in comparison to the difficulties raised by the biblical institution of *eved Cana'ani*. Here, Jewish law apparently accepts the existence of classical slavery within Jewish society. And yet, through an intricate web of edicts, the Torah seems to mandate "slavery with a difference."

These are some of the key laws that govern the status of the *eved Cana'ani*:[11]

1. Unlike an *eved Ivri*, an *eved Cana'ani* is physically sold to a master and becomes that master's property.

2. An *eved Cana'ani* can be bought and sold from household to household and the *eved* is bequeathed, upon the master's death, to the master's heirs.

3. An *eved Cana'ani* may be assigned any type of work and may be physically disciplined. Numerous halachic authorities, however, record ethical obligations to treat all *avadim Cana'anim* with kindness and compassion, to provide them with every type of food available to other members of the household, to feed them before other family members and to refrain from embarrassing or insulting them.

4. Upon acquiring a non-Hebrew slave, a master must present that slave with the choice of entering Jewish society *l'shem avdut* (for the purpose of servitude). If the slave agrees, he or she then undergoes an attenuated conversion process consisting of the same ritual steps found in a full

---

11. Rambam, *Mishneh Torah*, Hilchot Avadim 5–9; Shulchan Aruch, Yoreh Deah 267; Aruch Hashulchan 267:1–135.

conversion to Judaism. This conversion raises the slave to the official status of *eved Cana'ani* and obligates the slave to all positive non-time-bound commandments and to all negative commandments of Jewish law. Only a slave who voluntarily agrees to accept these obligations and to undergo the requisite conversion process becomes an official *eved Cana'ani*, enjoying the rights and privileges associated with that status (see below). A new, unique strata is thus created within the Israelite community through the formation of a subgroup comprised of *avadim Cana'anim*.

If the slave refuses to undergo this conversion he may remain in the Israelite household for twelve months in the hope that he will recognize, during that time, the benefits of entering into the covenant with God. If after that period, he still refuses to convert, he is to be sold back out of the Jewish community. (Some authorities maintain that if the slave initially agrees of his own accord to enter the Jewish household but forgo conversion, he may do so. According to these scholars, conversion *l'shem avdut* is not a prerequisite for remaining within a Jewish household. The slave who opts not to convert, however, foregoes many of the specific rights afforded to an official *eved Cana'ani*.)

5. One is forbidden, in the normal course of events, to free his *avadim Cana'anim*. Exceptions to this rule are made, however, under certain conditions, some of which are enumerated below. Upon attaining freedom, an *eved Cana'ani*, through an additional abridged conversion process, can become a full Jew.

6. Automatic freedom is granted to an *eved Cana'ani* who sustains a deliberate injury causing permanent loss of limb (even a tooth) at the hands of his master.

7. A master who directly causes the death of his *eved Cana'ani* is liable to the death penalty.

8. An *eved Cana'ani* enjoys a series of rights and privileges concerning his personal situation, including:

An *eved Cana'ani* who wishes to move to the land of Israel can force his master to do so or sell the *eved* to someone who will.

A Jew living in the land of Israel who wishes to move to the diaspora cannot force his *eved Cana'ani* to accompany him.

An *eved Cana'ani* who flees from the diaspora to Israel may not be returned to his master in the diaspora.

A Jew is forbidden to sell his *eved Cana'ani* to a non-Jew. If he does, he must pay up to ten times the slave's value to redeem him and the slave earns his automatic freedom.

If a Jew living in the land of Israel sells his *eved Cana'ani* to another Jew living in the diaspora, the second master is forced to grant the slave immediate freedom.

— **B** ————————————————————————————

The picture painted by these and other laws governing the status of an *eved Cana'ani* is complex, even contradictory.

On the one hand, the institution of *eved Cana'ani* clearly reflects many of the characteristics of classical slavery. The *eved Cana'ani* is his master's property to be owned, bequeathed, bought and sold.

On the other hand, the *eved Cana'ani* occupies a unique place within the strata of Jewish society. He enters this position through a voluntary conversion process and is afforded rights and privileges not possessed by slaves in any other culture. While not a full member of the Jewish community, the *eved Cana'ani* is nonetheless a member, entering into a covenant with God and acquiring the protection of God's law.

What is the Torah trying to accomplish through the creation of this unique subpopulation within Jewish society known as *eved Cana'ani*?

— **C** ————————————————————————————

From our vantage point, we wonder with discomfort why God would not simply prohibit slavery entirely. We cannot, however, ignore the historical context within which the Torah is given.

The nation of Israel is born into a world where slavery is accepted as a matter of course, openly practiced by all surrounding nations. Considered mere chattel, slaves are treated with barbaric cruelty and contempt, their lives forfeit to the whim of their masters.

Thrust into this environment, the Israelites must meet the twofold promise/challenge divinely transmitted at the dawn of their history to the patriarch, Avraham: "And I will make of you a great nation; I will bless you…and you shall be a blessing…. And all the families of the earth shall be blessed through you."[12]

Not only must the Israelites become a "blessed" nation, avoiding the

————————————
12. Bereishit 12:2–3.

brutal practices of their neighbors, they must also positively affect those around them. Surrounded by suffering, they must find a way to mitigate that suffering in real and concrete ways.

In light of this challenge, the two seemingly obvious ethical choices available to the Israelites emerge as either impractical or fundamentally unethical:

1. *The Torah could have prohibited slavery in its entirety and commanded the Israelites to work towards the freedom of all surrounding slaves.*

This attractive option is, of course, unworkable in practice. The ability of the Israelites to have any real impact upon the policies of surrounding nations would have been negligible.

2. *The Torah could have simply prohibited the Israelites from owning slaves themselves.*

While the selection of this option would certainly have made a powerful ethical statement, the historic mandate of the Israelites to better the lives of those around them in concrete ways would have been sorely constrained. By creating a system in which the Israelites could not purchase slaves from the surrounding nations, the Torah would have, through mandated inaction, effectively confined those very slaves to the inhumane conditions in which they now found themselves. In effect, ethics would have been preached but not practiced, as the Israelites would have remained unable to alleviate the pain surrounding them.

— D —

God, therefore, chooses a different, more nuanced path for His chosen people.

Israelites may, indeed, acquire slaves from surrounding cultures. These acquisitions, however, carry the clear responsibility to better the lives, both spiritually and physically, of those who enter Israelite homes. The *eved Cana'ani* must be offered the right to convert to a new status within the Israelite society. In this position he moves beyond his pagan origins and enters into a unique covenant with God, accepting a level of Torah observance consonant with his new standing. At the same time, he gains a new physical reality, with protections, rights and privileges of which he could heretofore have hardly dreamt.

A critical balance, however, must be struck. This approach to slavery carries significant dangers for the newborn Israelite nation itself. *An in-*

flux of foreigners from different cultures and backgrounds, many of whom are entering the society only to escape their current reality, can seriously undermine the stability of the community. History has shown, in the form of slave rebellions in ancient times and until today in the struggle of dealing with immigrant populations, the challenges created by the sudden introduction of disparate subgroups into a society.

Balancing the rights of these *avadim Cana'anim*, therefore, are continuing safeguards ensuring their subservience to the population as a whole. Limited opportunities for full freedom will exist. As a rule, however, these newcomers and their children will remain *avadim Cana'anim*.

—— **E** ————————————————————————————

Based on our analysis, the institution of slavery within the Jewish nation remains dependent upon the existence of such slavery outside the nation. In a world where such cruelty is unknown, these laws will have little or no practical application.

With intricate care and concern, the Torah thus mandates a humane approach to an inhumane practice for as long as necessary.

Points to Ponder

Our analysis of the overwhelmingly difficult topic of biblical slavery raises another significant issue worthy of note and further discussion.

What balance should be struck between eternality and temporal context when it comes to general study of Torah text? What is the relationship between the timelessness of the text and the particular time and world into which it was given?

Our tradition clearly maintains both the divine origin and the eternal applicability of the Torah. The Torah is God's word designed to be relevant to all times and places.

At the same time, however, we cannot deny that the Torah was revealed to a specific people in a specific era. Clearly, God spoke to the Israelites within the context of their times as He laid out His eternal messages.

Where do we draw the line, looking back, millennia later?

Can the argument of temporal context be used, as we have suggested, as the basis for an approach to the institution of *eved Cana'ani*? If so, where and when else can such arguments be applied? Can issues of context be raised without undermining the timeless nature of the Torah?

Two examples from traditional sources might prove instructive.

In his major halachic work, the *Mishneh Torah*, the Rambam refers to *korbanot* (biblical sacrifices) as edicts of God which cannot be understood.[13] In his *Guide to the Perplexed*, however, this scholar takes a dramatically different stance. Building upon earlier Midrashim,[14] he maintains that the *korbanot* were decreed because "you cannot take a people from one extreme to the other."[15] The Israelites were immersed in a culture and in a world where the only mode of communication with God considered possible was through sacrificial rite. God, therefore, mandates sacrifices within the Torah so that His people will feel able to relate to Him.[16]

The Ramban, for his part, suggests that the garments of the High Priest, described in detail in Parshat Tetzave,[17] were modeled after the imperial garments of royalty of the day.[18]

Both of these authorities, however, while accepting the possible contextual origin of these phenomena, maintain that, once decreed, they become everlasting. The Rambam clearly speaks of a return to sacrifices in messianic times and, in fact, dedicates a great deal of text to laws concerning the rituals of *korbanot*.[19] The Ramban, likewise, fully recognizes the eternal nature of the priestly garments plainly indicated within the Torah text itself.[20]

Clearly, temporal context and perpetual legacy should both be considered as we continue to study the Torah text. The beauty of the text lies in its unique ability to blend the ancient with the timeless. The balance created by these two forces helps us understand both the origin and complex nature of God's word.

---

13. Rambam, *Mishneh Torah*, Hilchot Me'ila 8:8.
14. Yalkut Shimoni, Acharei Mot 247:579.
15. Rambam, *Moreh Nevuchim* 3:32.
16. Ibid.
17. Shmot 28:2–43.
18. Ramban, Shmot 28:2.
19. Rambam, *Mishneh Torah*, Sefer Avoda, Sefer Korbanot.
20. Shmot 28:43.

2 When the Torah Does Not Say What It Means

Context

Commenting on one of the most well-known legal passages in the Torah, the rabbis overrule the seemingly clear intent of the text.

The Torah states, in its discussion of the laws of personal injury: "*...And you shall award a life for a life, an eye for an eye, a tooth for a tooth, a hand for a hand, a foot for a foot, a burn for a burn, a wound for a wound, a bruise for a bruise.*"[1]

In the book of Vayikra, the text is even clearer: "*And if a man shall inflict a wound upon his fellow, as he did so shall be done to him. A break for a break, an eye for an eye, a tooth for a tooth; as a man shall inflict a wound upon a person, so shall be inflicted upon him.*"[2]

The rabbis in the Talmud, however, maintain that the Torah never intended to mandate physical punishment in personal injury cases. Instead, they say, the text actually authorizes *financial restitution*. The oft-quoted phrase "an eye for an eye," for example, means that the perpetrator *must pay the monetary value commensurate with the victim's injury*.

All the other cases cited in these passages are to be understood similarly, in terms of financial compensation.[3]

So great is the gap between the face value of the Torah text and the legal conclusion recorded in the Talmud, that the Rambam, in his halachic magnum opus the *Mishneh Torah*, feels the need to stress that the decision to levy monetary compensation in personal injury cases is not the result of later rabbinic legislation: "All this is law given to Moshe in our hands, and thus did our ancestors rule in the court of Yehoshua and in the court of Shmuel from Rama and in each and

---

1. Shmot 21:23–25.
2. Vayikra 24:19–20.
3. Talmud Bavli Bava Kama 83b–84a.

179

every court which has stood from the time of Moshe, our teacher, to this day."[4]

In an unbroken tradition from the time of Revelation onward, the halachists insist that *Torah law itself mandates financial restitution, not physical punishment*, in cases of personal injury.

Questions

Why doesn't the Torah simply say what it means?

Over the ages, the "eye for an eye" formula has been cited by critics as proof of the vengeful, primitive nature of Mosaic law. If the Torah never meant to mandate physical punishment in cases of personal injury, why wasn't the text more clearly written?

A great deal of misunderstanding, misinterpretation and trouble could have been avoided had the Torah simply stated, *"The court shall levy the appropriate compensatory payment in cases of personal injury."*

Approaches

—— **A** ——

An easily missed phrase in the Rambam's above-cited codification of the law provides a glimpse into the Torah's true intent:

> The Torah's statement "As a man shall inflict a wound upon a person, so shall be inflicted upon him" does not mean that we should physically injure the perpetrator, *but that the perpetrator is deserving of losing his limb and must therefore pay financial restitution.*[5]

Apparently the Rambam believes, as do many other scholars who echo the same sentiment, that the Torah confronts a serious dilemma as it moves to convey its deeply nuanced approach to cases of personal injury: *using the tools at its disposal, how can Jewish law best reflect the discrepancy between "deserved" and "actual" punishment?*

The gravity of the crime is such that, on a theoretical level, on the level

---

4. Rambam, *Mishneh Torah*, Hilchot Chovel U'mazik 1:6.
5. Ibid., 1:3.

of "deserved punishment," the case belongs squarely in the realm of *dinei nefashot* (capital law). The perpetrator truly merits physical loss of limb in return for the damage inflicted upon his victim. Torah law, however, will not consider physical mutilation as a possible punishment for a crime. The penalty must therefore be commuted into financial terms.

Had the Torah, however, mandated financial payment from the outset, the full gravity of the crime would not have been conveyed. The event would have been consigned to the realm of *dinei mamonot* (monetary crimes), and the precious nature of human life and limb would have been diminished.

The Torah therefore proceeds to express, with delicate balance, both theory and practice within the law. First, the written text records the "deserved punishment" without any mitigation: "…an eye for an eye, a tooth for a tooth…" In this way, the severity of the crime is immediately made clear to all. Then, however, the actual monetary punishment must also be conveyed, as well. Concerning this task, the Oral Law serves as the vehicle of transmission. The practical interpretation of the biblical passage – commuting the penalty into financial terms – is divinely revealed to Moshe. This interpretation is then preserved and applied in an unbroken transmission, from the time of Revelation onward.

Jewish law thus finds a way to memorialize both the "deserved" and the "actual" punishments within the halachic code.

— **B** —————————————————————————

A few sentences further in Parshat Mishpatim, an even more glaring example of the discrepancy between theory and practice in the realm of punishment emerges. In this case, however, both variables are recorded in the written text itself. As the Torah discusses the laws of a habitually violent animal, two conflicting consequences appear in the text for the very same crime.

The Torah states that, under normal circumstances, if an individual's ox gores and kills another human being, the animal is put to death but the owner receives no further penalty. Such violent behavior on the part of a domesticated animal is extremely rare and could not have been predicted.[6]

---

6. Shmot 21:28.

If, however, the animal has shown clear violent tendencies in the past – to the extent that the owner has been warned yet has failed to take appropriate precautions – the Torah emphatically proclaims, "…The ox shall be stoned *and even its owner shall die*."[7]

The matter, however, is not laid to rest with this seemingly definitive declaration. Instead, the text continues, "If a ransom shall be assessed against him [the owner of the violent ox], *he shall pay as a redemption for his life whatever shall be assessed against him*."[8]

In this case, the written text itself seems bewilderingly contradictory. On the one hand, the Torah clearly states that the owner of a violent animal "shall also die." Then, however, the text offers the condemned man an opportunity to escape his dire fate through the payment of a financial penalty assessed by the court.

Nowhere else does the Torah allow avoidance of capital punishment through the payment of a "ransom." The very idea, in fact, is anathema to Jewish thought. In discussing the laws of murder, the Torah clearly states, "You shall not accept ransom for the life of a murderer who is worthy of death, for he shall certainly be put to death."[9]

Why, then, if the owner of the ox is deserving of death, is he offered the opportunity to ransom his life?

To make matters more complicated, many authorities maintain that what the Torah seems to present as a choice really is not. The ransom payment is mandatory.[10] No one is ever put to death as punishment for the actions of his violent animal.

In partial explanation, the Talmud does maintain that the death sentence mandated in this case refers to death "at the hands of heaven" rather than execution decreed by an earthly court.[11] Monetary payment enables the owner of the ox only to escape a divine decree. No ransom would ever be accepted as an alternative to true capital punishment determined through due process of law, in a human court.

The question, however, remains: if the punishment in this case is uniformly monetary, why doesn't the Torah say so in the first place? Why pro-

---

7. Ibid., 21:29.
8. Ibid., 21:30.
9. Bamidbar 35:31.
10. Rashi, Shmot 21:30; Rambam, *Mishneh Torah*, Hilchot Nizkei Mamon 10:4.
11. Talmud Bavli Ketubot 37b.

nounce a death sentence on the owner that will not actually be carried out, even at the hands of heaven?

Once again our questions can be answered by considering the distinction between "deserved" and "actual" punishment.

The Torah wants us to understand that, on a theoretical level, the owner of the ox deserves to die. His negligence has directly resulted in the loss of human life. On a practical level, however, this sentence cannot be carried out. Halacha only mandates capital or corporal punishment in cases of active crimes. Crimes of "uninvolvement," consisting of the failure to do something right, cannot carry such penalties in an earthly court. The owner who fails to guard his dangerous animal can only be fully punished through heavenly means.

There is, therefore, an available corrective, a way for the condemned man to escape the divine decree. God, Who "truly discerns the soul and heart [of man],"[12] will forgive a perpetrator in the face of real penitence and change.

Through payment of the fine levied by the court, the animal's owner actively proclaims a newfound willingness to take responsibility for his past failure. In effect, he corrects the omission that led to tragedy by admitting his involvement in the crime. This admission, if heartfelt, suffices to avert a merciful God's decree.

Through carefully balancing the textual flow, the Torah manages to convey a complex, multilayered message of personal responsibility in a nuanced case of "uninvolvement."

Points to Ponder

The practice of studying and quoting passages from the biblical text "out of context" has become common, not only among those who seek to attack the divine authority and character of the Torah, but even among those who claim to respect it. Conclusions and lessons are often drawn from words and phrases in isolation, without attention paid to their surrounding framework.

As the above discussions clearly demonstrate, true Torah study must be contextual in the fullest sense of the word. Failure to consider context inevitably leads to misinterpretation and misrepresentation of the text.

---

12. Yirmiyahu 11:20.

Each phrase of the Torah must be analyzed against the backdrop of surrounding textual flow, other sources in the written text and related Oral Law. Only such complete, comprehensive study reveals the true depth and meaning of the biblical text.

3 Measuring the Immeasurable

The main body of Parshat Mishpatim consists of a series of fundamental laws, wide-ranging in their scope. A full study of these edicts leads to an appreciation not only of the brilliance of Jewish law, but of its timeless applicability.

This study, in which one such area of law is chosen for analysis, is meant to serve as a paradigm, demonstrating the uncanny manner in which all of halacha speaks across the ages.

Context

As noted in the previous study, Torah law instructs the court to levy a monetary penalty upon an individual found guilty of injuring another (see Mishpatim 2).

Questions

What are the parameters for determining the financial penalties levied in personal injury cases? How does Jewish law suggest that we measure the "immeasurable" and fully compensate victims of serious injury?

Are the penalties eventually suggested in the halachic code the result of original rabbinic legislation or do the rabbis base their conclusions upon sources in the written text?

Approaches

—A—

The Mishna records the following formula for computing the financial obligation in personal injury cases: "An individual who injures another is liable for five things: *nezek* (damages), *tzaʾar* (pain and suffering), *ripui* (healing), *shevet* (loss of wages) and *boshet* (humiliation)."[1]

— **B** —

Elaborating on the Mishna, the Talmud explains that these five component payments are not created anew by the rabbis but, rather, derived from specific passages in the Torah text. Four of these sources are found in Parshat Mishpatim while the fifth is found in the book of Devarim.

The Mishna and Talmud also discuss, at great length, the method of computing each payment. While there are differences of opinion reflected in the Talmudic discussion, what follows is a brief review of the halachic conclusions according to most authorities.

1. *Nezek* (damages): "…an eye for an eye…"[2]

The rabbis view the phrase an "eye for an eye" as the source for the specific payment of damages – the concrete loss in the "monetary value" of the victim as a result of the injury. The phrase is thus interpreted as "the value of an eye for an eye."[3]

Damages are computed by comparing the asking price the victim would have fetched had he been sold as a slave before the injury with the price he would bring now, after the injury. The differential between these two sums constitutes the payment of damages.[4]

Clearly, any special skills lost through the injury must be taken into account. A gifted artist who loses the fine motor skills of his hands, for example, will merit a greater payment of damages than another individual who sustains the same harm.

2. *Tzaʾar* (pain and suffering): "…a burn for a burn…"[5]

Pain and suffering can, of course, result from an injury even in the absence of lasting physical damage. According to the scholars, the phrase "a burn for a burn" refers to such a circumstance – where the event results in no permanent physical harm and, consequently, no decrease in the "monetary value" of the victim (e.g., a burn on one's fingernail that causes no lasting wound). In this case, although no damages are assessed against

---

1. Talmud Bavli Bava Kama 83b.
2. Shmot 21:24.
3. Talmud Bavli Bava Kama 83b–84a.
4. Ibid., 83b.
5. Shmot 21:25.

the perpetrator, he must, nevertheless, compensate his victim for "pain and suffering."[6]

The payment of *tza'ar*, however, is not limited to cases where there is no permanent injury. This penalty is also levied, when appropriate, as an additional payment to damages in a case of lasting harm (as are the other payments listed in the Mishna).[7]

Tza'ar is computed in one of two ways:

a. In a case of no lasting harm: We assess how much an individual would demand to be paid to willingly endure the pain associated with this passing injury.[8]

b. In a case of permanent injury (where the victim is already being compensated for his enduring loss through the payment of damages): We factor out the value of *tza'ar* by considering the following hypothetical situation: A king has decreed that an individual similar to the victim must lose the limb in question. We assess the amount the individual, facing the unavoidable punishment, would be willing to pay in order that the procedure be done painlessly. This sum defines the payment of *tza'ar*.[9]

3–4. *Shevet* (loss of employment); *ripui* (healing): "...Only for the loss of employment shall he pay and he shall provide for healing..."[10]

The payments of *shevet* and *ripui* are both derived by the rabbis from the above passage found in Parshat Mishpatim in conjunction with an injury caused by a quarrel.[11]

In a case where no permanent injury results and the victim will eventually be able to return to his former profession, *shevet* is determined directly by computing the value of his lost wages over the period of recuperation. In a situation of lasting injury, however (where the victim is already being compensated through the payment of damages for his permanent disability), the additional payment of *shevet* remunerates the victim at minimum wage level until he can return to some form of employment.[12]

Ripui is determined by assessing the cost of providing independent

---

6. Talmud Bavli 83b.
7. Ibid., 84b–85a.
8. Ibid., 83b.
9. Ibid., 85a.
10. Shmot 21:19.
11. Talmud Bavli Bava Kama 85a.
12. Ibid., 83b,85b; Rambam, *Mishneh Torah*, Hilchot Chovel U'mazik 2:11.

expert medical care to the victim. This payment is limited to the medical needs directly associated with the injury.[13]

5. *Boshet* (humiliation): "…and she stretches out her hand and grasps his private place, you shall cut off her hand…"[14]

The fifth, final payment in cases of personal injury is in many ways the most difficult.

Boshet is the only payment not drawn from a passage in Parshat Mishpatim. It derives, instead, from a troubling text in the book of Devarim where the Torah discusses the case of a woman who, in the course of defending her husband, strikes his assailant in a publicly humiliating fashion.[15]

The rabbis are quick to explain that (as was the case concerning the passage "an eye for an eye"; see Mishpatim 2) the pronouncement "you shall cut off her hand" is not meant to be understood literally. Instead, they maintain, the punishment is to be assessed in monetary terms and only applied if the woman could have avoided the public spectacle by assisting her husband through other means.[16]

The financial penalty applied in this case serves as the source for the payment of *boshet* in all applicable cases of personal injury. However, complexity surrounds not only the origin of the payment of *boshet* but its practical assessment and application as well. The Mishna itself underscores the subjective nature of this penalty by stating, "*Boshet*? It is all according to the humiliater and the humiliated."[17]

The rabbis go on to explain that the payment of *boshet* is assessed according to the status and current situation of both the perpetrator and victim. One who humiliates a minor, for example, will be liable for a lesser payment than one who humiliates an adult.[18]

Finally, *boshet* differs from the other four component payments in personal injury cases in one other significant way. The payments of damages, suffering, loss of wages and health are applied whether or not the injury

---

13. Talmud Bavli Bava Kama 83b,85a; Rambam, *Mishneh Torah*, Hilchot Chovel U'mazik 2:14, 18.
14. Devarim 25:11–12.
15. Talmud Bavli Bava Kama 86a.
16. Ibid., 28a.
17. Ibid., 83b.
18. Ibid., 86a.

was the result of intent or negligence on the part of the perpetrator. *Boshet* is only assessed if the injurious action was committed intentionally.[19]

——— **C** ———

The sophistication of Torah law is nowhere more evident than in its legislation concerning cases of personal injury. A review of the payments mandated by halacha finds these payments to be singularly complete in their approach and strikingly consistent with "modern" views concerning reimbursement in similar circumstances.

Meeting the test of time, the ancient law of Sinai remains remarkably "on point" to this day.

---

19. Ibid., 86b; Shulchan Aruch, Choshen Mishpat 421:1.

3b My Son, the Doctor...

Even the "spin-off" from a full halachic discussion is often filled with far-reaching significance and meaning.

This short addendum is meant to demonstrate exactly that point through the further consideration of one biblical phrase central to our previous study (see Mishpatim 3).

We have all heard the pride-filled anecdotes, humorous and otherwise, concerning the emotional attachment of the Jewish community to the noble profession of medicine. More so than with perhaps any other calling, having a doctor in the family has been a source of satisfaction within Jewish homes for as long as we can remember.

Things, however, could well have been drastically different. Consider the following Talmudic comment, presented almost as an afterthought, on the textual source for the payment of *ripui* (see Mishpatim 3, *Approaches* B3–4): "'...And he shall provide for healing';[1] From here [we learn] that permission is given to a doctor to cure."[2]

This seemingly simple declaration enables us to avoid a monumental philosophical and practical abyss. Judaism could well have adopted a different attitude towards the practice of medicine. Our tradition could have followed the path of other religious groups, such as Christian scientists and Seventh-day Adventists, and viewed illness as an expression of God's will, not to be tampered with.

The rabbis thus contend that "permission" had to be granted by God to allow for healing intervention.

Even after this Talmudic pronouncement is issued, however, discussion

---

1. Shmot 21:19.
2. Talmud Bavli 85a.

and debate on the subject continue. No less a scholar than Avraham Ibn Ezra entertains the possibility that since the phrase "and he shall provide for healing" refers to treatment of external, man-caused injuries, only such wounds are open to medicinal healing by man. The remediation of internal, naturally caused illnesses, he posits, may well remain in God's hands.[3]

Mainstream Jewish thought chooses otherwise, of course, in line with our tradition's general approach to man's partnership with the divine. God grants us the opportunity to use all means at our disposal to better our lives and the lives of those around us. Technological advancements and scientific discoveries are to be viewed as newly acquired tools in the quest to achieve these goals.

Accompanying our striving, however, our tradition urges that we maintain an ever-present sense of humility and an awareness of the God-given nature of our growing skills.

The Rambam, an accomplished physician, saw the mandate of his profession in a particularly telling light. The *obligation to cure*, he maintains, is an extension of the general mitzva of *hashavat aveida* (returning a lost object). Just as one, if given the opportunity, must return a misplaced item to its original owner, so, too, an individual who has the ability and opportunity to return health to another is obligated to do so. The noble medical profession is, in the eyes of one of its most renowned practitioners, simply another way of restoring to another that which is rightfully his own.[4]

Thank God we live in a time when new avenues for the advancement of human health are constantly being uncovered. We would do well to remember, however, that the knowledge, ability and, yes, *even the right to cure*, are God-given gifts, never to be taken for granted.

---

3. Ibn Ezra, Shmot 21:19.
4. *Peirush Hamishnayot L'haRambam*, Nedarim 4:4.

4 The Truth, The Whole Truth and Nothing But...

Context

The Torah issues two general directives concerning the avoidance of falsehood.

Here, in Parshat Mishpatim, the text states, "Distance yourself from a false matter [or: a false word]."[1]

In Parshat Kedoshim in the book of Vayikra, on the other hand, the Torah simply proclaims, "And you shall not deal falsely with one another."[2]

Questions

Why, in Parshat Mishpatim, does the Torah use the unusually expansive phrase *"distance yourself from"* to express its concern over falsehood? This language is not used with regard to any other transgression in the Torah.

What is the distinction between the two differently worded prohibitions concerning the avoidance of falsehood? Why are both of these prohibitions necessary?

Approaches

According to rabbinic interpretation, the Torah's issuance of two separate commandments concerning the avoidance of falsehood is a response to the subtleties of life. Different settings and circumstances demand different approaches to our relationship with the "truth."

—A—

Based upon textual context, the Talmud indicates that the commandment in Parshat Mishpatim, "Distance yourself from a false matter," focuses

---

1. Shmot 23:7.
2. Vayikra 19:11.

primarily on matters of jurisprudence. The two sentences that surround this pronouncement in the text and, more importantly, the other half of the sentence itself, are all clearly directed towards those involved in court-room proceedings.

From a halachic perspective, settlement and compromise are possible, even desirable, before the wheels of justice have turned. In the determination of the law, however, truth – and only truth – becomes our goal.[3]

So great, in fact, is the need for truth in judgment, say the rabbis, that any possibility of seeming or potential impropriety must be avoided at all costs. The Torah thus states, "Distance yourself from a false matter." *Avoid any act in the process of jurisprudence which might lead to or give the appearance of falsehood.*

Reflecting their concern for truth in judgment, the Talmudic sages derive a long list of practical directives from this Torah passage, including the following examples:

1. A judge who has begun to doubt his conclusions should not continue to defend them simply because he is embarrassed to admit his error.[4]

2. A judge and a witness who are convinced of an individual's guilt should not conspire to convict that individual without due process.[5]

3. A judge who suspects that witnesses in a specific case are lying but cannot prove his suspicions should recuse himself from the case.[6]

4. A student who observes his teacher erring in judgment is obligated to speak up.[7]

5. A court must ensure that the litigants appearing in a case before them are clothed in garments of equal value (so that the verdict will not be influenced by external appearances).[8]

6. A court should not hear the testimony of a litigant outside the presence of his adversary.[9]

7. A student who is instructed by his teacher to attend a courtroom proceeding – so that the judges will erroneously interpret the student's

---

3. Talmud Bavli Sanhedrin 6b; Rambam, *Mishneh Torah*, Hilchot Sanhedrin 22:4.
4. Talmud Bavli Shevuot 30b; Rashi, ibid..
5. Talmud Bavli Shevuot 30b.
6. Ibid.; Rambam, *Mishneh Torah*, Hilchot Sanhedrin 24:3.
7. Talmud Bavli Shevuot 31a.
8. Ibid.
9. Ibid.

mere presence as testimony on the teacher's behalf – must refuse. The student should decline even if he is convinced of the veracity of the teacher's claim and even if he would not be required to say a word in support of that claim.[10]

These and other rabbinic injunctions underscore halacha's deep commitment to the integrity of the judicial process. The legal system is too precious to be endangered through artificial maneuvering, no matter what the reason or rationale. Under any and all circumstances, in and surrounding the courtroom, we must "distance [ourselves] from a false matter."

—— B ——

In contrast to the expansive approach adopted by the halacha concerning the avoidance of falsehood in the sphere of jurisprudence, the Torah's attitude to the same concern in other areas of life is apparently a bit more complex.

As Nehama Leibowitz notes, the operant text outside the courtroom is not "Distance yourself from a false matter" but the more limited prohibition, "You shall not deal falsely with one another."[11]

Certainly, truth-telling must be the order of the day in all spheres of human experience. The halachic system is, in fact, replete with specific laws mandating honesty in the marketplace and in other social settings. Often, even the appearance of impropriety is prohibited.[12]

There are times, however, when other concerns override the need to "tell the whole truth." *In particular, when the forces of "truth" and "peace" collide, Jewish thought is willing, albeit reluctantly, to set truth aside.*

The rabbis note a few such cases:

1. When three angels appear before Avraham and Sara with the news of Yitzchak's impending birth, Sara laughs and privately exclaims: "After I have waxed old, shall I have deep satisfaction? *And my husband is old!*" God, however, repeats Sara's words to Avraham in the following abbreviated fashion: "Why did Sara laugh, saying, 'Shall I then in truth bear *when I have become so old?*'"[13]

---

10. Ibid.
11. Nehama Leibowitz, *Studies in Shmot* (Jerusalem: World Zionist Organization, 1976), p. 438.
12. Shulchan Aruch, Choshen Mishpat 228.
13. Bereishit 18:12–13.

God omits Sara's derogatory reference to Avraham in order to preserve the peace between husband and wife.[14]

2. After Yaakov's death, Yosef's brothers fear that Yosef will now feel free to exact vengeance upon them for their past misdeeds. They therefore approach their brother and state: "*Your father gave orders before his death, saying*: 'so shall you say to Yosef: Please forgive the iniquity of your brothers and their sin for they have done you evil.'"[15]

There is, however, no independent textual corroboration that these orders were actually given by Yaakov. The rabbis therefore entertain the possibility that Yosef's brothers lied by putting words in their father's mouth, in order to preserve peace within the family.

This episode teaches us, the rabbis continue, that one is allowed to misrepresent the facts in order to establish peace.[16]

3. As noted earlier (see Shmot 5, *Approaches* D), a striking contrast is reflected in the personalities of the two brothers, Aharon and Moshe. While Moshe's worldview is reflected in the maxim "Let the law cut through the mountain," Aharon is described as a man who "loved peace, pursued peace and created peace between man and his friend."[17]

The rabbis explain that Aharon's efforts to establish interpersonal harmony took concrete form. Whenever a dispute developed between two Israelites, Aharon sat with the protagonists individually and convinced each that he himself had witnessed the overwhelming regret of the other party involved in the quarrel. So convincing were Aharon's fabrications that each of the adversaries invariably set his grievances aside and, as a result, the parties ultimately met in peaceful embrace.

Through his efforts Aharon became more beloved to the Israelites than even his brother, Moshe. Remarkably, this love is reflected in the deeper mourning exhibited by the nation upon the passing of Aharon than upon the passing of Moshe.[18]

Clearly, the world outside the halls of justice is not painted in black and white, but in shades of gray. Conflicting needs and concerns must be factored into every human interaction, with an eye towards the true

14. Talmud Yerushalmi Peah 1:1.
15. Bereishit 50:15–17.
16. Talmud Bavli Yevamot 65b.
17. Talmud Bavli Sanhedrin 6b.
18. Bamidbar 20:29; Devarim 34:8; Avot D'Rabi Natan 12:3.

purpose and ultimate effect of each word and deed. *While a step off the path of truth should never be taken lightly, there are times when that step must, nevertheless, be taken.*

— C —

So powerful are the issues dividing the courtroom from the outside world that the point of intersection between these two realms becomes the focus of deep halachic controversy.

The Talmud records two diametrically opposed opinions concerning the issue of judicial compromise. Recognizing that compromise often results in a conclusion which is not factually "true," the rabbis ask, is a court allowed to attempt settlement of a case or must justice take its course?

> Rabbi Eliezer the son of Rabbi Yossi Hagalili states: "It is forbidden to compromise! One who compromises is a sinner! One who blesses a compromiser mocks [the Lord]!"
>
> Rabbi Yehoshua ben Korcha states: "It is a mitzva to compromise! [This is proven by the proclamation of the Prophet Zechariah:] 'Execute the judgment of truth and peace in your gates.'
>
> "[How can this be accomplished?] Is it not true that where there is judgment there is no peace [for one of the litigants is bound to be disappointed] and where there is peace there is no judgment? *What, then, is judgment which contains peace? Compromise!*"[19]

Powerful warring forces lie at the core of this debate. From Rabbi Eliezer's point of view, once the litigants approach the court there can be neither compromise nor settlement. The court's only task is to arrive at the "truth."

Rabbi Yehoshua, on the other hand, maintains that potential harmony between the litigants still remains our preferred objective. Judges, themselves, are certainly bound by the search for truth in deciding a case. Before reaching their conclusion, however, they may still encourage a peaceful, albeit "untrue" resolution.

In his codification of the law, the Rambam records that it is a mitzva to encourage compromise upon the litigants' initial approach to the court.

---

19. Talmud Bavli Sanhedrin 6b.

Such compromise, he continues, is desirable up until the point that a verdict has been announced. Once that verdict is proclaimed, however, settlement is no longer possible. The truth of "judgment" must then rule the day.[20]

The halachic tension between "truth" and "peace" in everyday life is mirrored in a fascinating dispute between the House of Shammai, whose scholars were known for their strictness in the application of the law, and the House of Hillel, whose members had a reputation for kindness and sensitivity.

The Talmud asks:

Keitzad merakdin lifnei hakalla? (How should one dance before the bride? [meaning, "What praises should we sing as we dance before a bride?"])

The scholars of Beit Shammai say that [one should praise the bride honestly,] as she is.

The scholars of Beit Hillel, on the other hand, maintain [that one should universally exclaim:] *Kalla na'a v'chasuda!* (How beautiful and charming is the bride!)[21]

As the Talmudic discussion continues, the sages of Beit Shammai express their discomfort over the possibility of lying in a case where it is clear to all that the bride is undeserving of such praise. "After all," they argue, "does not the Torah state, 'Distance yourself from a false matter'?"

Beit Hillel respond that we are under no obligation to underscore the negative, even through omission, if only harm will result. Unless we praise all brides uniformly, they maintain, deep embarrassment at a most sensitive moment is bound to occur.[22]

Underlying this seemingly quaint argument courses the serious issue of truth-telling and its boundaries. Beit Shammai, true to their demanding nature, depart from the Talmudic sources cited above and apply the expansive phrase, "Distance yourself from a false matter," beyond the courtroom. Even in the festive setting of a wedding feast, they believe, falsehood cannot be countenanced. Only the truth can be told.

---

20. Rambam, *Mishneh Torah*, Hilchot Sanhedrin 22:4.
21. Talmud Bavli Ketubot 16b–17a.
22. Ibid., Tosafot, ibid.

Beit Hillel, on the other hand, ever sensitive, refuse to embarrass the bride and groom, even if an outright fabrication must be proffered.

The halachic verdict concerning this dispute is reflected in a beautiful practice recorded in the *Shulchan Aruch*.[23] No traditional wedding is complete without a dance set to the words *Keitzad merakdin lifnei ha'kalla?* "How should one dance before the bride?"

And, as the dance unfolds at each and every celebration, the response of Beit Hillel unfailingly rings through the air: *Kalla na'a v'chasuda!* "How beautiful and charming is the bride!"

Several authorities, still uncomfortable with an outright lie, struggle to base this practice on a foundation of factual truth. Every bride, after all, they say, has something beautiful and charming about her.[24]

Many other scholars, however, accept Beit Hillel's, and consequently our, apparent willingness to "stretch the truth" at face value. *Sometimes the truth need not be told. For the sake of harmony we choose to live in a world in which every bride is beautiful (even if she is not)!*[25]

---

23. Shulchan Aruch, Even Ha'ezer 65:1.
24. Beit Shmuel, Even Ha'ezer 65:2.
25. Ritva, Ketubot 17a.

5 Sealing the Deal

Context

In an abrupt and striking departure from the legalistic content which, in general, characterizes Parshat Mishpatim, the parsha returns towards its close to a scene of spiritual revelation at Sinai.

God commands Moshe to ascend the mountain, accompanied partway by Aharon, Aharon's two oldest sons (Nadav and Avihu) and seventy elders from among the nation.

Prior to ascending the mountain, Moshe informs the people of God's instructions and laws and receives their assent, writes down "God's words," builds an altar and twelve pillars (representing the twelve tribes) at the foot of the mountain, instructs the "youths" from among the nation to offer sacrifices, reads the "book of the covenant" to the nation, eliciting the dramatic response, "Everything that God has spoken we will do and we will hear,"[1] and symbolically seals a covenant between God and the people.

Moshe and his entourage then ascend partway up the mountain. There, they experience a majestic vision of God. The Torah testifies that, as the vision unfolds, "Against the great men of the Israelites He did not stretch out His hand – they gazed at God, and they ate and they drank."[2]

Questions

What is the significance of the multiple events prior to and during Moshe's ascent partway up Mount Sinai together with Aharon, Aharon's sons and the seventy elders?

When did these events occur? The rituals performed by Moshe before

---

1. Shmot 24:7.
2. Ibid., 24:1–11.

ascending the mountain seemed to be preparatory in nature. Shouldn't they therefore have been performed at the beginning of Revelation, before the transmission of the Ten Declarations of Parshat Yitro and the detailed laws of Parshat Mishpatim?

What exactly did Moshe record in the "Book of the Covenant" and then read to the Israelites?

What is the meaning of the bewildering statement, in conjunction with the vision on Sinai, "Against the great men of the Israelites, He did not stretch out His hand…"? Why would we have assumed that God would have "stretched out His hand against" the great men of Israel?

Upon seeing the vision of God, the participants on Sinai "gaze at God and eat and drink." Is this an appropriate response to a majestic spiritual experience?

Approaches

So deep is the mystery surrounding the narrative in question that strikingly disparate positions develop among the scholars concerning every aspect of the text's unfolding, from its chronology to its ultimate significance. Discussions surrounding this passage thus form a case study in traditional interpretation, mirroring the vastly different points of view which can develop within rabbinic literature surrounding a single section of Torah text.

—— **A** ——

Numerous commentaries, applying the tool of *Ein mukdam u'me'uchar ba'Torah* (the Torah does not necessarily follow chronological order; see Yitro 1: *Approaches* A), maintain that the events recorded towards the end of Parshat Mishpatim actually occur prior to the onset of Revelation. Rashi, for example, basing his position on an earlier tradition quoted in the Mechilta, dates the narrative as beginning on the fourth day of Sivan, two days before the transmission of the Ten Declarations. Combining this text with earlier texts, Rashi develops the following chronology.

On the fourth day of Sivan, Moshe

1. instructs the people concerning the imperative of *hagbala* (creating a boundary around Mount Sinai; see Yitro 2, 3);

2. reiterates the Seven Noachide Laws and all other already revealed edicts;

3. records those edicts and the entire Torah narrative from Bereishit until Revelation in the "Book of the Covenant."

On the fifth day of Sivan, Moshe

1. erects an altar and twelve pillars at the foot of Mount Sinai;

2. instructs the "youths" to offer sacrifices;

3. reads the "Book of the Covenant" to the nation, eliciting the dramatic response, "Everything that God has spoken we will do and we will hear";

4. symbolically seals a covenant between God and the people;

5. ascends partway up Mount Sinai together with Aharon, Nadav, Avihu and the seventy elders, where they experience a majestic vision of God.

Once these preparatory acts are performed, Revelation finally begins on the sixth day of Sivan.[3]

According to Rashi and those who follow his lead, the narrative towards the end of Parshat Mishpatim, when combined with earlier text, chronicles a series of essential steps prior to *Matan Torah. Through a carefully planned amalgam of education, ritual and majestic spiritual vision, God readies His people for their moment of closest contact with the divine.*

——— **B** ———

Numerous other commentaries, including the Ramban, adamantly disagree. Unwilling to invoke a nonchronological rendering of the text, these scholars maintain that the events recorded in Parshat Mishpatim occur exactly in the order in which they are written.[4]

From the perspective of these scholars, the proceedings in question are not preparatory to Revelation, but an integral part of the process itself. *Revelation becomes participatory, as Moshe and the Israelites "seal the deal" that God has proposed.*

The Ramban, in addition, maintains that the "Book of the Covenant" which Moshe writes and then reads to the nation includes the detailed laws of Parshat Mishpatim which God has just revealed.[5] In contrast to those who place the Israelite's acceptance of Torah before the onset of Revelation, the Ramban and his colleagues are thus able to view the people's

---

3. Rashi, Shmot 24:1–7.
4. Ramban, Shmot 24:1, Rashbam, Shmot 24:1–3.
5. Ramban, Shmot 24:1.

concurrence as *knowledge based*. When the Israelites exclaim "We will do and we will hear" they are not accepting the tradition on blind faith, without any understanding of its parameters. Through the detailed laws which have begun to unfold, the people have gained a true glimpse of the nature of the obligations that will now be theirs. Volumes more certainly remain to be learned, but the nation already possesses enough knowledge to make an informed decision. The rituals performed by Moshe and the people symbolically represent and solidify that decision.

— C —

Whatever position we adopt concerning the timing of these events, however, the vision granted to Moshe and his entourage partway up Mount Sinai remains fraught with mystery. In particular, fierce debate breaks out among the commentaries as they attempt to explain the bewildering statement "Against the great men of the Israelites He did not stretch out His hand – they gazed at God, and they ate and they drank."

Rashi interprets the passage as a reflection of serious sin on the part of those who accompany Moshe and Aharon partway up Mount Sinai. Granted a momentous vision of God's presence, Aharon's sons and the seventy elders respond irreverently by indulging in food and drink. Although this reaction earns them the death penalty, God temporarily stays His hand so as not to mar the joy of Revelation. Eventually, however, this divinely decreed sentence is carried out when, on separate occasions, the seventy elders and, later, Nadav and Avihu are consumed in heavenly fires.[6]

The Rambam perceives an even deeper spiritual failing on the part of Aharon's sons and the elders. In stark contrast to Moshe, who initially hides his face when confronted with God's presence,[7] these individuals impetuously venture into esoteric realms for which they are unprepared. As a result, their experience of God is imperfect and they attribute corporeal attributes to the divine, as the Torah states, "They saw the God of Israel, and *under His feet* was the likeness of sapphire brickwork…"[8] This flawed, partly physical vision further leads them to an inappropriate physical response through food and drink.

---

6. Rashi, Shmot 24:10–11.
7. Shmot 3:6.
8. Ibid., 24:10.

From the Rambam's perspective, the episode on Sinai thus emerges as a cautionary tale, warning that an individual must prepare and perfect his knowledge before contemplating realms of spiritual mystery.[9]

At the other end of the spectrum are those scholars who explain the text before us in a positive light, attributing no sin or failing to those who ascend Mount Sinai.

Onkelos, for example, in his interpretive translation of the Torah, explains that Aharon's sons and the elders did not actually eat and drink at all. Instead, the text informs us that their joy upon experiencing God's presence was so profound that it compared to the greatest of physical pleasures.[10]

Both the Rashbam and the Ibn Ezra interpret the phrase "And against the great men of Israel He did not stretch out His hand" to mean that Aharon's sons and the elders were spared from the usual danger that accompanies direct confrontation with the divine.[11] The Rashbam explains that these individuals then, appropriately, ate the portions of their sacrifices set aside for human consumption.[12] The Ibn Ezra adds that the eating and drinking represented a joyous celebration in response to the majestic heavenly vision.[13] Likewise, Rabbeinu Bachya compares their celebration to the festive feast sponsored by the Kohen Gadol (High Priest) immediately after Yom Kippur marking his safe emergence from the Temple's Holy of Holies during Judaism's most sanctified day.[14]

— **D** —————————————————————

The approach of the Sforno to this mysterious episode, however, is perhaps the most intriguing.

This Italian commentator remains true to his oft-stated position that the highest form of prophetic vision occurs when the prophet remains rooted in "reality." *Moshe is the greatest of prophets specifically because his encounters with God do not demand the suspension of his physical faculties.* While other *Nevi'im* (prophets) experience the divine through dreams and

---

9. Rambam, *Moreh Nevuchim* 1:5.
10. Targum Onkelos, Shmot 24:11.
11. Rashbam, ibid.; Ibn Ezra, ibid.
12. Rashbam, ibid.
13. Ibn Ezra, ibid.
14. Rabbeinu Bachya, ibid.

visions, Moshe "sees God face-to-face":[15] awake, in full possession of his senses.[16]

The Sforno even claims that the Revelation at Sinai was orchestrated in part to allow the nation to briefly and temporarily experience "Moshe-like prophecy," to encounter God while still rooted in the physical world. This experience enables the fulfillment of God's promise to Moshe: "And also in you [Moshe] will they believe forever."[17] Through their encounter with God at Sinai, the Israelites learn that it is possible to experience the divine while remaining fully sentient.[18]

Analogously, maintains the Sforno, the passage "Against the great men of the Israelites He did not stretch out His hand – they gazed at God, and they ate and they drank" actually testifies to the towering level of prophecy achieved by Moshe's entourage during their meeting with the divine. God does not "stretch out His hand" to remove them from their physical reality. They remain rooted in their world, experiencing "Moshe-like prophecy" to a deeper extent than the rest of the nation. In the aftermath of this majestic encounter, Aharon's sons and the seventy elders "eat and drink" – appropriately celebrating God's manifestation within a material setting.[19]

Through the Sforno's eyes, the phenomenon of prophecy remains remarkably consonant with Judaism's general attitude towards man's search for the divine. As we have noted (see Shmot 3, *Approaches* D, E; Yitro 2, *Approaches* C, D), normative Jewish thought maintains that the greatest iteration of God's Presence is not found in distant esoteric realms, but in man's own investiture of the physical world with sanctity through the fulfillment of God's will. *Even mystical encounters with God, says the Sforno, reserved for the select few chosen as prophets, achieve their highest level when experienced within the context of the natural world.*

Points to Ponder

Which of the vastly different approaches to the events recorded towards the end of Parshat Mishpatim is true?

The halachic maxim *Eilu ve'ilu divrei Elokim chaim*, "These and these

---

15. Shmot 33:11.
16. Sforno, ibid.
17. Shmot 19:9.
18. Sforno, ibid.
19. Sforno, Shmot 24:11.

are the words of the living God,"[20] applies within the interpretive realm as well. Each of the rabbinic approaches to this passage teaches us lessons consonant with Jewish thought and idea. Each of these approaches is, therefore, "true."

One day, God will reveal to us exactly what really happened on those monumental days as the Jewish nation stood at the foot of Sinai. Until then, we are meant to draw lessons from all the possibilities.

---

20. Talmud Bavli Eruvin 13.

Teruma

תרומה

CHAPTER 25:1–27:19

פרק כה:א-כז:יט

Parsha Summary

Sanctified architecture…

In yet another abrupt transition, God lays the next foundation of Jewish thought and law at Sinai, as He moves the focus from the courtroom to the sanctuary.

Parshat Teruma opens as God instructs Moshe to collect offerings of various materials for the creation of the Mishkan, the portable sanctuary in the desert and the precursor of the Temples in Jerusalem.

With the dramatic commandment "And they shall make for Me a holy place, and I will dwell within them," God then launches the plans for the Mishkan's construction.

The parsha first outlines in great detail the plans for the various utensils to be used in the Sanctuary service, including the Aron (Ark), the Kaporet (Ark Cover), the Keruvim (Cherubs), the Shulchan (Table) and the Menora (Candelabrum). The text then discusses the construction of the Sanctuary itself and closes with a description of the Mizbeiach (Altar) and the Sanctuary courtyard.

1 Why Build It At All?

Context

As the Israelites stand rooted at Sinai, yet another major foundation of their eternal heritage is divinely laid. God turns to Moshe and commands, "And they shall make for Me a holy place, and I will dwell among them."[1]

The construction of the Mishkan, the portable sanctuary that will accompany the Israelites during their desert travels, is thus launched. This sanctuary serves as the precursor to the Beit Hamikdash, the Holy Temple, eventually erected in Jerusalem.

One can scarcely imagine Judaism without the concept of the Beit Hamikdash. No single symbol has been more fundamental to the Jewish people than the Temple, representing their eternal connection to God.

Just as the Mishkan serves as the focal point of the Israelite encampment during its desert wanderings, so too, the first and second Batei Mikdash each become the central feature of the corresponding Jewish commonwealth in the Land of Israel. Twice destroyed, the Temple lives on in the hearts and minds of Jews throughout the world who pray daily for its rebuilding.

Questions

Why does God command that the Mishkan be built in the first place?

Judaism introduces to the world the concept of a unified, omnipresent God Who can be related to and worshiped at any time and in any place. If God is omnipresent, why then does He require a "central address"? Are we not limiting a limitless God by creating a Temple for His worship? To quote the objections of the Abravanel: "Why would God command the creation

---

1. Shmot 25:8.

of the Sanctuary, as if He were defined in corporeal terms and bounded by specific location? This is the opposite of the truth!"[2]

Approaches

A multitude of approaches, some of them revolutionary, are suggested by the classical scholars as they struggle to unravel the mysteries surrounding one of Judaism's most enduring and central symbols. Their suggestions can be divided into two contrasting global positions.

─── **A** ───────────────────────────────

One position is that the creation of the Mishkan is a divinely ordained response to the sin of the *egel hazahav* (the golden calf). This astounding possibility is first suggested in the Midrash and later adopted by numerous authorities, including Rashi.[3]

The Torah, however, introduces the Mishkan a full two and a half parshiot before the narrative of the golden calf. The Midrashic approach to the sanctuary, therefore, requires the reordering of the text through the application of the principle *Ein mukdam u'me'uchar ba'Torah* – the Torah text does not necessarily follow chronological order (see Yitro 1, *Approaches* A). The Midrash thus suggests that, textual flow of the Torah notwithstanding, God did not command the construction of the Mishkan until after the sin of the golden calf.

Why do the rabbis struggle so mightily to place the origin of the Mishkan after the sin of the golden calf? Because, it would seem, this chronological reordering allows for new light to be thrown on the complex symbolism of the Temple.

Through the eyes of the Midrashic scholars, the Mishkan is *not* an integral part of God's original plan for His newly formed nation, but rather a response to their weakness and failing. God has no need for the sanctuary and, in fact, does not initially include it as a component in His relationship with the Israelites. Once the people demonstrate their inability to relate to Him directly, however, God decrees the creation of the Mishkan as an act of remediation.

Some within the Midrash view the creation of the Sanctuary as a

───────────

2. Abravanel, ibid.
3. Rashi, Shmot 31:18, 33:11.

healing gesture on the part of God towards the nation. The people find themselves, as a result of the *chet ha'egel* (sin of the [golden] calf), hopelessly distanced from their Creator. God, therefore, reaches across the chasm to show them a way back.[4]

Other Midrashic sources consider the Sanctuary public testimony to the world of the enduring connection between God and His people, a connection that survives the tragedy of the golden calf. [5]

Most foundational, however, is the approach, based on the Midrashic chronology, which interprets the creation of the Mishkan as a divinely designed response, calculated to counteract the root causes of the *chet ha'egel*. At the core of this seminal sin lies the nation's inability to worship God directly without the benefit of intervening tangible symbols. This inability drives the Israelites, upon Moshe's perceived disappearance, to create the golden calf as a proposed intermediary between themselves and God. Recognizing the people's need for physical symbols, God, therefore, decrees the creation of the Mishkan and all of its associated rituals and utensils. *The fundamental concept of the Beit Hamikdash thus originally emerges as a concession to the Israelites' limitations.*[6]

——— **B** ————————————————————————————————————

At this point, we must digress for a moment to consider an overarching issue raised by this Midrashic approach to the Mishkan.

How are we to understand the concept of trial and error in association with God's will and actions? Mortal man is often forced to resort to "Plan B" when "Plan A" fails. An infallible God, however, should not encounter such difficulty. God knows in advance that the Israelites will sin through the golden calf. Why not, then, short-circuit the process and provide the nation with the symbolism it needs by issuing the commandments concerning the Sanctuary from the outset?

As we have noted before (see *Bereishit*, Noach 1, *Approaches* A), trial and error does not exist on God's part but on man's. God creates a world based upon free will, and the existence of free will is predicated on the possibility of human failure. In this case, God knows from the very beginning

---

4. Midrash Rabba Shmot 33:3.
5. Midrash Tanchuma Shmot, Teruma 8.
6. Sforno, Shmot 24:18.

the Israelites will sin, but He does not interfere. Instead, He retreats to allow them room to succeed or fail on their own.

God, in addition, wants the people to learn from their own failure. Had God initially commanded the erection of the sanctuary, the Midrash contends, the Israelites would never have discovered the nature of their own limitations. Like a child, the infant nation must be allowed to stumble and fall, if only to learn to rise again.

—— c ——

One other troubling issue, however, must be raised concerning the Midrashic approach to the Mishkan.

If, as we have suggested, the sin of the golden calf was caused by the nation's inability to relate to God without the benefit of a physical intermediary, isn't the proposed "cure" a perpetuation of the problem? *God simply seems to substitute the symbolism of the Sanctuary for the symbolism of the golden calf.* In what way is this beneficial? Shouldn't God, instead, train the nation towards the fact that such symbols are unnecessary – that man is capable of establishing a direct relationship with the divine?

On a basic level, we might simply answer that, in contrast to the golden calf, the Sanctuary and its rituals are divinely ordained. Through difficult experience at Sinai, the nation is taught that symbolic worship is allowed in Judaism when, and only when, the symbols involved flow from God's command.

In a deeper sense, however, the Sanctuary is not a replacement for the golden calf at all but a true antidote for its root causes. Through the creation of the golden calf, the Israelites attempt to establish *distance* between themselves and their Creator. Frightened by the perceived loss of Moshe and firmly convinced of their inability to relate to the divine directly without a go-between, the nation erects the golden calf to act as an intermediary between themselves and God (see Ki Tissa 2, *Approaches* b). In contrast, as will become clear in the next two studies (see Teruma 2, 3), the Mishkan represents man's ability to *draw close* to God. Properly understood, each and every detail of the Sanctuary and its associated rituals and utensils carries the message of God's accessibility to man. In a brilliant stroke, God not only responds to the *chet ha'egel* but prominently weaves the corrective to that failing into the very fabric of Jewish tradition.

—— **D** ————————————————————

In spite of the attractiveness of the Midrashic approach as a rationale for the creation of the Sanctuary, numerous other scholars, such as the Ramban,[7] demur.

Unwilling to accept the notion that the central concept of the Beit Hamikdash could possibly have emerged after the fact, as a concession to the weakness of the Israelites, these authorities maintain that God intended all along to create a central location for his worship.

In the words of Nehama Leibowitz, these scholars

> reject the idea that the Sanctuary was in any way an afterthought, a cure for their [the Israelites'] sickness, atonement for sin, or compromise between the idea of spirituality and the reality of man's material conceptions, demanding a form of worship limited to a definite space-time dimension. *On the contrary, the institution of the Sanctuary was there from the beginning, a deliberate act of divine grace and thoughtfulness designed to strengthen the immanence of His presence* [my italics].[8]

The Ramban and his colleagues maintain that the Mishkan and, therefore, the entire concept of a Beit Hamikdash are much too significant not to have been part of God's initial plan for His people. Far from being the source of the Mishkan, the sin of the golden calf actually threatens its creation. Only God's forgiveness for that sin reinstates His full relationship with the Israelites and enables the Sanctuary to be built.

—— **E** ————————————————————

Another benefit, of course, accrues to this approach.

The chronology of events at Mount Sinai unfolds exactly as recorded in the text. The commandments concerning the erection of the Mishkan are divinely transmitted to Moshe prior to the *chet ha'egel*. After that tragic event, God conveys His willingness to forgive and to reestablish His relationship with the nation. Moshe consequently perceives, of his own accord,

---

7. Ramban, Shmot 35:1, Vayikra 8:2.
8. Leibowitz, *Studies in Shemot*, p. 467.

that the previously given directives associated with the Sanctuary still apply. He therefore proceeds to share them with the nation.[9]

The Ramban, among others, thus remains consistent in his general reluctance to uproot the sequence of events as they are recorded in the text. "Why," he asks, in an attack on Rashi concerning this issue, "should we overturn the words of the living God?"[10] Unless the text itself indicates otherwise, maintains the Ramban, events in the Torah actually unfold in the order in which they are recorded.[11]

— **F** ————————————————————————————————

Those scholars who view the Mishkan as part of God's original blueprint for His chosen people also maintain that the Sanctuary is in no way meant to be perceived as an intermediary between the Israelites and their God. *Man's ability to relate to his Creator directly is, after all, a hallmark of Jewish faith.* The Mishkan, its symbols and its rituals are, instead, tools, carefully devised to assist the Israelites in the enterprise of seeking the divine.

Various theories are offered by the commentaries as to exactly how the Sanctuary achieves this goal.

Some, such as the Ba'al Hachinuch, author of the *Sefer Hachinuch*, suggest that the Mishkan provides the Israelites with the setting in which they can regularly perform personally beneficial acts of prayer and sacrifice. Such repeated action, says the Ba'al Hachinuch, makes a positive impact upon each supplicant, serving to purify his thoughts and refine his character.[12]

Others focus on the minute details of the rituals and utensils associated with the Sanctuary. Each of the many details recorded in the Torah, they suggest, carries its own specific lessons concerning the relationship between God and man.[13]

As will become even clearer over the next studies, neither the Mishkan nor the Beit Hamikdash, no matter their origin, is "God's home." Each of these central institutions is, instead, divinely designed to teach how we can successfully "bring God home to us."

———————————

9. Ramban, Vayikra 8:2.
10. Ibid.
11. Ramban, Bamidbar 16:1.
12. Sefer Hachinuch, mitzva 95.
13. Rabbi Shimshon Raphael Hirsch, Abravanel, Alshich, Akeidat Yitzchak and others, in their commentaries on Parshat Teruma and elsewhere.

2 Interpreting God's Blueprint

Context

As previously indicated (see Teruma 1, *Context*), God initiates the creation of the Mishkan (the portable Sanctuary in the desert) with the seemingly straightforward directive, "And they shall create for me a *mikdash* (a holy place), and I will dwell within them."[1]

Questions

Two linguistic issues emerge upon careful review of the commandment concerning the Mishkan.

Why does God state, "and I will dwell *within them*"? Parallel structure would have mandated that the sentence read: "And they shall make for Me a holy place, and I will dwell *within it*."

Why does the Torah use the generic term *mikdash* (holy place) in this commandment? This is the only occasion in the text where the portable desert Sanctuary is not referred to by its specific name: *Mishkan*.

Approaches

—A—

In light of our previous discussion concerning the Mishkan (see Teruma 1), the apparent non-parallel structure of this commandment makes abundant sense. The Torah does not state "and I will dwell *within it*," because *God does not dwell in the Mishkan nor will He dwell later in the Beit Hamikdash*.

Centuries later, in his historic address on the occasion of the First Temple's dedication in Jerusalem, *Shlomo Hamelech* (King Solomon) makes this point clear:

---

1. Shmot 25:8.

Will God indeed dwell on the earth? *Behold, the heaven and the heaven of heavens cannot contain You; how much less this house that I have built? Turn, therefore, to the prayer of Your servant and to his supplication… that Your eyes will be open towards this house night and day…. And You will listen to the supplication of Your servant and of Your nation Israel that they shall pray towards this place…*[2]

Shlomo's sentiments are thus foreshadowed in the Torah text with the very first introduction of the Mishkan, the precursor of both Temples. The Torah states, "and I will dwell *within them*," to stress that the purpose of the Sanctuary is to bring God into the lives of the people. Whether a sign of God's reconciliation with the nation after the sin of the golden calf or a corrective for that sin or an originally mandated symbol of continued divine presence, the Sanctuary serves to represent God's constant accessibility to man.

Some commentaries, including the Malbim, go a step further in their interpretation of the phrase "and I will dwell within them." The Israelites are commanded, they say, to build not only a physical sanctuary in the midst of the camp, but an internal spiritual sanctuary within each of their souls. They are thus instructed to create a place for God to "dwell within them" – in the hearts of the individual Israelites and their descendents.[3]

— **B** —

Concerning the text's use of the generic term *mikdash*, in place of the more specific Mishkan, a number of scholars maintain that the chosen terminology reflects the continuing character of the obligation. The nation is commanded from the outset to erect a *mikdash* (a holy place), not only at this point in their history, but also when they successfully establish a presence in their homeland.

The Rambam codifies this eternal mitzva as follows: "It is a positive commandment to build a 'House for the Lord'…as it states, 'And they shall make for Me a holy place…'"[4]

---

2. Melachim (Kings) I 8:27–30.
3. Malbim, Shmot 25:8.
4. Rambam, *Mishneh Torah*, Hilchot Beit Habechira 1:1.

— c ——————————————————————————

The Ohr Hachaim derives a beautiful additional lesson from the text's use of the word *mikdash*.

The sequence within the sentence "And they shall make for Me a holy place, and I will dwell within them," he claims, is counterintuitive. One would expect the Sanctuary to become "holy" only after the investiture of God's presence. By referring to the Sanctuary immediately as a *mikdash*, a holy place, the Torah conveys that the Temple is holy *from the moment that the Israelites create it* – even before God fulfills His commitment to "dwell" within the nation.[5]

The commandment to build the Temple thus reconfirms the fundamental truth repeated over and over again, in different ways, during the critical period of our nation's birth (see Shmot 3, *Approaches* D, E; Yitro 2, *Approaches* C, D): *Sanctity is created in this world when man acts in accordance with God's will. Man, as God's partner, invests the Sanctuary with holiness.*

Points to Ponder

Two points for consideration concerning the term *mikdash*:

1. If the commandment to build the *mikdash* is ongoing, are we not obligated to construct the Third Temple in Israel in our day? While numerous positions concerning this issue are staked out by the halachists, the approach presented by the *Sefer Hachinuch* is particularly intriguing.

The Ba'al Hachinuch explains that the parameters of the obligation to build a "holy place" shift dramatically with the building of the first permanent Temple in Jerusalem (tenth century BCE). From that time on, the commandment is effective only when the majority of the Jewish nation is living in the Land of Israel.

An immediate challenge to the Ba'al Hachinuch's position, however, emerges from a clear historical reality. The Second Temple was erected at the end of the Babylonian exile, when the vast majority of "exiles" tragically opted to forgo a return to Zion and remain in Babylon. Why, then, was the Second Temple built by the minority who did return?

Rabbi Yehoshua of Kotno defends the Ba'al Hachinuch with a bold contention: the Jews of Babylon remained in "exile" of their own choice. They

—————————————

5. Ohr Hachaim, Shmot 25:8.

therefore effectively ceded their rights to the Temple and could no longer, through their absence, prevent its rebuilding.[6]

The Ba'al Hachinuch's basic contention and Rabbi Yehoshua's further observation highlight the historic opportunities and challenges of our day. As the balance of Jewish life inexorably shifts from the diaspora to the State of Israel, we are rapidly approaching the point when the majority of Jews will be living in their homeland. Will we be biblically obligated at that point, political exigencies aside, to commence rebuilding the Temple?

Even further, an argument might be made that the "tipping point" concerning the Temple has already been reached. The majority of diaspora Jews today, like the Babylonian Jews of the Second Temple period, live in an "exile of choice" with the opportunity of return to the Land of Israel fully available. Have those of us in the diaspora lost our "rights" to the Temple? If so, should the Beit Hamikdash be built today, even in our absence?

The question remains academic given the political realities as well as other philosophical/halachic concerns. The issues raised, however, certainly should give us pause as we consider the momentous times in which we live. For the first time in nearly two thousand years we approach the point when, after centuries of wandering, a majority of the Jewish nation will be "home." What halachic, philosophical and psychological changes should occur within our nation's psyche as a result of this new reality? How are we meant to mark our momentous transformation from a "people of exile" to a "people of return"?

And what of those of us who choose not to participate fully in this new historic national adventure – we, who, yet today, live our lives outside of the Land of Israel?

We are quick to criticize, in retrospect, the Babylonian exiles who failed to return to Zion. How, we must honestly wonder, will history judge us?

Our excuses are many – some, perhaps, more valid then others. But the question must be asked: what "rights" do we lose when we voluntarily *choose* not to return home?

2. A refrain often sounded in today's Jewish community bemoans the lack of "spirituality" in traditional practice and worship. Pulpit rabbis regularly hear, "Rabbi, I fail to be 'moved' by the *tefilla* (prayer service)… The daily ritual leaves me empty."

---

6. Yeshuot Malko, Shmot, Parshat Teruma.

Responding to the challenge, numerous religious schools, synagogues and communal institutions have instituted studies and programs designed towards making age-old ritual personally relevant to their constituents. Federations have commissioned studies with an eye towards "reinventing the synagogue"; synagogues, themselves, have initiated programs, from prayer services featuring the poignant tunes of Rabbi Shlomo Carlebach to innovative adult education classes; schools regularly design and implement new curricula for the teaching of prayer and ritual.

On an individual level, frustrated by the perceived lack of meaning in "ordinary" Jewish practice, many Jews find their search leading to more esoteric areas of their tradition. Kabbalists and mystics – some of them authentic and some less so – become frequent visitors to "modern Orthodox communities," with claims of easy access to sacred realms. Sophisticated members of the Jewish community treasure questionable symbols – such as the "red *bendlach*" (red threads worn on the wrist purportedly to ward off the "evil eye," often received from beggars at the Western Wall) – with greater intensity than they do normative Jewish rituals.

While communal creativity (within halachic boundaries) is certainly laudable, and authentic spiritual search is essential to Jewish tradition, Judaism offers no shortcuts to religious meaning. Spiritual "quick fixes" are alien to our tradition. In a world marked by instant gratification, *Judaism preaches that spirituality is ultimately found only as a result of hard, continuing work.*

An individual, for example, who expects to be spontaneously and passively "moved" by weekly synagogue prayer, without the investment of true effort into that prayer, is doomed to disappointment. *Tefilla* is neither theater nor spectator sport. Prayer becomes meaningful only as a result of study of text, honest personal introspection, wrenching self-assessment and a continuing evaluation of our relationship with God.

As the Mishna proclaims: "One should not stand to pray without full and serious intent. The righteous of old would deliberate a full hour before beginning to pray, in order to direct their hearts towards the Almighty."[7]

Consider, in contrast, the hurried, preoccupied nature of so much of our *tefilla* today.

Like *tefilla*, all the daily rites and rituals of Judaism are filled with

---

7. Mishna Brachot 5:1.

significance readily available to those motivated, committed and industrious enough to explore the familiar. Within and through this regular ongoing observance, we are meant to find true religious meaning in our lives.

Centuries ago, God launched the central symbol of Jewish worship with the commandment "And they shall make for Me a holy place…" Only we, as God's partners, generate holiness in this world. Only we, through conscientious effort, can create sanctity and attain spirituality in our lives.

3 Law and Reason

Context
The Torah records God's instructions concerning the construction of the Sanctuary and its utensils in painstaking detail.[1]

Questions
Why are all these details necessary?

Is there independent meaning to each element of the Mishkan and its utensils or are these particulars simply subsidiary components with no significance of their own?

If each detail is independently significant, can we hope to determine its meaning without clear information from the text?

On a more fundamental level, the issue of the Sanctuary's details clearly relates to a series of much broader questions: What are the parameters of our intellectual relationship to Jewish law? Are each of the mitzvot based on a specific logical reason meant to be understood by man or are some of the commandments simply "divine decrees"? Does man attain a higher form of worship through blind obedience to the law or through rational search for each commandment's meaning?

Approaches

——A——

As a first step in their discussion of these basic issues, the scholars distinguish between two different types of Torah law:

1. *Mishpatim*: logical laws whose usefulness is evident (e.g., the prohibition of murder or theft)

---

1. Shmot 25–27.

2. *Chukim*: edicts whose purpose is not evident (e.g., forbidden mixtures of plants, animals, materials, etc.)[2]

Once agreeing upon that distinction, however, the commentaries part ways as they continue to debate the intellectual basis of the mitzvot.

—— **B** ——————————————————————————————

At one end of the spectrum lie Rashi and those who follow his lead. In his commentary on Vayikra, Rashi boldly proclaims: "*Chukim* are edicts of the king which have no reason."[3] *Chukim*, says this scholar, must be viewed not only as laws beyond our comprehension but as *edicts which have no intrinsic purpose.*

At the same time, however, by referring to *chukim* as "edicts of the King," Rashi effectively grants these laws general purpose as a group. *Chukim*, he concludes, exist to develop man's loyalty to God.

If a king commands ten laws to his subjects and they respond, "Nine of your edicts make sense; those we will observe," the subjects are not showing loyalty to the king. They are showing loyalty solely to their own intellect. Only through the observance of the tenth, illogical law do these individuals evidence true fealty to their monarch. In similar fashion, Rashi infers, *loyalty to God is most clearly expressed through the observance of laws "which have no reason."*

Rashi's position finds apparent support in a number of Talmudic sources, most notably a passage in the tractate of Megilla where the authorities chastise the individual who suggests a logical explanation for the mitzva of *shiluach hakein* (sending the mother bird away before taking its young).[4]

True to his principles, Rashi eschews any discussion of the meaning behind the Mishkan's detailed construction in his commentary on Parshat Teruma. He limits himself to clarifying the physical details outlined in the text.

—— **C** ——————————————————————————————

A fascinating intermediate position concerning intellectual examination

---

2. Rambam, *Mishneh Torah*, Hilchot Me'ila 8:8.
3. Rashi, Vayikra 19:19.
4. Talmud Bavli Megilla 25a.

of the mitzvot is offered by the medieval philosopher and poet Rabbi Yehuda Halevi:

> It is God's Torah and he who accepts it completely, without any inves-
> tigation and without any contemplation, is greater than one who
> becomes more knowledgeable and investigates.
>
> The individual, however, who has turned from this higher level to-
> wards the path of investigation should find a reason for these things…
> rather than leaving them and turning to incorrect thoughts and doubts
> that lead him to be lost.[5]

While disagreeing with Rashi's fundamental premise that a divine mitzva
could be "purposeless," Rabbi Yehuda Halevi nonetheless maintains, like
Rashi, that *blind obedience to the commandments, without intellectual search,
represents the highest level of relationship with the divine.* Only those unable
to relate on this highest plane, according to Rabbi Yehuda, should engage
in rational investigation of the mitzvot.

— **D** —

The Ramban, commenting on the same passage in Vayikra as Rashi, strenuously objects to Rashi's contention that "*Chukim* are edicts of the king which
have no reason": "The intent is not [that we should believe] that any edict
of the King of Kings is without reason…; rather, the *chukim* of the Heavenly One Blessed Be He are His secrets…; *all of them, however, are with
good reason and full purpose.*"[6]

The Ramban and the many scholars who follow his lead are unwilling
to consider the possibility that a perfect God would command a "reason-
less" law even for the purpose of honing man's loyalty. Man should, they
maintain, make every effort to understand the fundamental reason behind
each mitzva in order to reach more complete understanding and observance of God's will.

Obviously, these scholars will argue, failure to determine a reason for
a specific commandment should not lead us to treat that mitzva lightly.
In addition, any reason we find may or may not be accurate, given the

---

5. Hakuzari, second *ma'amar.*
6. Ramban, Vayikra 19:19.

limitations of our own intellectual abilities. *Our goal, however, should be the full comprehension of each mitzva and its divinely ordained purpose.*

The Ramban, in fact, proceeds, in the very same source, to offer rationales for the puzzling series of *chukim* delineating the prohibitions of *kilayim* (forbidden mixtures).[7]

As one would expect, the Ramban's commentary throughout the Torah is filled with discussion on the underlying philosophical significance of *chukim* such as elements of the Temple service.

— **E** ———————————————————————————

For his part, the Rambam not only agrees that every law given by God is reasoned and purposeful, but also maintains that man should "contemplate the laws of the Holy Torah…to know the end of their subjects to the extent of his ability."[8]

From the perspective of this great philosopher, the very act of "contemplating" the purpose of the mitzvot brings an individual closer to God even if no firm conclusion is reached. By stressing that this contemplative process should be performed by each individual "to the extent of his ability," the Rambam also allows for the possibility that different explanations will be arrived at by different "seekers." We have no way of knowing whether an explanation determined is objectively "true" or not. Nonetheless, an explanation is worthwhile as long as it is consonant with Jewish thought and enhances the meaning of the mitzva for the individual.

There are limits, however, the Rambam declares, to rational examination of the mitzvot. He draws a clear distinction between the commandments themselves, whose purpose should be studied and explored, and the myriad details embedded within the mitzvot. The study of such details, he proclaims, is futile and should be avoided at all costs.

> The mitzva obligating us to bring offerings [to God] has great purpose…. Why, however, one offering must be a lamb while another a ram, why a fixed number must be brought, we simply cannot say.
>
> Anyone who attempts to find reasons for such details enters, in my eyes, into the realm of absurdity…. Whoever claims that these detailed

---

7. Ibid.
8. Rambam, *Mishneh Torah*, Hilchot Me'ila 8:8.

rules have specific reasons [which he can identify] is as distant from the truth as those who assume that the whole law has no purpose.[9]

How fascinating that the Rambam, whose very lifework epitomizes intellectual, rational religious search, should proclaim the limitations of such search and the clear dangers of going "too far."

True to his principles, while the Rambam carefully records the details of the Sanctuary's construction in his halachic compendium, he steers clear of suggesting deeper philosophical significance to those details.[10]

— **F** —

Finally, there are those scholars, such as Rabbi Yitzchak Arama[11] and Rabbi Shimshon Raphael Hirsch,[12] who openly disagree with the Rambam's imposed limitations. *These scholars emphatically maintain not only that the mitzvot themselves are reasoned and purposeful but that each detail of every commandment is fraught with meaning.*

Thus Arama, after discussing the general symbolism of the Menora in the Sanctuary, turns towards its details and declares:

> Consider how meticulous divine wisdom was in the construction of the Menora – its form, its shape, its dimensions, and its image. *It is inconceivable that these matters could possibly have been recorded in the divine law by chance.* Bear in mind that if one letter of a Torah scroll is missing, or one letter is superfluous, the entire Torah is disqualified. Far be it from the God Who fashioned us to command us to record in His perfect Torah all these details…simply for the sake of human adornment.[13]

As can be expected, Arama, Hirsch and others who follow their lead wax eloquent on each particular recorded in Parshat Teruma, as the Torah outlines the intricate instructions concerning the construction of the Mishkan and its utensils (see Teruma 4).

---

9. Rambam, *Moreh Nevuchim* 3:26.
10. Rambam, *Mishneh Torah*, Hilchot Beit Habechira.
11. Akeidat Yitzchak Shmot, sha'ar 49.
12. Rabbi Shimshon Raphael Hirsch, *Nineteen Letters*, letters 10–14.
13. Akeidat Yitzchak Shmot, sha'ar 49.

Points to Ponder

The continuing discussion concerning the relationship between intellectual exploration and Jewish law serves, once again, to remind us that there is a place for all within Jewish thought and practice. Clear, authentic support can be found for the widest range of intellectual paths – from those who view blind observance of halacha as the highest iteration of religious devotion to those driven to find meaning in each nuance of the law.

We are each challenged to find the personal path of intellectual inquiry most meaningful to us and to refrain from criticizing the paths chosen by others.

In its brilliantly structured flexibility, Jewish tradition provides us with options as we approach the law, giving us each the space we need to find our own way.

4 Delving into Details

As indicated in the previous study, a wide-ranging debate rages among the scholars concerning our right and our ability to determine the purpose behind each detail of Torah law. While some authorities reject such intellectual search, others embrace it.

This study will depart from our usual question and answer format. Instead we will temporarily adopt a position in the above debate by featuring a sampling of suggestions made by Midrashic and other authorities who maintain that significance can be found in each detail of the Sanctuary and its utensils. Some original ideas, in this vein, will be offered, as well.

This far from exhaustive sampling is presented to provide examples of an approach that finds spiritual and ethical meaning in each nuance of Jewish law. While some of the observations included certainly fall into the realm of Midrash (rabbinic commentary that moves away from direct explanation of the text), all convey invaluable ethical and moral teachings deeply rooted in Jewish thought.

Context
As Parshat Teruma unfolds, God reveals in detail the construction plans for the Sanctuary and its various utensils.[1]

---

1. Shmot 25–27.

Approaches

——**A**————————————————————————

"And you shall cover it [the Aron (Ark)] with pure gold, from within and without shall you cover it."[2]

The rabbis maintain that the Aron was covered with gold both externally and internally to convey that any sage who is not as pure internally as he appears externally is not a true sage.[3]

——**B**————————————————————————

"And you shall insert the poles in the rings on the sides of the Aron, with which to carry the Aron. The poles shall remain in the rings of the Aron; they may not be removed from it."[4]

All of the utensils and components of the Mishkan were designed to be portable and were moved from place to place through the use of staves inserted into rings attached to each element. These poles were removed from their rings when the Mishkan was at rest – with one singular exception. The Aron poles remained in the rings. Their removal was expressly prohibited in the text and counted among the negative prohibitions of the Torah.

Why does the Torah prohibit the removal of the Aron poles?

The Ba'al Hachinuch offers an approach based on *pshat*. The honor due to the Aron and to the Torah within, they say, warranted that the staves remain in place. In this way, if a sudden journey became necessary there would be no danger that the Aron would be improperly moved.[5]

Others, however, see this prohibition in symbolic terms.

The Meiri, for example, suggests that the poles symbolize man's physicality, in contrast to the spirituality represented by the Aron and its contents. The poles, he says, remain in place to teach us that man's physical and spiritual dimensions are meant to be fused, so that his entire being is guided by the Torah.[6]

Other authorities suggest that the Aron poles represent individuals

---

2. Ibid., 25:11.
3. Talmud Bavli Yoma 72b.
4. Shmot 25:14–15.
5. Sefer Hachinuch, mitzva 96.
6. Meiri, quoted in Nachshoni, *Hagot B'parshiot HaTorah* p. 333.

within the community who "support" (financially and otherwise) the study of Torah. The poles remain in the Aron rings to symbolize the pivotal role these individuals play and to reflect the deep continuing benefit that they, themselves, derive from the very Torah they support.[7]

A beautiful suggestion is offered by Rabbi Shimshon Raphael Hirsch in his commentary on the Torah. The presence of the staves in the rings of the Aron, he says, symbolizes the Torah's "portability." Unlike other symbols of our tradition which are rooted in our homeland, the Torah exists above place. Wherever we have traveled as a people, the Torah has traveled with us. The Aron poles remain in place to remind us that although the Torah may seem at rest in any one location, it is not bound to that site.[8]

An additional explanation might, perhaps, be offered. Our relationship with the Torah and its law is dynamic, never at rest. We are constantly meant to study its contents and apply its laws to ever-changing circumstances. To symbolize that the Torah is philosophically always "in flux," even when the Aron is stationary, the staves must remain in the rings.

C

"And you shall make a Kaporet (Ark Cover) of pure gold…"[9]

The Ark Cover was called the Kaporet, the rabbis claim, because it served to atone (*l' kaper*) for the sins of the Israelites.[10]

Carrying this idea one step further, the Talmudic authorities maintain that the Kaporet was specifically forged out of gold so that "the gold of the Kaporet would atone for the gold of the sin of the golden calf."[11] (See Teruma 1, *Approaches* A for a discussion of the relationship between the Sanctuary and the golden calf.)

This last contention, however, is problematic in light of another well-known rabbinic observation connecting gold in the Sanctuary to the gold of the golden calf.

The Talmud in the tractate of Rosh Hashana explains that the Kohen Gadol (High Priest) doffs his royal priestly garments on Yom Kippur, in

---

7. Midrash Lekach Tov Shmot 25:14; Chafetz Chaim, *Perush al Hatorah*, Shmot 25:14–15.
8. Rabbi Shimshon Raphael Hirsch, Shmot 25:14–15.
9. Shmot 25:17.
10. Midrash Tanchuma Vayakhel 10.
11. Talmud Yerushalmi Shekalim 1:1.

favor of garments of white linen, because "the prosecuting attorney cannot become the defense attorney." Gold, which figured prominently in the sin of the golden calf, the event which necessitated the forgiveness of the first Yom Kippur,[12] cannot now be used in defense of the Jews on that sanctified day.[13]

If gold is rejected on Yom Kippur because of the *chet ha'egel*, how, then, can the gold of the Kaporet atone for that very sin?

The answer may well lie at the core of the sin of the golden calf. As we have noted and as we will explain in greater detail, the Israelites, frightened by the perceived loss of Moshe, create the golden calf as a proposed intermediary between themselves and God (see Teruma 1, *Approaches* C, F; Ki Tissa 2, *Approaches* B).

The danger exists that the High Priest's role will be similarly misunderstood – that he will be perceived as an intermediary between God and the people, rather than as the nation's representative within the Temple.

Allowing the Kohen Gadol to enter the Holy of Holies on the most sanctified day of the year, royally bedecked in garments of gold and other precious materials, could well perpetuate this misconception. The Kohen Gadol thus "dresses down" and enters the Holy of Holies wearing simple garments of white linen to underscore his mortality and equality with the people.

Gold, worn by the Kohen Gadol on Yom Kippur, would improperly elevate the High Priest in the eyes of the nation and effectively carry on the sin of the golden calf. Gold, on the other hand, dedicated to the Kaporet – a symbol of man's direct relationship to his Creator – serves as "atonement" and a corrective for that very sin.

The symbolism of the Kaporet thus reminds us that no element of the natural world that surrounds us is inherently evil. Gold is not rejected from the Sanctuary simply because it was used to create the golden calf. *Material elements are amoral – their ethical value is determined by how we use them.*

— **D** —

"And you shall make two Keruvim (Cherubs) of gold…from both ends of

---

12. Midrash Tanchuma Ki Tissa 31.
13. Talmud Bavli Rosh Hashana 26a.

the Kaporet…. And the Keruvim shall be with wings spread upward, sheltering the cover with their wings, and their faces shall be towards one another; towards the Kaporet shall be the faces of the Keruvim."[14]

No element of the Sanctuary's construction is more complex or more philosophically problematic then the Keruvim. Found at the center of the Mishkan, hewn out of the Kaporet itself, identified as the markers of the location from which God will speak to Moshe,[15] these jarring figures seem to starkly contradict the clear prohibition against "graven images" divinely transmitted at Sinai.

Rising to meet the challenge presented by the Keruvim, the rabbis offer a variety of suggestions.

Some authorities adopt a straightforward approach and explain that these golden images actually represent the celestial beings that worship God in the heavens. The inclusion of the Keruvim in the Sanctuary serves to strengthen belief in the existence of the spiritual entities they represent (see *Bereishit*: Vayeitzei 4, *Approaches* A for a discussion of celestial beings in Jewish thought).[16]

Many other authorities, however, from Talmudic times onward, view the Keruvim not as representations of supernatural beings, but as powerful symbols of the eternal relationship between God and His people.

One Talmudic tradition, adopted by many authorities, suggests that the Keruvim bore the faces of children.[17] This imagery was chosen, some commentaries maintain, to convey God's deep love for His people, reflective of the love of a parent for a child.[18] Even further, other sources continue, the very placement of the Keruvim at the center of the Mishkan serves to underscore that no power on earth is greater than the power of children engaged in Torah study: "the world exists on their account and they will eventually cause God to be fully revealed."[19]

Elsewhere the Talmud records that the two Keruvim were individually forged –one in male and one in female form.

---

14. Shmot 25:18–20.
15. Ibid., 25:22.
16. Midrash Hagadol Shmot 25:18; Rambam, *Moreh Nevuchim* 3:45; Rabbeinu Bachya, Shmot 25:18.
17. Talmud Bavli Chagiga 13b.
18. Rabbeinu Bachya, Shmot 25:18.
19. Introduction to the Zohar 1b.

"When Israel would ascend [to the Temple] on the Pilgrim festivals, the priests would push aside the curtain, show them the Keruvim…and proclaim, 'Recognize your preciousness before the Holy One, like the reciprocal love of a man and a woman.'"[20]

Rabbi Ovadia Sforno weaves a beautiful interpretive tapestry connecting the Aron, the Kaporet and the Keruvim. The Aron, he says, represents the human body. The Kaporet symbolizes the divine spirit invested in man. This spirit is an independent entity (just as the Kaporet covers the Aron but is not connected to it). Finally, the Keruvim with their outstretched wings represent man's intellectual search for his Creator as he directs his wisdom towards determining God's ways. The faces of the Keruvim, the Sforno continues, are turned both towards each other and towards the Kaporet[21] to emphasize that the source of man's wisdom is the Torah and that man should use that Torah wisdom to guide his interactions in this world. [22]

Numerous other commentaries and scholars wax eloquent in their description of the lessons learned from the symbolism of the Keruvim.

—— **E** ————————————————————————

"And their [the Keruvim's] faces shall be *one towards his brother*; *towards the Kaporet* shall be the faces of the Keruvim."[23]

At first glance, this sentence seems internally contradictory. Did the Keruvim face each other or did they face the Kaporet? Most commentaries simply explain that the Torah speaks of an angled, inwards-downwards glance. The language of the text, however, remains problematic. If the gaze was angled, why doesn't the Torah connect the two elements of the Keruvim's gaze by stating, "And their faces shall be one towards his brother *and* towards the Kaporet shall be the faces of the Keruvim"?

So troubled are the Talmudic scholars by the question of the Keruvim's gaze (which they find further complicated by a source in Divrei Hayamim [Chronicles] which indicates that the Keruvim in Shlomo's Temple faced inward towards the Sanctuary's interior[24]) that they claim the Keruvim miraculously moved in response to the people. When the nation followed

---

20. Talmud Bavli Yoma 54a.
21. Shmot 25:20.
22. Sforno, Shmot 25:8–9, 20–22.
23. Shmot 25:20.
24. Divrei Hayamim II 3:13.

God's will, the Keruvim faced one another. When, on the other hand, the people rebelled against their Creator, the Keruvim's gaze shifted away.[25]

One final explanation might be offered for the Torah's contradictory description of the Keruvim's gaze.

A true vision of God in this world can best be achieved by glimpsing the "godliness" in each other. *Our mutual gaze and our reciprocal care for each other reveal God's presence in our lives.*

By looking at each other, the Keruvim "see" the Kaporet and gain a glimpse of their Creator. That is why the Torah states that God appears to Moshe in the midst of the mutual gaze of the Keruvim.[26]

The Torah thus states, "And their faces shall be one towards his brother… [and, by definition] towards the Kaporet shall be the faces of the Keruvim."

—— **F** ——————————————————————————————

"And you shall make a Shulchan of acacia wood…"[27]

The Shulchan (Table) in the Sanctuary, and later in the Temple, held twelve specially baked loaves of "show-bread" at all times, arranged in two columns of six loaves each.[28] The nation's prosperity, say the rabbis, was ensured by the rituals associated with the Shulchan.[29]

The Ramban offers a fascinating interpretation of the mechanism through which the sustenance of the Israelites is assured by the Temple's show-bread. Referring to a principle elucidated in his commentary on Bereishit, this scholar explains that after the close of the six days of creation, God no longer creates ex nihilo (something from nothing).[30] *He instead blesses what already exists* by causing it to reach its full potential. "This is the secret of the Shulchan…: God rested His blessing upon [the show-bread] and from it sustenance flowed for all of Israel."[31]

The show-bread served, according to the Ramban, as the ever-present

---

25. Talmud Bavli Bava Batra 99a.
26. Shmot 25:22.
27. Ibid., 25:23.
28. Vayikra 24:5–6.
29. Rabbeinu Bachya, Shmot 25:23.
30. Ramban, Bereishit 1:1.
31. Ramban, Shmot 25:24.

physical source from which God would actually "create" provisions for the
entire people.

—— **G** ——————————————————————————————

"And you shall make a Menora of pure gold, beaten out of one piece shall be
the Menora; its shaft, its cups, its knobs and its blossoms shall be [beaten]
from it. Six branches shall emerge from its sides, three branches of the Menora from one side and three branches of the Menora from the second side.
Three cups engraved like almonds on one branch, a knob and a flower…"[32]

No component of the Mishkan is described in greater detail than the
Menora. So complex was its construction, maintain the rabbis, that Moshe
was unable to comprehend what was required until God showed him a miraculous model Menora of fire, to illustrate its particulars.[33]

Given the great detail of the Menora's description, a wide array of symbolic interpretations is suggested by the rabbis.

The Abravanel, for example, maintains that, while the Shulchan represents the material reward bestowed upon the righteous, the Menora symbolizes the prize of wisdom and the attainment of spiritual heights. The
seven branches correspond to seven types of wisdom embedded in the
Torah. The flames all pointed inward towards the center flame, which, in
turn, was directed towards the Holy of Holies to show that true wisdom
must be consistent with the foundations of the Torah housed in the Aron.
The Menora itself was fashioned of pure gold to illustrate that true wisdom
must not be tainted by alien ideas. The cups, knobs and flowers symbolize
the various sciences which branch out from each other. The entire Menora,
however, including these decorations, was "beaten" of one piece of gold, to
signify that all of these disciplines emerge from one common source.

Rabbeinu Bachya suggests that, on the level of *pshat*, the Menora's
beautifully intricate construction served to instill in the beholder a respect
for the Sanctuary as a whole. For this reason the Menora was placed outside the Holy of Holies for all to see. This external placement, in addition,
illustrated that the Torah, its own independent source of "light," had no
need for the illumination provided by the Menora.

Rabbeinu Bachya then proceeds to offer two Midrashic approaches to

---

32. Shmot 25:31–33.
33. Talmud Bavli Menachot 29a; Rashi, Shmot 25:40.

the Menora's construction. In the first of these, he develops ideas similar to those later presented by the Abravanel (see above), while, in the second, he moves in an entirely different direction. The seven branches of the Menora, he suggests, correspond to the seven stars which, under God's direction, govern the cycles of nature. The middle flame specifically relates to the solar cycle, central to the world's survival.[34]

Countless other explanations are offered by the rabbis for the detailed construction of the Menora, from the Alshich's contention that the complex candelabra symbolizes aspects of man's natural being and life challenges[35] to mystical Kabbalistic interpretations that relate the sum of the Menora's components to the number of verses that begin each of the five books of the Torah.[36]

Each of these interpretations adds to our appreciation of one of the most enduring symbols of our tradition.

— **H** —————————————————————————————————

Centuries ago, God outlined detailed plans for a Sanctuary which would symbolize His eternal presence within the people of Israel. As the comments cited above demonstrate, those detailed plans continue to capture the imagination of our people to this day, as we seek to learn the lessons that may well be embedded within.

---

34. Rabbeinu Bachya, Shmot 25:31.
35. Torat Moshe, Shmot 25:31–40.
36. Yalkut Reuveini, Teruma 75.

Tetzave

Parsha Summary

An honored position, a heavenly wardrobe…

    After detailing the plans for the construction of the Sanctuary, God turns His attention to those who will serve within its walls.

    Parshat Tetzave introduces the concept of the kehuna *(priesthood), as* God designates Aharon as Kohen Gadol (High Priest) and his sons as Kohanim (priests). *They are to serve as representatives of the people within the Sanctuary and, later, within the Temple.*

    God then commands Moshe concerning the fashioning of the bigdei kehuna, *the divinely designed garments to be worn by Aharon and his sons respectively as they engage in the Sanctuary service.*

    The parsha closes with a description of the rituals to be performed by Moshe during the seven days of preparation prior to the inauguration of the priesthood and during the inauguration ceremony itself. This ceremony will be recorded again in detail, as it occurs, in the book of Vayikra.

1 An Absentee Role

Context

For the first and only time since his introduction in the beginning of Parshat Shmot, Moshe's name is omitted from an entire parsha.[1]

Questions

Why is Moshe's name omitted from Parshat Tetzave?

The question is compounded by the fact that the omission seems clearly deliberate. Over and over again, the Torah creates settings in the parsha where Moshe's name, by all rights, should appear – only to exclude it from the text on each occasion.

For example, the first sentence of the parsha does not begin with the usual formula, "And the Lord *said to Moshe* saying, speak unto the children of Israel and say…"

In place of this familiar opening we find the abrupt directive, "*And you* [Moshe] shall command the children of Israel…"[2]

This phenomenon repeats itself throughout the parsha.

Approaches

A

A fascinating Midrashic tradition connects the omission of Moshe's name in Parshat Tetzave to a dramatic encounter between this great leader and his Creator, chronicled in the next parsha, Ki Tissa.

In the aftermath of the sin of the golden calf, Moshe turns to the Israelites and proclaims, "You have committed a grievous sin, and now I will ascend to the Lord; perhaps I can atone for your sin."

---

1. Shmot 27:20–30:10.
2. Ibid., 27:20.

239

Moshe then ascends Mount Sinai where he confronts God and declares: "I beseech you! This people have committed a grievous sin and have created for themselves a god of gold. And now, if you will forgive their sin – and if not, *erase me from Your book which You have written!*"

God responds, "*Whoever has sinned against Me, I shall erase from My book…*"[3]

The rabbis are deeply puzzled by this interchange. To what "book" does Moshe refer when he bargains with God for the people's forgiveness?

One Talmudic tradition, quoted by many later authorities, maintains that Moshe refers to the books of judgment which are opened on Rosh Hashana (the beginning of the year), when God determines the fate of His creations.

If You will not forgive the Israelites, Moshe essentially says to God, *then, erase me from the heavenly books of judgment, that I may die…*[4]

Others, however, suggest that when Moshe exclaims, "erase me from Your book which You have written," he is speaking of the Torah.

If You will not forgive the Israelites, he argues, *then, count me out! Erase me from the entire Torah text! I no longer want to be part of Your unfolding divine plan.*[5]

God's response makes it abundantly clear that He has no intention of erasing Moshe from "His book." A problem, however, emerges. So significant are the words spoken by the righteous that, "the curse of a sage, even when conditionally stated (and even when the conditional clause fails to be met), is never completely abrogated."[6]

Moshe has decreed his own fate and God cannot ignore that decree. Some "erasure" of this great leader's name must occur. To fulfill the curse that Moshe has placed upon himself, therefore, God deliberately omits Moshe's name from the entire parsha of Tetzave.[7]

While this Midrashic approach is poignantly powerful, it fails to address an obvious question: why, of all the parshiot of the Torah, is Parshat Tetzave chosen as the setting for Moshe's absence? Even putting aside the chronological difficulty raised by the fact that Parshat Tetzave precedes

3. Ibid., 32:30–33.
4. Talmud Bavli Rosh Hashana 16b.
5. Midrash Rabba Shmot 47:9.
6. Talmud Bavli Makkot 11a.
7. Midrash Hane'elam Zohar Chadash 60; Rabbeinu Bachya, Shmot 32:32.

the dialogue recorded in Ki Tissa, why is Tetzave the appropriate parsha through which to fulfill Moshe's self-imposed erasure? (See Yitro 1, *Approaches* A, for a discussion of chronology and the Torah text.)

Are the rabbis simply engaging in an intellectual exercise, associating two phenomena in arbitrary fashion when no real association exists?

A closer look at the dramatic encounter between God and Moshe in Parshat Ki Tissa reveals a fascinating possibility. The rabbis perceive a powerful connection between that encounter and the philosophical theme of Parshat Tetzave.

During the critical, turbulent moments following the sin of the golden calf, Moshe apparently makes a fundamental error in his own assessment of his leadership role – an error which must be emphatically and immediately corrected by God.

The episode begins as Moshe turns to the Israelites and says, "You have committed a grievous sin, and now I will ascend to the Lord; perhaps I can atone for your sin." *You have distanced yourselves from God and can no longer approach Him on your own… I will ascend to meet Him; perhaps I can secure atonement for you.*

Ascending Mount Sinai, Moshe confronts his Creator: "I beseech You! This people have committed a grievous sin and have created for themselves a god of gold. And now if You will forgive their sin – and if not, erase me from Your book that You have written!" *If You will not forgive the Israelites, allow me to atone for them. Punish me in their stead.*

God's response is swift and emphatic: "Whoever has sinned against Me, I shall erase from my book." *Moshe, in spite of all that has happened, you still miss the point. I will accept no intermediary or substitute when it comes to personal responsibility. You cannot effect atonement for others. Those who have sinned must directly pay the price.*

Understood in this way, Moshe's dramatic interchange with God following the *chet ha'egel* reflects the critical lessons learned from that event. Even Moshe has to be reminded that he cannot serve as the intermediary between God and His people. Once again, the Torah conveys the fundamental truth that is transmitted over and over again during the unfolding events at Sinai: *the hallmark of divine worship is direct, personal encounter between man and God.*

We can now understand the connection drawn in the Midrash between this event and the omission of Moshe's name in Parshat Tetzave.

Parshat Tetzave is dedicated exclusively to the topic of the *kehuna* (priesthood). Within this parsha's boundaries the Torah introduces the concept of the *kehuna*, outlines the detailed instructions for the fashioning of the priestly garments and discusses plans for the eventual investiture of Aharon and his descendents into their eternal roles as Kohanim.

As we have already noted, the very concept of the priesthood carries the potential danger that the Kohen will be perceived, erroneously, as an intermediary between the people and their God rather than as the nation's representative within the Temple (see Teruma 2, *Approaches* C). To clarify that no leader should ever perceive himself or be perceived as an essential go-between between the people and their Creator, Moshe's name is omitted specifically from Parshat Tetzave. There could be no more appropriate response for the momentary, yet critical, lapse on Moshe's part recorded in Parshat Ki Tissa – the instance, when, due to the unimaginable pressures of the moment, Moshe attempts to take upon himself the atonement of others.

—— **B** ——

An alternative explanation for Moshe's "absence" from Parshat Tetzave is offered by some scholars, based upon a Talmudic tradition rooted at the burning bush, the scene of Moshe's call to leadership.

There, God repeatedly overrules Moshe's objections concerning his election to leadership, until, finally, the Torah states: "And the anger of God was kindled against Moshe and He said: 'Is there not Aharon your brother, the Levi? I know that he will gladly speak…. He shall speak for you to the people…"[8]

Rabbi Shimon bar Yochai, noting God's anger and the sudden introduction of Aharon, explains that at this point Moshe loses an honored opportunity. Moshe was originally destined to be not only *Moshe Rabbeinu*, the lawgiver, teacher and political leader of the Israelites, he was to be the Kohen Gadol, as well. Due to Moshe's continued reluctance at the burning bush, however, God relieves him of that honor and bestows it upon his brother, Aharon.[9]

To mark this lost opportunity, Moshe's name is omitted from Par-

---

8. Shmot 4:14–16.
9. Talmud Bavli Zevachim 102a.

shat Tetzave, the parsha that introduces the concept of the *kehuna* (priesthood).[10]

— C ————————————————————————

As intriguing as the Midrashic explanations for Moshe's "absence" in Parshat Tetzave may be, a much simpler, yet equally powerful, *pshat* explanation can be offered.

Parshat Tetzave is "Aharon's parsha," the section of biblical text which introduces the glorious role that Aharon and his descendents will assume across the ages. In recognition of the fact that this is his brother's "moment," Moshe is forced to take a step back out of the limelight. Moshe is certainly present, playing an essential role in the proceedings. Aharon, however, is center stage.

Even Moshe, the greatest leader our people has known, must at times step aside, to allow others to shine.

Points to Ponder

Although it was almost thirty years ago, I can clearly remember the evening when my wife and I attended the first "back to school night" for our oldest son, Avi. He was, at the time, in kindergarten. After the teacher briefly reviewed her curriculum, she turned to the parents in attendance and asked for questions.

There was silence for a moment, and then a flurry of hands shot up:

"What is your reading readiness curriculum?"

"What topics in science are you teaching the children?"

"What about social studies?"

Astounded, I turned to my wife and whispered: "What's wrong with me? I just want to know how he's getting along… Is he kicking the kid next to him? *After all, it's only kindergarten!*"

Many of us are so driven, in today's modern Jewish community, towards our children's academic success, that we rob them of their childhood. Tutors and extracurricular programs proliferate as we strive to ensure that each child is "well rounded" and given the full opportunity for success. "Free time" disappears in their overprogrammed world and pressures increase to

———————
10. Paneiach Raza, Shmot 27:20.

the point where the process of getting into a yeshiva high school of choice feels similar to what getting into medical school felt like years ago.

Even more significantly, as we push our children towards personal success, we often forget to teach them the lessons of belonging, of being part of a surrounding community and society:

You don't always have to be the best and the brightest in everything. That goal is, in fact, not only unhealthy but impossible.

The world doesn't revolve around you.

You don't always have to be the star.

You can't always get the highest grade on the test.

True success is often achieved through the enabling of others to reach their goals – and happiness often rests in the enjoyment of their accomplishments.

Sometimes it's appropriate to pass the ball and not take the shot.

While these messages may sound self-evident when they are so openly stated, we should ask ourselves whether or not we communicate them clearly enough to our children. Certainly against the backdrop of the other messages we transmit, we cannot assume that these ideas are automatically understood.

Centuries ago, God forces Moshe to take a step back and allow his brother, Aharon, to take "center stage." For the sake of our children's well-being, we should regularly convey the same lesson.

2 A Partnership of Brothers

Context

The concept of the *kehuna* (priesthood) is introduced as Aharon and his sons are designated to assume this honored role. The details of the *bigdei kehuna* (priestly garments) are then outlined, with special emphasis placed upon the vestments of Aharon (who is to serve as the Kohen Gadol).[1]

Questions

Why is Aharon chosen to serve as the Kohen Gadol? Why couldn't Moshe, already chosen for leadership, assume this role along with his other responsibilities?

What lessons are to be learned from this "partnership of brothers" which shapes the earliest leadership configuration in the history of the Jewish nation?

Approaches

—A—

As noted in the previous study, the Tannaitic sage Rabbi Shimon bar Yochai maintains that the high priesthood was originally Moshe's to lose and that he, indeed, loses this role during the initial moments of his leadership career.[2] Responding to Moshe's repeated objections at the burning bush, God is "angered" and transfers the *kehuna* from Moshe to his brother, Aharon.

---

1. Shmot 28:1–43.
2. Ibid., 4:14–16.

Moshe's reluctance to accept the challenges of leadership ultimately results in the limitation of his public role.[3]

— B —

Disagreeing adamantly, the majority of Rabbi Shimon bar Yochai's colleagues maintain that *Moshe was never meant to serve permanently as the Kohen Gadol.* That role was reserved from the outset for Aharon, while the *kehuna*, as a whole, was likewise designated for Aharon's descendents.

Moshe, however, does assume the position of High Priest temporarily, specifically during the days of preparation that immediately precede Aharon's inauguration into the priesthood. During that seven-day period, the plans for which are described in Parshat Tetzave, Moshe performs the preparatory rituals relating to Aharon and Aharon's sons.

Moshe's tenure as Kohen Gadol, according to this mainstream position, is limited to the role of an enabler. He serves only to usher his brother and his brother's progeny into their honored roles.[4]

— C —

Finally, a third, minority position recorded in the Talmud references the phrase in Tehillim (Psalms), *"Moshe and Aharon are among His priests and Shmuel among those who call His name…"*[5] and suggests that Moshe serves throughout his lifetime alongside Aharon as High Priest. In contrast to Aharon's descendents, however, Moshe's progeny do not inherit the *kehuna*.[6]

— D —

A fundamental question emerges according to the majority position which maintains that Moshe was never meant to receive the priesthood permanently. *Why is Moshe denied this honor in favor of his brother, Aharon?*

The commentaries propose a variety of suggestions.

One solution offered by the Ibn Ezra, for example, is simple and straightforward. Moshe's overwhelming role as the leader, teacher and judge of the people denies him the time necessary to perform the complex

---

3. Talmud Bavli Zevachim 102a.
4. Ibid.
5. Tehillim 99:6.
6. Talmud Bavli Zevachim 102a.

rituals required of the Kohen Gadol. The two positions are temporally in-
compatible.[7]

The Malbim, in his discussion of the issue, underscores God's ability to
determine the inner qualities of every human being. Upon reviewing the
attributes of all those alive at the time of the inauguration of the *kehuna*,
God finds Aharon most fit for the task. Different roles require different
attributes and talents. Without being specific, the Malbim maintains that
Aharon is chosen over Moshe for the priesthood simply because he is more
suited to the task.[8]

The renowned preacher the Maggid of Dubno is more explicit in his
analysis of the personal characteristics that make Aharon a more appropriate choice for the priesthood than Moshe.

The role of the Kohen, says the Maggid, is to educate and lead the people through example – to be a role model for the nation. Moshe, however,
towers over the Israelites. So distant does he seem from their personal reality that they are unable to emulate his example. God, therefore, chooses
Aharon, a man of the masses, an individual who relates to all,[9] to serve as
the first Kohen Gadol. Through this choice, God underscores the educative role which is to be the Kohen's across the ages.[10]

—— **E** ———————————————————————————

A wider perspective on Aharon's ascension to the *kehuna* can be gained by
focusing upon the *collaboration* created by his selection. By designating
both Moshe and Aharon for leadership at the dawn of Jewish history God
forges a formative "partnership of brothers." This partnership is marked
by a delicate political and personal equilibrium, setting the stage for Jewish governance across time.

1. *Political partnership*: from the outset, by selecting both Moshe and
Aharon for their respective roles, God creates a *balance of power* meant to
be maintained within the Jewish nation. The political and judicial seat of
power is separated from the ritual hierarchy to ensure that total control is
never invested in any one source.

The deep dangers of combined ritual and political authority in one seat

---

7.   Ibn Ezra, Shmot 28:1.
8.   Malbim, Shmot 28:1.
9.   Talmud Bavli Sanhedrin 6a.
10. Ohel Yaakov, Tetzave.

are evidenced not only by the "Ayatollahs" of our time but also by a tragic period of ancient Jewish history.

During the years following the heroic Chanuka rebellion against the Syrian Greek Empire, the priestly family that led that revolt assumes the monarchy of the Jewish commonwealth, establishing the century-long Hasmonean dynasty.

In short order, Hasmonean rule descends from its heroic origins into political excess and corruption, eventually setting the stage for Roman entry into the governance of the Jewish commonwealth. The historical passage from Matityahu and his son Yehuda "Maccabi" (the leaders of the revolt against the Syrian Greeks) to the final Hasmonean rulers, Aristoblus and Hyrcanus, is a tragic journey of assimilation into the very culture against which the first Hasmoneans had so bravely fought.

While the moral decay of the Hasmoneans was the result of many forces, their control of both the priesthood and monarchy played a major role in that decline.[11] A dynasty that never should have been reminds us of the wisdom of the divinely ordained separation of leadership powers.

2. *Personal partnership*: on a personal level, the balance created by the partnership between Moshe and Aharon is equally striking. As we have noted before, based upon the evidence of the text, the personalities and leadership styles of these brothers could not have been more different (see Shmot 5, *Approaches* D; Mishpatim 4, *Approaches* B3).

Moshe emerges from the Torah as forthright and uncompromising, a man whose worldview, according to the rabbis, is summed up in the maxim "Let the law cut through the mountain." Blunt and honest almost to a fault, Moshe is a leader who pursues truth and justice at all costs.

Aharon, on the other hand, exemplifies a very different leadership model. He is, above all, a man of the people who "loves peace, pursues peace and creates peace between man and his friend." Negotiation, compromise and flexibility are the tools of his trade as he pursues interpersonal harmony within the nation.

Which of these leadership models is correct? Obviously, both – dependent upon the circumstances. There are times when a leader must be uncompromising in his pursuit of right. At other times, however, flexibility for the sake of harmony and accord is the order of the day. A true leader

---

11. Talmud Bavli Yoma 8b; Rashi, ibid.

must learn to apply the proper approach to the appropriate time and circumstance.

At the dawn of Jewish history, as Jewish authority begins to take root, God establishes a partnership of brothers which enables us to see each of these two leadership styles in their purity. If Moshe had been more like Aharon he would have been, by definition, a "lesser Moshe." His characteristics and skills would not have emerged with full clarity. The same, of course, is true for Aharon in the opposite direction. God, therefore, places these two very different men at the helm of the fledgling Jewish nation so that their respective qualities will emerge as a beacon across the ages.

The lesson, however, does not end there. Fascinatingly, the two men who ultimately inherit the roles of Moshe and Aharon are, seemingly, their polar opposites. This is certainly clear in the case of Pinchas, Aharon's grandson, who according to many authorities earns the high priesthood for his progeny[12] through an act of justified but violent religious zealotry.[13] How different this ascension to the *kehuna* is from that of his grandfather!

Yehoshua, Moshe's faithful student, who assumes the mantle of political leadership after Moshe's death, is painted less clearly in the Torah. On more than one occasion in the text, however, Moshe finds it necessary to encourage his successor with the words *Chazak ve'ematz*, "Be strong and of courage,"[14] a charge which, tellingly, God reiterates to Yehoshua four times in swift succession after Moshe's death.[15] This repeated encouragement seems to indicate that this student who "would not part from the tent [of Moshe]"[16] was a less forceful personality than his illustrious teacher.

Of particular interest in this regard, as well, is the fact that during the pivotal sin of the spies, recorded in the book of Bamidbar, Calev ben Yefuna rises first to speak in defense of Moshe and entering the land, only then to be joined by Yehoshua. Yehoshua's hesitancy to speak up immediately may indicate a natural softness, as compared with Moshe's, and even Calev's, forcefulness. In addition, in advance of that critical event, Moshe changes Yehoshua's name from the original Hoshea to Yehoshua. He does

---

12. Ibn Ezra, Bamidbar 25:12.
13. Bamidbar 25:6–15.
14. Devarim 31:7; 31:23.
15. Yehoshua 1:6, 7, 9, 18.
16. Shmot 33:11.

so, suggest the rabbis, as an implicit prayer for Yehoshua's protection from
the "counsel of the spies."[17] Moshe is aware, perhaps, of a "gentleness" in his
beloved student's character that requires "toughening" as Yehoshua faces
his first real test of leadership.

In the generation following Moshe and Aharon, the leadership styles
are reversed, clearly indicating that both styles are at times appropriate for
both roles. By clearly highlighting the delicate balance that shapes the origin of Jewish governance, God challenges us to merge the varied attributes
of leadership and establish a model that will succeed at all times.

Points to Ponder

The human drama coursing through the Torah should never be far from our
minds as we study the text. We have noted before that the Torah presents
real stories about real people – people who possess a full range of human
emotions, strengths, weaknesses, successes and failings. The heroes of the
Torah are not divine. Their very humanity makes them great and enables
us to learn from them (see *Bereishit*: Lech Lecha 2, *Approaches*).

The partnership between Moshe and Aharon is a perfect case in point.
This powerful collaboration, so critical to the birth of the Jewish nation,
was probably not always an easy one. As we have seen, Moshe and Aharon
were two very different individuals. Success was clearly dependent upon
their ability to compromise and cooperate and, even more importantly,
upon their mutual love and respect.

The rabbis are not afraid to contemplate possible tensions that could
well have developed.

How, for example, does Aharon feel in the face of Moshe's overwhelming leadership role, which in many ways towers over his own? Aharon is,
after all, the older brother. Rashi notes that Aharon's potential internal conflict is hinted at with the very first mention of his appointment to leadership.
At the burning bush, God informs Moshe that his brother will partner with
him and states: "Behold he is going out to meet you *and when he sees you
he will rejoice in his heart*."[18] God feels compelled to tell Moshe that Aharon

---

17. Talmud Bavli Sota 34b.
18. Shmot 4:14.

will rejoice at their meeting, Rashi says, because of Moshe's concern that Aharon "might begrudge Moshe's rise to leadership."[19]

How, on the other hand, does Moshe feel when he performs the preparatory rituals that usher his brother's family into the priesthood? If we accept Rabbi Shimon bar Yochai's position that Moshe loses the priesthood at the burning bush, we naturally wonder whether he now regrets that loss. Even if he was never destined for the priesthood, does he envy his brother at the moment of the *kehuna's* inauguration? Conflicting Midrashic traditions hint at possible divergent emotions that may have coursed through Moshe's heart.[20]

Even more devastating for Moshe must have been the dawning realization that his own children would fail to play a role in the continuing leadership of the nation while Aharon's sons would remain front and center. Tragically, Moshe's descendents eventually fade into historical oblivion while his brother's progeny remain identifiable as Kohanim to this day.[21]

Only by recognizing the potential pitfalls and dangers that might have marked the personal and professional relationship of these two brothers can we fully appreciate their shared accomplishment. In stark contrast to the intrigue of "royal families" across the ages, Moshe and Aharon forge a partnership marked by cooperation, understanding, respect and love. Their example sets the standard for us all.

The hatred of Yaakov's sons towards their brother, Yosef, results in our descent into slavery. The brotherly love of Moshe and Aharon leads to our redemption.

---

19. Rashi, Shmot 4:14.
20. Midrash Rabba Shmot 2:6, 37:4; Torat Moshe, Shmot 27:20–21.
21. Bamidbar 3:1–2.

3 Do Clothes Make the Man?

Context

God outlines in great detail the garments to be worn by Aharon in his role as Kohen Gadol,[1] vestments which, the Torah states, are to be created "for glory and for splendor."[2]

After describing the garments to be worn by Aharon's sons, as well,[3] the Torah declares: "And they [the priestly garments] shall be on Aharon and his sons when they enter the Tent of Meeting or when they approach the Altar…*and they shall not bear a sin and die*; it shall be an eternal decree for him [Aharon] and his descendents after him."[4]

Numerous authorities deduce from this passage that the priest who serves in the Temple without wearing the priestly garments is liable to death.[5]

Questions

What was the ultimate purpose of the vestments created for Aharon and his sons and why does the Torah record the plans for their fashioning in such detail?

Why are these garments so essential to the priestly service that they must be worn, according to many authorities, on pain of death?

What eternal lessons, if any, can be learned from the creation of these garments to which the Torah dedicates so much text?

Approaches

Numerous commentaries analyze each of the intricate details of the *bigdei*

---

1. Shmot 28:2–43.
2. Ibid., 28:2.
3. Ibid., 28:40–43.
4. Ibid., 28:43.
5. Midrash Tanchuma Acharei Mot 6; Rashi, Shmot 28:43.

kehuna, discerning within them symbolic lessons similar to those found within the various elements of the Sanctuary itself (see Teruma 4).

Other scholars, however, focus on the big picture – on the subject of the *bigdei kehuna* in general terms – in an attempt to uncover the overall purpose of these garments created, in the Torah's words, "for glory and for splendor."

From this latter discussion a variety of lessons emerge.

—**A**————————————————————————

Some scholars see the priestly garments primarily as catalysts designed to instill awe and respect in the heart of the beholder.

The Netziv, for example, explains that Aharon's segregated, honored position within Israelite society rests upon the maintenance of a nuanced relationship with the rest of the nation. On the one hand, the people must come to recognize that Aharon's exalted station raises him above the rest of the population. At the same time, however, Aharon's position must be seen as divinely ordained, not self-determined. The *bigdei kehuna*, fashioned at God's command, serve as ever-present reminders that God has appointed Aharon and his descendents to this exalted role.[6]

Centuries earlier, the Ramban offers a bold suggestion concerning the origin of the priestly garments. *God models the* bigdei kehuna, *he says, after royal garb of the day.* These vestments, described in such intricate detail within the Torah text, mirror the clothing worn by non-Jewish monarchs at the time of the Torah's codification. The *bigdei kehuna* are thus familiar to the Israelites and serve to create an aura of "majesty" surrounding Aharon and his divinely ordained role.[7]

The Ramban is unafraid to consider the possibility that God "borrows" from the beauty of outside society in order to enhance the glory of his own eternal tradition.

—**B**————————————————————————

Based upon the Torah's fundamental requirement that the *bigdei kehuna* be created "for glory and for splendor" and upon later Talmudic discussion,[8]

---

6. Ha'amek Davar, Shmot 28:2.
7. Ramban, ibid.
8. Talmud Bavli Zevachim 18b, 88b.

the Rambam moves beyond the clear requirements outlined in the Torah text. In the *Mishneh Torah*, he codifies the law as prohibiting *any aesthetic imperfection at all* in the priestly garments:

> The priestly garments must be new and beautiful…for the text states "for glory and for splendor." If they are ragged, dirty, too long or too short for the wearer…the service performed [by the Kohen who wears them] is null and void.
>
> If any of the priestly garments become soiled, they may not be cleaned or laundered. They are, instead, set aside for use as wicks and new garments are worn…[9]

The *bigdei kehuna* are invalid not only if they are missing a divinely ordained detail, but also if they fail to meet the standards that apply to all attire. It is apparently self-evident, according to the Rambam, that the comportment of every individual should meet certain minimum criteria. These criteria become even more important, of course, in the case of the Kohen Gadol.

— C ————————————————————————

In contrast to those authorities who stress the impact of the *bigdei kehuna* on the outside observer, the Ba'al Hachinuch focuses on their effect upon the wearer:

> Man is affected by his own deeds, and his consciousness and intent is forged by them. The "atoning messenger" (High Priest) must direct his thoughts and entire consciousness totally towards the [Temple] service. It is therefore appropriate that he don clothing specific to that service. [In this way] as he gazes upon any part of his body, he is immediately reminded – and his heart becomes aware of – before Whom he stands.[10]

Clothing, says the Ba'al Hachinuch, plays a critical role in shaping the wearer's own self-image, thoughts and actions. This power is put to deliberate use in the case of the Kohen Gadol.

---

9. Rambam, *Mishneh Torah*, Hilchot Klei Hamikdash 8:4–5.
10. Sefer Hachinuch, mitzva 99.

—— **D** ——————————————————————————————

Finally, a fascinating viewpoint on the *bigdei kehuna* is offered by the nineteenth–twentieth-century German scholar Benno Jacob, who places the phenomenon in global perspective. Jacob notes that mankind's first garments come from God Himself as He clothes Adam and Chava following their initial sin. This divine act indicates that clothing is much more important than might first appear:

> Clothing is not merely protection against the cold; nor is it simply ornamentation. It is the first identifiable, essential symbol of human society. In man's moral conscience, clothing raises him above the beast.
>
> The status and glory of man are reflected in the nature of his attire. The fundamental purpose of clothing is to lend dignity to man. The Kohanim are thus given garments "for glory and for splendor"…[11]

God, in His glory, clothes Adam and Chava in garments that He provides, clearly indicating that clothing is not simply social convention but a continuation of the work of creation.

Benno Jacob's words allow us to bring our discussion of the *bigdei kehuna* to an appropriate close. The *bigdei kehuna* are an extreme manifestation of a phenomenon that touches all our lives.

Clothing is much more than a covering against the elements; it is a fundamental reflection of who we are. *We say much about ourselves – both to ourselves and to others – through our attire. Even more importantly, what we wear affects and shapes our own personal behavior.*

The lesson of the *bigdei kehuna* reminds us that on a real level, clothes do help make the man.

Points to Ponder

One of the concepts within Jewish tradition that has fallen upon hard times in many segments of the Jewish community today is *tzniut* (modesty), particularly in the area of attire.

The very introduction of the subject of *tzniut* automatically conjures

---

11. Benno Jacob, *Das Buch Exodus* (Stuttgart, 1997), translated as *The Second Book of the Bible: Exodus* (Hoboken, NJ: Ktav, 1992), Bereishit 3:21.

up images of an old-world, shtetl mentality, and engenders protests that the topic is hardly relevant to our modern world.

Nothing could be further from the truth. Specifically today, when we are surrounded by a society that so often preaches that "anything goes" in dress and comportment, we need to reassess the issue of proper attire for ourselves and for our children.

As we have seen above, dress is not neutral. Our clothing is a mirror of our souls, speaking volumes about who we are and affecting our very thoughts and actions.

What, for example, do our teenage and even preteen daughters say about themselves when they walk outside our doors? Does what they wear advertise availability and invitation? Have we taught them to recognize that their value as people is defined by *so much more* than the externals that they show to others?

Are the young men of our community attired in a manner that reflects the values we expect them to emulate? Are the styles and fads which they adopt from an outside society compatible with and reflective of our traditional ideals?

And we – in the workplace, in our synagogues and at social events – do we dress in a fashion which mirrors who we should aspire to be? What does our own attire announce – to others, to our children and to ourselves?

Proper garments were an integral component in the Kohen's service before God. We, constant emissaries of God in this world, should give serious thought to our own dress each day.

Ki Tissa

CHAPTER 30:11–34:35

כי תשא

פרק ל:יא-לד:לה

Parsha Summary

Monumental majesty, frightening failure, wrenching reconciliation…

Breaking the smooth flow of the parshiot rooted at Mount Sinai, Parshat Ki Tissa presents a complex tapestry of majestic vision, overwhelming sin and ultimate resolution.

As the parsha opens, God, speaking to Moshe on the summit of Mount Sinai, issues commandments concerning

- an indirect census to be taken of the Israelite males, twenty years old and over, through individual contributions of half shekels;
- the creation of the laver, the anointment oil and the incense to be used in association with the Sanctuary;
- the appointment of Betzalel ben Uri ben Chur and Oholiav ben Achisamach to supervise the construction of the Sanctuary;
- Shabbat observance.

At the conclusion of these directives, God presents Moshe with the two Tablets of Testimony (inscribed with the Ten Declarations).

Meanwhile, at the foot of Mount Sinai, the Israelites grow uneasy with Moshe's prolonged absence. They turn to Aharon and demand: "Rise up, make for us gods who will go before us, for Moshe – this man who brought us out of the land of Egypt – we do not know what has become of him!"

Aharon instructs the people to contribute their gold earrings, which he fashions into a molten calf. He then declares: "A festival for the Lord tomorrow!" The Israelites rise early the next morning to celebrate.

God informs Moshe, who is still on the summit of Mount Sinai, of the sin which has been perpetrated at its base. God threatens the nation with immediate extinction, relenting only in response to Moshe's impassioned pleas.

Moshe descends the mountain with the Tablets of Testimony. When he *sees the revelry unfolding in the Israelite camp, however, he throws the tablets from his hands in anger, smashing them at the foot of the mountain. Moshe then burns the calf, grinds the remains into powder which he sprinkles into water and forces the Israelites to drink, takes Aharon to task for his involvement in the sin, and directs the Leviim (who rally to his side) to execute those most directly involved in the transgression.*

The next morning Moshe reascends Mount Sinai in an attempt to secure atonement for the nation's crime. God informs Moshe of his intent to punish the surviving perpetrators and proceeds to strike down these individuals.

God commands Moshe to lead the people to the land of Canaan. He states, however, that His presence will no longer accompany the people. In His place, an angel will lead the nation to victory. When the people hear of God's decision, they respond with mourning. Mirroring God's withdrawal, Moshe pitches his own tent outside of the Israelite encampment.

Moshe beseeches God to return His presence to the people and asks for a clearer understanding of God's ways. God informs Moshe that He will reconcile with the nation but that Moshe will only be granted an indirect vision of God's essence.

God commands Moshe to carve a second set of tablets to replace the ones that Moshe destroyed. On this new set of tablets God will, once again, inscribe the Ten Declarations.

After carving the new set of tablets, Moshe ascends Mount Sinai where he experiences, as God had promised, an indirect encounter with the Divine Presence. Moshe again requests and receives reassurances that God will continue to journey in the midst of the nation. God commands Moshe concerning the avoidance of idolatry upon entry into the land of Canaan and issues a series of additional directives, including the observances of the yearly festivals.

At God's command, Moshe remains on Mount Sinai for an additional forty days and forty nights to record and renew the covenant between God and the people. At the end of this forty-day period, Moshe descends from the summit of the mountain with the second set of Tablets of Testimony, his face supernaturally radiant from the encounter with God.

1 Making the Count

Context

God commands Moshe to take a census of the Israelite males, twenty years old and over, through individual donations of a half shekel each. The proceeds are to be dedicated towards the communal offerings within the Mishkan.

Each of the collected half shekels will serve, the text states, as a *kofer nefesh* (soul atonement) for each of the contributing Israelites. By conducting the census in this manner, the Torah continues, Moshe will enable the nation to avoid a plague.[1]

Questions

Questions abound as we consider this puzzling, divinely ordained census.

Why couldn't the nation be counted directly? Why does God direct Moshe to count the people through donations of half shekels?

Why are the half shekels referred to as "soul atonements" for the Israelites? For what sin is the nation atoning?

Why were the Israelites under the threat of a plague?

Approaches

As the rabbis rise to answer the obvious questions listed above, they paint varied pictures of a national census fraught with eternal meaning and message.

—— **A** ——

Addressing the need for the half-shekel contribution, some of the commentaries focus on the moral lessons learned from a straightforward reading of the text.

---

1. Shmot 30:11–16.

Rabbi Shimshon Raphael Hirsch, for example, is among those who focus on the twin messages of *equality* and *unity* embedded in the half-shekel donation. God mandates an equivalent contribution on the part of every Israelite, rich or poor, to demonstrate that the involvement of each individual is equally precious to Him. At the same time, the amount commanded is a *half* shekel because, alone, no one individual is "whole." To be personally "complete" each Israelite must join with those around him. On a communal level, only through the combined effort of the entire community will the nation achieve its goals.[2]

In his discussion of the half-shekel mitzva, the Ba'al Hachinuch translates the message of equality into more concrete terms:

> The roots of this commandment reflect the desire of the Holy One Blessed Be He…that the contributions to the [communal] sacrifices brought before Him be equivalent…and that all, both poor and wealthy, be equal in this one mitzva…[3]

Finally the most basic lesson emerging from a straightforward reading of the text is self-evident: communal affiliation in Jewish tradition is not a passive phenomenon. Simply "being there" does not earn you a place among the numbered Israelites. *In order to be counted as a member of the Jewish community, you must actively do something that "counts."*

God therefore transforms the census itself into an act of participation. Inclusion is not automatic – it must be earned through the contribution of the half shekel towards the Sanctuary.

—— **B** ——————————————————————————

Concerning the identification of the half-shekel contribution as *kofer nefesh* (soul atonement), some authorities accept the opinion, first voiced by Rabbi Yehuda in the Midrash, that the half shekels serve as "atonement" for the looming sin of the golden calf, recorded later in Parshat Ki Tissa.[4] God prescribes these donations preemptively as a way of mercifully providing the "cure" before the "illness."

---

2. Rabbi Shimshon Raphael Hirsch, Shmot 30:13–15.
3. Sefer Hachinuch, mitzva 105.
4. Midrash Hagadol Shmot 30:12.

Others, including Rashi and the Chizkuni, suggest that the element of atonement associated with the half shekels refers to the ritual offerings that are ultimately acquired through these donations. Each half shekel is a "soul atonement" because it will be used to purchase *korbanot* (sacrifices) designed to secure expiation for the nation's sins.[5]

Many scholars maintain, however, that the "atonement" of the half shekels addresses a *potential failing embedded in the very act of counting*, a failing that could result in the biblically mentioned threat of plague. These authorities disagree, however, as to what this "failing" might be.

Rabbeinu Bachya suggests that the act of counting momentarily *separates* each individual unit from the whole. Standing alone, each entity is instantly vulnerable, robbed of the physical and spiritual protection afforded by the collective. God, therefore, prohibits the direct counting of the Israelites so that they will not be separated from each other – even for a moment – and, in that moment, become susceptible to danger.[6]

The vulnerability of which Rabbeinu Bachya speaks brings to mind the scene of the patriarch Yaakov, alone in the darkness, open to the attack of the mysterious stranger who struggles with him throughout the night. There, the Torah testifies: "*And Yaakov was left alone, and a man wrestled with him until the break of dawn.*"[7] *We are at risk, the Torah states, when we stand alone* (see *Bereishit*: Vayishlach 2, *Approaches* B).

The Sforno perceives a different kind of spiritual exposure highlighted by the act of counting. The requirement for periodic censuses, he says, is driven by man's mortality. As individuals age and die, the need arises for regular population updates. This personal transience, the Talmud testifies, is itself directly attributable to the existence of sin.[8] *To counteract, therefore, the element of sin rooted at the core of the need for every census, God mandates the collection of the half shekels as "atonement."*[9]

A beautiful, exquisitely simple, additional interpretation is offered by Rabbi Moshe Chaifetz in his eighteenth-century work *Melechet Machshevet*. God commands the uniform contribution of the half shekels in order to forestall the strife and jealousy that inevitably characterize communal

---

5. Rashi, Shmot 30:15; Chizkuni, Shmot 30:12.
6. Rabbeinu Bachya, Shmot 30:12.
7. Bereishit 32:25.
8. Talmud Bavli Shabbat 55a.
9. Sforno, Shmot 30:12.

fundraising and projects. The Torah thus testifies, "And there shall be no plague." *By insisting that each participant contribute a half shekel, God enables the nation to avoid the plague of divisiveness and dispute.*[10]

—— **C** ——————————————————————————————

Another possible explanation for the atoning nature of the half shekels might be deduced through a closer look at the word *kofer* (atonement), used to characterize the nature of the donation. This term is certainly familiar as the root of the word *kapara* (atonement), and appears in many variations throughout the Torah.

Here, however, the word acquires specific additional meaning. The *kofer* of the half-shekel donation is a "monetary atonement," or, as some translate, a "ransom," apparently paid to avoid a more severe penalty. In this form, the term *kofer* appears only three other times in the entire Torah text.

Two consecutive sentences in the book of Bamidbar explicitly prohibit the acceptance of a *kofer* from someone convicted of either murder or manslaughter. The Torah mandates capital punishment for the individual found guilty of premeditated murder, while exile to a "city of refuge" is the penalty for one convicted of negligent homicide. The text goes out of its way to state that these individuals cannot "pay off" their responsibilities monetarily. They must, instead, be punished to the full extent of the law.[11]

In contrast, however, as we have seen (see Mishpatim 2, *Approaches* B), a strange passage in Parshat Mishpatim mandates the *acceptance* of a *kofer*. The Torah states that if a domestic animal, known to be dangerous, kills a human being, the owner of that animal "deserves to die." He may, however (some authorities say he *must*[12]) pay a *kofer* (a financial penalty) in order to escape his dire fate.[13]

The defining line as to when a monetary *kofer* is legally acceptable seems clear. Crimes of "involvement," such as murder and manslaughter – when the perpetrator is guilty of an active, direct crime – cannot be addressed through the payment of a "ransom." A monetary payment is insufficient to atone for active participation in such a transgression. Crimes of

---

10. Melechet Machshevet, Shmot 30:12.
11. Bamidbar 35:31–32.
12. Rashi, Shmot 21:30; Rambam, *Mishneh Torah*, Hilchot Nizkei Mamon 10:4.
13. Shmot 21:29–30.

"uninvolvement," however –as when an individual fails to properly guard his dangerous animal – can result in the payment of a *kofer*. The very payment of the *kofer* is an admission of new awareness of one's involvement in, and responsibility for, the event. The *kofer* thus emerges as an appropriate corrective for the crime itself.

If the payment of a *kofer* elsewhere in the Torah is a corrective for crimes of uninvolvement, perhaps that is its role in the Ki Tissa census, as well. Specifically, the half-shekel *kofer* is designed to address inevitable lapses in the sphere of communal connection.

The Torah recognizes that every individual invariably falls short of fulfilling his communal obligations. Life's pressures, the exigencies of the moment, prevent us from fully participating in our shared responsibilities. As each individual pays his half shekel, therefore, he connects to the community and openly atones for the times when he had the opportunity to connect communally yet did not.

The half-shekel payment to the national coffers serves as a corrective for the crime of "communal uninvolvement" – for all the contributions, monetary and otherwise, which could have and should have been made.

— **D** ——————————————————————————

In addition to all the above approaches, no discussion of the half-shekel payment would be complete without mention of a puzzling, even troubling, concept within Jewish tradition: the concept of *ayin hara* (the evil eye). Commenting on the phrase "and there shall be no plague among them,"[14] Rashi immediately pronounces that during a census the participants become vulnerable because "the evil eye rules during counting."[15] He then continues by referring to an occasion during the reign of King David when a plague actually broke out among the people – apparently because of an improperly performed census.[16]

Once introduced, the concept of *ayin hara* cannot be ignored. On the one hand, Jewish thought clearly accepts the existence of this esoteric, unlucky, damaging force. Literally hundreds of sources in traditional Jewish literature make it clear that real danger lies at the center of an *ayin hara*

---

14. Ibid., 30:12.
15. Rashi, Shmot 30:12.
16. Shmuel II 24:1–15.

gaze. And yet, an argument could well be made that the very concept of an evil eye runs directly counter to the clear prohibition against superstition found in the Torah text.[17]

While a full discussion of the concept of *ayin hara* is well beyond the scope of this study, one pattern is worthy of mention. The phenomenon of *ayin hara* emerges when an individual openly behaves in a way that is bound to incur the jealousy of others. The rabbis warn against ostentatious conduct of any sort on the grounds that it raises the specter of the evil eye.[18]

Even more telling, perhaps, is the use of the term *ayin hara* at the opposite end of the equation. The rabbis draw a distinction between two potential character traits: the laudable characteristic of an *ayin tova* (a "good eye") and the negative trait of an *ayin hara* (an "evil eye"). The Mishna, in fact, proclaims:

> [Those who possess] *a good eye*, a humble spirit and a retiring soul are of the disciples of Avraham, our forefather. [Those who possess] *an evil eye*, an arrogant spirit and a greedy soul are disciples of the wicked [sorcerer] Bilam.[19]

Numerous authorities explain that the possessor of a "good eye" is satisfied with his lot and is not envious of others, while the possessor of an "evil eye" jealously craves what he does not possess.[20]

A reciprocal balance is apparently struck within Jewish tradition.

An individual who is constantly envious of others possesses the trait of an ayin hara (*an evil eye*). An individual, on the other hand, who acts in such a way as to incur the jealousy of others becomes vulnerable to the mysterious, damaging force of an *ayin hara*. Our tradition maintains that just as we potentially benefit, on a spiritual level, from the good wishes, amity and blessings of others, so, too, we can be spiritually endangered by any ill will and jealous sentiments that may come our way.

The puzzling, mysterious concept of *ayin hara* thus conveys a moral message which is clearly comprehensible:

---

17. Vayikra 19:26.
18. Talmud Bavli Sanhedrin 29b; Rashi, ibid.; Shulchan Aruch, Orach Chaim 141:6; Shulchan Aruch, Even Haezer 62:3.
19. Pirkei Avot 5:19.
20. Rashi, ibid.; Rambam, *Peirush Hamishnayot*, ibid.

Just as it is wrong and personally damaging to be jealous of others, it is also wrong and personally damaging to consciously incur the jealousy of others. While an individual has every right to fully enjoy the largesse that God may bestow upon him, he should never flaunt it. We must always remain sensitive to the potential impact of our good fortune upon those less fortunate than we.

Points to Ponder

Consider the oft-repeated refrain: "Careful, you don't want to give yourself an *ayin hara!*" We do not count people directly to this day, we are a little uncomfortable blithely speaking about good news, we fear just a bit when things are going too well…

All of this is understandable, given the emphasis within our tradition upon the potential dangers of incurring an *ayin hara*, the mysterious force known within our tradition as an "evil eye."

Perhaps, however, we are missing the point…

The ultimate purpose of Jewish ritual and belief is to shape the way we think and act. The ethical lessons embedded in even the most esoteric of our traditions should, therefore, not be ignored. *To avoid an ayin hara we must not only superstitiously seek ways to escape its wrath; we must actively refrain from the behavior that gives rise to this "force" in the first place.* By judging ourselves and each other through standards more meaningful than material gain, by seeking to promote harmony rather than ill will among those around us, we deny an *ayin hara* the very possibility of developing.

Not by accident does the Prophet Micha proclaim: "He [God] has told you, o man, that which is good; and that which the Lord requires of you, but to do justly, and to love true loyalty *and to walk humbly with your God.*"[21]

Conspicuous consumption, the flaunting of material wealth, the desire for others to be aware of and covet our success – all phenomena so prevalent in our day – are *antithetical to Jewish thought and to our overall spiritual health.* That is the real lesson of *ayin hara*, and one we ignore at our own peril.

---

21. Micha 6:8.

2 A Sin for the Ages

Context

Rooted at the base of Sinai, the Israelites grow restive as they wait for Moshe to descend from the mountain's summit. Turning to Aharon, they demand, "Rise up, make for us gods who will go before us, for Moshe – this man who brought us out of the land of Egypt – we do not know what has become of him!"

Aharon responds by instructing the people to contribute gold, which he fashions into a molten calf. He then proclaims, "A festival for the Lord tomorrow!" [Note: Aharon's role in this difficult episode will be examined in the next study.]

Rising early the next morning, people bring offerings and celebrate with food, drink and revelry.[1]

Even before Moshe descends from the mountain, God informs him of the sin of the golden calf and threatens the nation with immediate extinction, only relenting after Moshe's impassioned pleas.[2]

The perpetrators of the sin are punished and the rest of the nation earns forgiveness through repentance.[3] The sin of the golden calf remains, however, according to rabbinic thought, a seminal transgression that continues to affect the Jewish people in countless ways across the centuries.[4]

Questions

No event within Jewish history is more puzzling or more frightening than the *chet ha'egel.*

How could the people who experienced the Exodus from Egypt, the

---

1. Shmot 32:1–6.
2. Ibid., 32:7–14.
3. Ibid., 32:20–34:10.
4. Talmud Bavli Sanhedrin 102a.

parting of the Reed Sea, the defeat of Amalek, the gift of the manna and the powerful Revelation at Mount Sinai fail so completely in the very shadow of that mountain?

Forty days earlier, against the dramatic backdrop of God's manifestation at Sinai, the Israelites heard the clear commandment against idol worship.[5] How could they now, at the first sign of difficulty, create and deify a golden calf?

In a different vein, the rabbis maintain that the sin of the golden calf reverberates across the ages, affecting each era of Jewish history. And yet, the *chet ha'egel* seems irrelevant to our lives – an ancient event rooted in idolatrous practices distant from our experience. What possible eternal message might be contained in what the rabbis clearly perceive to be a formative, instructive tragedy?

Approaches

—**A**————————————————————

In spite of the apparent disconnect between the *chet ha'egel* and the backdrop against which it occurs, initial sources do view and identify this sin as *an outright case of idol worship.*

"By worshiping the calf, the Israelites clearly indicated their acceptance of idolatry," the Talmud proclaims,[6] mirroring a position which finds even earlier voice in a passage of Tehillim: "They exchanged their glory for the image of a bull that feeds on grass."[7] Similar opinions are found in the Midrash, as well.[8]

Some Talmudic authorities mitigate the crime by focusing on the plural tense of the Israelites' demand upon Aharon: "Rise up, *make for us gods who will go before us…*" With the sin of the golden calf, these rabbis explain, the Israelites do not attempt a total rejection of God. They instead endeavor to couple their worship of God with that of other idolatrous deities.[9] Rashi

---

5. Shmot 20:3–5.
6. Talmud Bavli Avoda Zara 53b.
7. Tehillim 106:20.
8. Pirkei D'Rabi Eliezer 45.
9. Talmud Bavli Sanhedrin 63a.

reflects this Talmudic position in his commentary when he states, "They [the Israelites] desired many gods."[10]

Even this softening of the sin, however, does not address the fundamental question: how could the Israelites turn their backs so quickly on all that they had recently experienced and learned? Forty days earlier, amidst the thunder and lightning of Revelation, God's declarations concerning His "oneness" were crystal clear:

> I am the Lord your God…. You shall have no other gods in my presence. You shall not make for yourself a carved image or any likeness of that which is in the heavens above or on the earth below or in the water beneath the earth; you shall not bow down to them nor shall you worship them…. [11]

How could those words now be totally ignored?

A powerfully insightful approach to the behavior of the Israelites at the foot of Sinai can be gleaned from the writings of the Rambam. In his *Guide to the Perplexed*, this great scholar develops the principle that human behavior does not change abruptly and that a people cannot journey immediately from one extreme to the other: "It is not in man's nature to be reared in slavery…and then 'wash his hands' and suddenly be able to fight the descendents of giants [the inhabitants of the land of Canaan]."[12]

The Rambam goes on to explain that the full transformation of the Israelites eventually requires a forty-year period of wandering and "schooling" in the wilderness – a period during which they acquire the traits necessary for successful nationhood.[13]

Abrupt events, no matter how miraculous and awe-inspiring, do not carry the power to make fundamental changes to human nature. True behavioral change is gradual. In spite of all they had seen and experienced, the Israelites standing at the foot of Sinai were unable to make the leap beyond their idolatrous origins. Battered by the fearful forces surrounding them, bewildered by Moshe's apparent disappearance, they return to the comfort of the familiar – and create an idol of gold.

---

10. Rashi, Shmot 32:1.
11. Shmot 20:2–5.
12. Rambam, *Moreh Nevuchim* 3:32.
13. Ibid.

The actions of the Israelites at the foot of Sinai are understandable and instructive, Nehama Leibowitz maintains, as she poignantly outlines the lessons to be learned:

> Therefore we should not be astonished – *but should, rather, learn and take to heart* [my italics] – that thousands of individuals from among those who stood at the base of the mountain and heard the voice of God speaking from the midst of the fire, forty days later created the golden calf.
>
> A one-time proclamation will not change man…even a clear Divine Revelation will not turn him from idolatry to the worship of God.
>
> Only prolonged exposure to a life of Torah and mitzvot…surrounding an individual on all sides – ordering his days, nights, weekdays and festivals; his life within the home and his existence outside; his dealings with his family and his interactions with others; his toil at home and his labor in the field; guiding him day by day, hour by hour – only such immersion will change a person and guard him from sliding back into the depths of darkness."[14]

---— **B** ————————————————————————————————

In stark contrast to those who view the actions of the Israelites at Sinai as classically idolatrous, numerous scholars offer radically different approaches to the *chet ha'egel*.

Rabbi Yehuda Halevi, for example, maintains that the Israelites are actually motivated by a desire to worship God effectively. Reared among religions that make extensive use of physical images, the Israelites feel unable to approach their God in the absence of a tangible symbol towards which to focus their devotion. The people fully expect that Moshe, with his descent from Mount Sinai, will bring such a symbol: the Tablets of Testimony (inscribed with the Ten Declarations). When they conclude that Moshe has failed to return with the tablets, the Israelites turn to Aharon and demand a substitute.

Rabbi Yehuda goes on to explain that the nation's transgression lies not

---

14. Nehama Leibowitz, *Iyunim Chadashim b'sefer Shmot* (Jerusalem: Hasochnut Hayehudit, 1970), pp. 399–400.

in their fundamental intent or assumptions, but in their methods. Symbols are certainly critical to Judaism, as can be seen from the extensive use of symbolic ritual in the building and operation of the Mishkan (see Teruma 4). Only symbols that flow from God's law, however, are acceptable. The Israelites have no right to devise and create their own mechanism through which to approach God. Their sin can be compared, says Rabbi Yehuda, to an individual who enters a doctor's dispensary and prescribes drugs – thereby killing the patients who would have been saved had they been given the proper dosage by the doctor himself.[15]

Numerous later authorities follow in the footsteps of Rabbi Yehuda Halevi's interpretation, some with attribution and some without.

In his work the *Beis Halevi*, Rabbi Yosef Dov Halevi Soloveitchik offers a slightly variant approach. The Israelites know that the ritual service will be performed by a specific individual, Aharon, and will be conducted in a specific location, the Mishkan. They therefore believe that they have the right to create their own "Tabernacle" as they see fit. They fail to realize, however, that each detail of the Sanctuary is purposeful, filled with divinely ordained mystery and meaning.[16]

Other commentaries, including the Ramban, Ibn Ezra and Rabbi Shimshon Raphael Hirsch, focus on the wording of the Israelites' demand of Aharon: "Rise up, make for us gods who will go before us, *for Moshe – this man who brought us out of the land of Egypt – we do not know what has become of him!*"[17]

The Israelites, they say, are not attempting to replace God. *They are, instead, attempting to replace Moshe.* Deeply frightened by Moshe's apparent disappearance (their fear exaggerated, the rabbis say, by an error they make in computing the days of Moshe's absence[18]), the people feel unable to approach God without the benefit of the only leader they have known. They therefore demand of Aharon that he create a new "leader."

The sin of the Israelites, says Hirsch, lies in the "erroneous idea that man can make, may make, must make a 'Moses' for himself…" The grave error in their thinking is their belief that in order to bridge the unimaginable chasm between man and the Divine, an intermediary is required. *This*

---

15. Hakuzari 1:97.
16. Beis Halevi, Shmot Parshat Ki Tissa.
17. Shmot 32:1.
18. Talmud Bavli Shabbat 89a.

suggestion is diametrically opposed to the fundamental Jewish belief in man's ability to forge his own direct and personal relationship with God.[19]

[Note: As will be explained in the next study, Hirsch maintains that while the nation's initial intent is not idolatrous, they quickly and inexorably do descend into actual idol worship.]

— C ————————————————————————————————

Finally, a puzzling passage rooted in the aftermath of the *chet ha'egel* may well provide the key towards a concrete understanding of the sin and its continuing relevance to our lives.

After punishing the perpetrators of the crime, God turns to Moshe and says:

Go, rise up from here, and the people whom you brought up from the land of Egypt – to the land which I promised to Avraham, Yitzchak and to Yaakov.... *And I will send before you an angel*, and I will drive out the *Cana'ani*, the *Emori*, the *Chitti*, the *Perizi*, the *Chivi*, and the *Yevusi* [the nations inhabiting the land of Canaan] – to a land flowing with milk and honey, *for I will not go up among you, for you are a stiff-necked people, lest I destroy you on the way.*[20]

The Israelites' reaction to this news is swift and emphatic:

"And the people heard this bad tiding and they *fell into mourning...*"[21]

At first glance, this interchange is bewildering.

What exactly is the nature of God's threat? He maintains that He will not "go up among the people." And yet, what will be the practical impact of His absence? Everything seems, on a concrete level, to stay the same! God's angel will go before the nation, the people will enter the land of Canaan, the current inhabitants of the land will be driven out...

What, then, exactly is the problem?

Furthermore, why does the nation respond so powerfully by descending into "mourning"? Given the possible eventualities that could have

19. Rabbi Shimshon Raphael Hirsch, Shmot 32:1.
20. Shmot 33:1–3.
21. Ibid., 33:4.

resulted from the sin of the golden calf, the news delivered by God to Moshe does not seem so devastating.

The answer to these questions lies in understanding that God, intent upon educating the people to the nature of their failing, responds to the nation's sin "measure for measure." In effect, He says to the people: *Be careful what you ask for, because you might get it!*

From the very beginning of Revelation, the Israelites consistently respond to God's presence with a desperate desire for "distance." Awed by the overwhelming scene accompanying the Ten Declarations, the people's reaction is clear – *retreat*:

> And the entire people saw the thunder and lightning and the sound of the shofar and the smoking mountain and they trembled and stood from afar. And they said to Moshe, "You speak with us and we will listen; and let not God speak with us, lest we die."[22]

As we have noted before (see *Bereishit*: Bereishit 3, *Approaches* D), this reaction stands in stark contrast to the nation's response just a few weeks earlier after the destruction of the Egyptian army in the Reed Sea. There, on the banks of that sea, the revelation of God's power is greeted with song and dancing, not with fear and retreat.[23] Why do the people react so differently now?

The Israelites are responding to two very different messages from God.

The message at the Reed Sea is "God will take care of you."

The message of Sinai is "God demands from you."

Faced with demands upon their behavior from a thinking God, the people opt for personal comfort rather than self-confrontation. They desperately seek distance from God and from His demands by insisting that Moshe speak in their stead.

And when, forty days later, Moshe apparently fails to return from the summit of the mountain at the expected time – and the people face the fact that they will now be required to interact with God directly, without the benefit of Moshe as their intermediary – this desperate desire for *distance*

---

22. Ibid., 20:15–16.
23. Ibid., 15:1–21.

from God becomes an overwhelming fear. The Israelites create a golden calf to take Moshe's place, to stand between them and their Creator.

Now, in the devastating aftermath of that crime, God responds to the nation's failing. He turns to the people and says, "I will send before you an angel…" *If it's distance you want, it's distance you will get.*

"For I will not go up among you, for you are a stiff-necked people, lest I destroy you on the way." *After all, you are right. If I remain close to you, you will be vulnerable. Therefore, I grant you your wish… You will achieve your national destiny but I will not be there with as you reach your goals.*

The question, however, remains: why is God's absence a problem if the nation's concrete goals will all eventually be met?

To understand, we must take a step back to recognize that the parameters which define our relationship with God often mirror the universal rules which govern interpersonal relationships.

Inevitably, the closer we grow emotionally to those around us, the more vulnerable we become. The possibility of personal pain increases geometrically as we open our lives to others. Conversely, safety is found in emotional "distance." An individual who goes through life avoiding close relationships effectively lives in "safety" – immune from potential heartache and pain.

And yet, such an individual never knows the deep beauty that is possible with closeness to another. Absent from his life are the wonders of true friendship and love. In his desire for "safety," this individual misses out on the very phenomenon that makes life truly worthwhile, the splendor that results when one heart touches another.

Here, then, is the essence of God's threat. *I will be absent from your lives. You will be safe, as you avoid the vulnerability that would inevitably accompany My close connection with you, but you will also miss out on the potential grandeur that would have resulted.*

In response, the nation mourns. For now they understand their fatal error. The distant relationship from God which they had so desperately craved might well be safe, *but it is also empty*; and that emptiness confronts them in the aftermath of the sin of the golden calf. Moshe is forced to plead with God that He return to the people – until God ultimately relents.[24]

God's actions following the *chet ha'egel* thus prove to be supremely

---

24. Ibid., 33:12–17.

educative, as He forces the nation to squarely face the failure that resulted from their deep-seated fear. Even more, God's response crystallizes the eternal significance of this seminal sin.

As He demanded of the Israelites at Sinai, God demands of us that we create a close relationship with Him in our lives – that we each risk our "safe" existence by drawing near to Him and to His Torah. Over and over again, we pull away, afraid that too much closeness with the Divine will upset our comfortable lives, afraid that we will be challenged to examine our decisions and actions…

And, when we pull away, we once again create the golden calf.

Points to Ponder

What does it mean to draw close to God – near enough to the fire of Sinai to feel the heat?

While the answers are potentially manifold, one clear manifestation of the tug of Sinai and of our resistance to that pull was driven home to me many years ago.

I had served as rabbi in a Modern Orthodox congregation for a few years, when a congregant approached me with upsetting news: "Do you know, Rabbi, that many of our congregants rationalize and 'eat out' certain foods in non-kosher diners? In fact, things have gotten so bad that those of us who want to patronize only kosher establishments feel pressured to relent in order to maintain our friendships."

Deeply disturbed, I dedicated my next Shabbat sermon to the topic of kashrut, outlining in clear, practical terms the halachic problems of eating even dairy foods in non-kosher restaurants.

I was totally unprepared for the resulting uproar. An avalanche of comments followed my presentation, including:

"Rabbi, don't you have more important things to speak about?"

"What right does the Rabbi have to tell us where to eat?"

"The Rabbi is only upset that we didn't invite him to the party at the Italian restaurant."

And even, bewilderingly: "The Rabbi didn't say that the food isn't kosher. He only said that it is *treif* [the Yiddish term for non-kosher]. If he really meant that it isn't kosher, he would have said it isn't kosher."

The next week, I delivered a second sermon in which I revisited the issue. After humorously reviewing the reactions to my first presentation, I made a simple point: "What you eat," I said, "is your business. At the very least, however, be both knowledgeable and honest. If you intend to eat at the diner tonight, then don't rationalize; don't call the food that you will eat kosher. Admit to yourself, 'Tonight I am going to eat *treif*.' If, upon that admission, you still want to go to the diner, go right ahead."

By all accounts, this second sermon had measurable impact.

More importantly, however, the experience underscored a fundamental truth about our relationship to Judaism.

Most of us choose to practice *comfortable* as opposed to *confrontational* Judaism (see *Bereishit*: Bereishit 3, *Points to Ponder*). We prefer "distance" from the demands of our tradition. Hiding behind rote ritual and habitual observance, we adhere to a religious structure that does not challenge our lives or test our commitments.

The members of my community reacted so strongly because I had touched a raw nerve. As long as I spoke about issues that demanded no change on their part, they did not object. As soon as I raised a concern, however, that directly challenged their ongoing behavior, a firestorm erupted.

My congregants and I relearned an important lesson on those Shabbatot. For Jewish belief to be a valuable component of our lives we must allow that belief to challenge and shape our existence. A dean of the American rabbinate, Rabbi Leo Jung, is quoted as having said, "The job of the rabbi is to comfort the afflicted – and to afflict the comfortable." In truth, that is not only the job of the rabbi, but the job of Judaism itself.

As God taught the Israelites centuries ago at Sinai: *comfortable Judaism eventually becomes, like every "distant" relationship, meaningless and empty. Only confrontational Judaism – only drawing near enough to God to risk change and growth – adds real meaning to our lives.*

3 What about Aharon?

Context

When Moshe ascends Mount Sinai to receive the first set of Tablets of Testimony, he leaves his brother Aharon, together with Chur, in charge of the people.[1] Nearly forty full days later, the Israelites grow restless over Moshe's prolonged absence and confront Aharon with the demand: "Rise up, make for us gods who will go before us, for Moshe – this man who brought us out of the land of Egypt – we do not know what has become of him!"

In response, Aharon directs the people to "Remove the rings of gold that are in the ears of your wives, sons and daughters, and bring them to me."

Aharon then takes the gold which he receives, fashions it with an engraving tool into a molten calf and proclaims: "A festival for the Lord tomorrow!"[2]

When Moshe descends the mountain, he confronts Aharon and exclaims: "What has this people done to you that you brought upon it such a grievous sin?"

Aharon responds by pleading with his brother: "Let not my master be angry, you know that this people is disposed towards evil."

Aharon then recounts the nation's demand and closes with the statement: "And I said to them, 'Who has gold?' They removed it and gave it to me, *I threw it into the fire, and this calf emerged.*"[3]

---

1. Shmot 24:14.
2. Ibid., 32:1–5.
3. Ibid., 32:21–24.

Questions

Aharon's behavior seems unconscionable!

Why does Moshe's brother apparently fail so miserably in his leadership role at the foot of Sinai?

Why does Aharon accede to the nation's demand without argument and create the golden calf? Should he not have attempted to dissuade the people from their ill-advised, destructive path?

When confronted by Moshe, how can Aharon defend his actions with the strange claim: "I threw it [the gold] into the fire, and this calf emerged"? The text clearly states that Aharon deliberately "fashioned" the gold which he received into a molten calf.[4]

In the aftermath of the *chet ha'egel*, the active perpetrators are executed and the entire nation is threatened with serious punishment. Aharon seems to escape, however, with only a reprimand. Even more, he continues to serve for forty years as High Priest and as partner with Moshe in the leadership of the people. How is this equitable?

Approaches

At face value, the textual evidence against Aharon seems overwhelming. At the same time, however, it is inconceivable that Aharon could be guilty of, at worst, involvement in the serious crime of idolatry and, at best, a misguided attempt to create an intermediary between God and the people – and escape unscathed. In the face of this overwhelming puzzle, a wide range of opinion emerges among the commentaries concerning the intentions and actions of this biblical hero at this critical moment of his career.

—**A**———————————————————————

Rashi, for example, who elsewhere defends biblical figures in the face of apparent wrongdoing (see Toldot 4, *Approaches* B), strenuously works to defend Aharon in this difficult circumstance, as well. He quotes a series of Midrashic traditions, each of which offers a different rationale for Aharon's behavior.

First, mirroring the position found in the Midrash Tanchuma,[5] Rashi claims that *Aharon is simply stalling for time.* Fully confident that Moshe

---

4. Ibid., 32:4.
5. Midrash Tanchuma Ki Tissa 19.

will shortly return, Aharon deliberately reacts to the people's demands by directing them to contribute "the rings of gold that are in the ears of your wives, sons and daughters." Aharon calculates that the women and children's reluctance to part with their cherished jewelry will delay the process long enough for Moshe to descend the mountain (the Midrash actually goes a step further by suggesting that Aharon knows that the women, more righteous than the men, will be unwilling to participate in the *chet ha'egel*). Aharon underestimates, however, the zealous desire of the perpetrators. When the women refuse to participate, the men immediately contribute their own jewelry towards the project.[6]

Rashi cites a second Midrashic tradition which even maintains that Aharon never actually fashions the golden calf, at all. As soon as Aharon throws the gold into the fire, sorcerers from among the "mixed multitude" who fled Egypt with the Israelites magically cause the golden calf to form. Aharon is thus able to later claim, "I threw it into the fire, and this calf emerged."[7]

Further in the narrative, Rashi notes a series of Midrashic observations on the phrase "And Aharon saw and he built an altar before it [the golden calf]."[8] What is it, the Midrash Rabba asks, that "Aharon saw"?

1. *Aharon "saw" the fate of Chur.* This tradition is based on Chur's mysterious disappearance. When Moshe ascends Mount Sinai to receive the first set of tablets he appoints Aharon and Chur to lead the nation in his absence. Chur, however, suddenly and completely vanishes from the scene and is not mentioned again. The Midrash explains that Chur actively objects to the creation of the golden calf and is killed by the people. After witnessing Chur's fate, Aharon decides to deal with the nation's demands differently. [The Midrash actually goes a step further and suggests that Aharon is not motivated by concern for his own safety but by fear for the nation. He believes that upon killing both a prophet (Chur) and a priest (Aharon), the people will become totally irredeemable.]

2. *Aharon saw the possibility of assuming responsibility.* It is preferable, Aharon reasons, that I build the altar rather than the people. I will then be responsible for the crime rather than they.

---

6. Rashi, Shmot 32:2.
7. Ibid., 32:4; Shmot 32:34.
8. Shmot:32:5.

3. *Aharon saw an additional possibility for delay.* Aharon realizes that if he allows the nation to build the altar as a group they will do so quickly. He therefore determines to build it himself, continuing to delay the process in the hope that Moshe will return.[9]

Finally, on the basis of *pshat*, Rashi defends Aharon through a careful reading of Aharon's proclamation after he builds the altar: *"A festival for the Lord tomorrow!"*[10] Firstly, Aharon further delays the nation's celebration until the next day. Secondly, Aharon uses the term *A-do-nai* (Lord), the title reserved for the God of Israel. Aharon's heart, claims Rashi, is directed at all times towards heaven. He is certain that Moshe will return and that the morrow's celebration will truly be "for the Lord."[11]

— B

So difficult are the issues surrounding Aharon's role in the *chet ha'egel* that many of those commentaries who normally eschew Midrashic interpretation, in favor of a rational approach to the text, in this case adopt elements of the Midrash in their interpretations.

Rabbi Shimshon Raphael Hirsch, for example, accepts as a given the Midrashic view that Aharon's main goal is *delay*. Rooting his position in the text, however, Hirsch notes that the very wording of Aharon's request for gold indicates an expectation of reluctance on the part of the people. In addition, the Torah's step-by-step description of the creation of the golden calf mirrors Aharon's slow, methodical response to the people's demands.[12]

Other *pashtanim* (commentaries who adhere to the *pshat* of the text), such as the Rashbam, are conspicuously silent on the issue of Aharon's role in the *chet ha'egel*, offering no explanation or excuse for Aharon's actions.[13]

— C

Some commentaries are able to mitigate Aharon's behavior through their acceptance of a less onerous approach to the entire episode of the golden calf. As we have noted (see Ki Tissa 2, *Approaches* B), the Ramban and Ibn

---

9. Midrash Rabba Vayikra 10:3.
10. Shmot 32:5.
11. Rashi, Shmot 32:5.
12. Rabbi Shimshon Raphael Hirsch, Shmot 32:2–4.
13. Rashbam, Shmot 32:2–5.

Ezra maintain that the Israelites' intent was not fundamentally idolatrous. Frightened by Moshe's apparent disappearance, the people demand the appointment (or the creation) of a new leader to take his place. Aharon feels that this request, while misguided, is not totally evil. He therefore determines to "play along" until Moshe returns.

Chizkuni, while adopting the same approach to the sin, offers a fascinating alternative insight into Aharon's reasoning: Aharon rationalizes, *The people are asking for a new leader. If I appoint another individual to leadership, when Moshe returns and that individual refuses to relinquish his power, deep division will result within the nation. If, on the other hand, I refuse completely, the people will appoint their own leader and even greater strife will ensue. Finally, if I accept the leadership myself, friction will develop between me and my brother. I will, therefore, occupy the people with various activities, none of which will have any real impact, until Moshe returns.*[14]

Rabbi Shimshon Raphael Hirsch is among those commentaries who paint a picture of developing disaster, as things proceed "from bad to worse." Aharon recognizes that the nation's original request is not idolatrous. He also realizes, however, that a thin line separates the people's initial intent from true idolatrous practice. If he resists and is killed for his efforts, he rationalizes, the people will, "over his dead body…give themselves up to their folly with still greater unrestrained license."[15] Aharon, therefore, both delays the process and attempts to limit the severity of the crime. On the next day, however, "Aharon sees" that the nation "has already passed across the narrow bridge from the notion of a divine intermediary to that of a real god." In spite of Aharon's attempts to forestall complete tragedy, the nation falls into idolatry.[16]

— **D** —

Finally, no analysis of Aharon's actions in conjunction with the sin of the golden calf would be complete without acknowledging the context to this situation, shaped by Aharon's personality. As we have previously explained (see Shmot 5, *Approaches* D; Mishpatim 4, *Approaches* B3; Tetzave 2, *Approaches* E2), Aharon is a behavioral "photographic negative" of his

---

14. Chizkuni, Shmot 32:2.
15. Rabbi Shimshon Raphael Hirsch, Shmot 32:2–4.
16. Ibid. Shmot 32:5–6.

brother. Whereas Moshe is direct and blunt almost to the point of being undiplomatic, Aharon is a soft compromiser who desires nothing more than harmony within the nation. How telling that the failures of each of these brothers take place at the extremes of their personalities. Moshe will lose his leadership at *Mei Meriva*, where, moved to anger by the people's demand for water, he will strike a rock rather than fulfill God's command by speaking to it. Aharon's low point of leadership occurs here, at the foot of Sinai, as *the great compromiser compromises once too often*. We cannot excuse Aharon's behavior, but, given his personality, we can understand.

— E —————————————————————————

When all is said and done, the issue of Aharon's involvement in the *chet ha'egel* is one of those cases where the questions are better than the answers. In such circumstances we are challenged to continue the search for understanding – even as we acknowledge that we may never know the "real truth" until God sees fit to reveal it.

4 Why Break the Tablets?

Context

God informs Moshe, on the summit of Mount Sinai, of the sin of the golden calf and commands him to descend the mountain and confront the nation. After beseeching God to forgive the people, Moshe complies, carrying with him the divinely created Tablets of Testimony upon which God has inscribed the Ten Declarations.[1]

When Moshe nears the Israelite encampment, however, and sees the nation dancing before the golden calf, he becomes enraged and "casts the tablets out of his hands and smashes them beneath the mountain."[2]

In the book of Devarim, nearly forty years later, when Moshe recalls this event before the nation, he emphatically declares, "I grasped the two tablets and threw them from my two hands, and I smashed them before your eyes."[3]

In the wake of the destruction of these tablets, God commands Moshe to carve a second set upon which: "I [God] will inscribe the words that were on the first tablets *asher shibarta* (which you shattered)."[4] The Talmudic sages perceive in the two words *asher shibarta* divine approbation of Moshe's actions: *Yiyasher kochacha sheshibarta*, "You are to be congratulated for shattering [the first set of tablets]." The rabbis thus identify the breaking of the tablets as one of three actions which Moshe performed of his own accord, to which God retroactively gives His stamp of approval.[5]

So powerfully does Rashi identify with this rabbinic observation that he cites it in his final commentary on the Torah.

---

1. Shmot 32:7–16.
2. Ibid., 32:19.
3. Devarim 9:17.
4. Shmot 34:1.
5. Talmud Bavli Yevamot 62a.

The Torah ends with the statement "Never again has arisen a prophet like Moshe, who knew God face-to-face; as evidenced by all the signs…and by the strong hand and great power that Moshe performed before the eyes of all Israel."[6] Rashi maintains that the very last words of the Torah, "…before the eyes of all Israel," allude to the breaking of the tablets, an event which Moshe describes as having occurred "before the eyes of the people."[7]

Questions

The classic, familiar image of Moshe breaking the Tablets of Testimony at the foot of Mount Sinai demands a second look.

Simply put, why does Moshe shatter the tablets? Why does he take out his seemingly misdirected anger upon an object of such overwhelming sanctity? The destruction of any sanctified object is a grievous sin; how much more so the shattering of the God-created Tablets of Testimony.

Compounding the problem is the apparent positive judgment of the rabbis concerning Moshe's actions. Why do the rabbis believe that God congratulates Moshe for breaking the tablets? Why, in addition, would Rashi see this action as so commendable and significant that he would cite it as his final comment on Moshe's life and close his monumental work on the Torah specifically by recalling this event?

Approaches

So serious are the issues raised by Moshe's breaking the first set of Tablets of Testimony, that a wide range of often diametrically opposed views concerning this event are proposed by the commentaries.

— **A** ——————————————

Strangely enough, it is the Rashbam, *pashtan* par excellence, who veers sharply away from the straightforward explanation of the Torah text. Maintaining that Moshe did not shatter the tablets at all of his own accord, the Rashbam states: "When Moshe saw the calf, his strength ebbed and he only

---

6. Devarim 34:10–12.
7. Ibid., 9:17; Rashi, Devarim 34:12.

had enough power to thrust the tablets far enough away that they would not damage his feet as they *fell* from his hands."[8]

As the Rashbam himself indicates, he builds his position on earlier statements found in the Midrash which postulate a sudden inability on Moshe's part to carry the tablets. A source in Pirkei D'Rabi Eliezer explains, for example, that the divine inscription on the tablets miraculously enables the stone to "carry itself and Moshe with it." When, however, the golden calf and the rejoicing Israelites come into view, the inscription "flies" from the tablets. With God's words gone, Moshe can no longer carry the heavy stone and the tablets fall from his hands.[9] Similar explanations are found elsewhere in Midrashic literature.[10]

While the Rashbam does translate these Midrashic traditions into less miraculous terms, he nonetheless seems to contradict the clear intent of the biblical text, both here and in the book of Devarim. The Torah indicates that Moshe does not drop the tablets but actively thrusts them from his hands, destroying them at the foot of the mountain. The Rashbam must have struggled deeply with the concept of Moshe consciously shattering the divinely created tablets, to have adopted a Midrashic position so clearly at odds with the straightforward meaning of the text.

— **B** —

The Ramban believes, like the Rashbam, that the breaking of the tablets simply could not have been a conscious, premeditated action on Moshe's part. Attempting to remain more clearly within the boundaries of the text, however, the Ramban maintains that Moshe is overcome not by physical but by spiritual and emotional weakness when he comes into sight of the celebrating Israelites: "Moshe did not hesitate to shatter the tablets, for he was so angered when he saw this evil deed, *he could not control himself.*"[11]

— **C** —

Numerous other authorities, however, are unwilling to accept the breaking of the tablets as an involuntary action on Moshe's part. Strange as it might seem, they claim, Moshe consciously destroys the Tablets of Testi-

---

8. Rashbam, Shmot 32:19.
9. Pirkei D'Rabi Eliezer 44.
10. Midrash Tanchuma Devarim Eikev 11.
11. Ramban, Shmot 32:16.

mony in response to the sin of the golden calf. For this deliberate act, they continue, Moshe receives the divine approbation recorded in the Talmud (see above).

While the sources agree, however, on the deliberate nature of Moshe's act, his motivations remain the subject of ongoing debate.

Some Midrashic authorities maintain that Moshe is motivated by a desire to protect the nation from the full effect of their sin. He reasons: *If I give the law to the people, they will be held fully culpable for their actions under that law. Far better that they should be judged as inadvertent rather than as deliberate sinners.*

Moshe, therefore, smashes the tablets to avoid presenting them to the Israelites.[12]

Another Midrash suggests that Moshe goes even further in a self-sacrificing attempt to save the nation. He deliberately sins by breaking the tablets so that his fate will be bound up with the fate of the Israelites.

True, Moshe says to God, *the people have sinned – but so have I. If You will forgive them, then forgive me as well. If You will not forgive them, then do not forgive me. Instead, "erase me from the book that You have written."*[13]

At the opposite end of the interpretive spectrum, Rashi sees Moshe's motivation as condemnatory of the Israelites actions. Moshe deliberates: *If the Torah states with regard to the Pesach sacrifice, which is only one mitzva, "no apostate may eat of it,"*[14] *now, when the entire Torah is involved and all of Israel are apostates, shall I give the Torah to them?*[15]

Yet other commentaries interpret Moshe's actions as consciously educative in intent. Moshe wants, through the smashing of the tablets, to shock the Israelites back to their senses. The Netziv goes so far as to claim that Moshe deliberately refrains from breaking the tablets at the summit of Mount Sinai, when God first informs him of the *chet ha'egel*. He instead bides his time and waits until his actions will have the greatest impact upon the people at the foot of the mountain. When the nation witnesses his destruction of these overwhelmingly sanctified objects, Moshe reasons, they

---

12. Midrash Rabba Shmot 43:1.
13. Shmot 32:32; Midrash Rabba Shmot 46:1.
14. Shmot 12:43.
15. Rashi, Shmot 32:19.

will be so shocked and aggrieved that they will, without objection, accept the punitive measures necessary in response to their sin.[16]

—— **D** ——————————————————

The broadest and boldest classical suggestion concerning Moshe's motivation in breaking the Tablets of Testimony is offered by the nineteenth–twentieth-century scholar, Rabbi Meir Simcha HaCohen of Dvinsk, in his insightful work the *Meshech Chochma*. Rabbi Meir Simcha maintains that Moshe wants to convey to the people one simple truth: *there is only one source of holiness in existence: God, Himself.*

Moshe recognizes that at the core of the sin of the golden calf lies the nation's erroneous belief in sources of sanctity outside of God. The Israelites perceive Moshe as inherently holy and essential to their relationship with the Divine. When Moshe apparently disappears they feel compelled to create another source of supposed holiness in an attempt to reach God – hence, the creation of the golden calf.

Realizing that he must try to cure the nation of its misconceptions, Moshe turns to them and effectively says: *I am not holy. I am a man just as you. The Torah is not dependent upon me. Even had I not returned, the Torah would have continued in my absence.*

The Sanctuary and its utensils are not intrinsically holy. Their sanctity derives from God's presence in our midst. If you sin, these objects lose their holiness.

Even these Tablets of Testimony – the word of God – are not holy, in and of themselves. Their sanctity derives from your relationship with God and your willingness to observe His law. Now that you have sinned, these tablets are mere stone, devoid of any sanctity. As proof of my point, I shatter them before you!

Moshe, Rabbi Meir Simcha continues, is deeply afraid that the Tablets of Testimony will be misused by the nation in its present state. He is concerned that the people will deify the tablets themselves. By shattering the tablets, therefore, Moshe directly addresses a root cause of the *chet ha'egel* as he teaches the Israelites that God, alone, is the source of holiness.[17]

———————————

16. Ha'amek Davar, Shmot 32:15–20.
17. Meshech Chochma, Shmot 32:19.

— **E** —

One final approach to Moshe's actions can be suggested if we consider the fundamental differences between the two sets of tablets received by Moshe on Sinai: the first set, destroyed as a result of the *chet ha'egel*, and the second set, mandated by God to take their place.

The most obvious distinction is that the first set of tablets were both carved and inscribed by God while the second set were carved by Moshe at God's command and then divinely inscribed on the summit of Mount Sinai.

A second, more subtle, yet fascinating distinction between the two sets emerges as part of Moshe's recollections in the book of Devarim. Recalling the flow of events at Sinai for the people, Moshe states that accompanying the commandments to carve the second set of tablets and to ascend the mountain with them was an added divine directive: "And make for yourself a wooden Ark [in which to place these tablets]."[18] So important is this Ark (which, strangely, is not mentioned at all when the events occur in the book of Shmot) in Moshe's mind, that he cites it no fewer than four times within the span of five sentences.[19]

Perhaps the message of the second tablets and the Ark into which they are placed is the *message of context*. The Torah is valueless in a vacuum. Its words are only significant when they find a ready home in the heart of man – only when those words are allowed to shape the actions of those who receive them.

Moshe, descending the mountain and witnessing the celebrating Israelites, recognizes that the tablets and the law they represent have no context within which to exist. The nation is simply unready to accept God's word. Were that word to be given to them in their present state, the Torah itself would become an aberration, misunderstood and even misused. Moshe, therefore, publicly destroys the Tablets of Testimony, and then, at God's command, begins the process of reeducating the people.

Central to that process of reeducation will be the symbolism of the second set of Tablets of Testimony, themselves. God will inscribe upon them His decrees but, this time, only on stone carved by Moshe. The tablets

---

18. Devarim 10:1.
19. Ibid., 10:1–5.

themselves will thus represent the word of God, finding a home in the actions of man.

These new tablets must also immediately be placed into a symbolic home, a simple Ark of wood. Only if the contents of those tablets find their home, as well, in the humble hearts of men – only if the Torah finds its context – will that Torah be worthy of existence.

Points to Ponder

One of the first personal mottos I developed for myself in the early years of my rabbinate was: *You can't judge Judaism by the Jews.*

This motto has, unfortunately, come in handy more times than I can count during the years since.

We cringe when we are confronted with individuals who claim to be observant Jews but whose actions belie their faith. "How," we are asked, or ask ourselves, "can a religious person act this way? If this is what Judaism produces…"

The appropriate responses to these challenges are, of course, clear. *If an individual behaves in a way that contradicts the values that Judaism represents, then that individual is not an observant Jew and, even more importantly, what he practices is not Judaism.* The problem is not with the law but with the context. Judaism cannot exist in a vacuum. For Jewish law to take concrete root in this world it must rest in the hearts and shape the actions of those whose very lives reflect its goals.

The partnership with which God challenges us is full and our relationship is, on some level, symbiotic. We are the vehicles divinely chosen to bring God's presence into this world. *Just as the law must give meaning to our lives, our lives must give meaning to the law.*

5 Bold, Enigmatic Requests – Momentous, Enigmatic Responses

Context

When God threatens to remove His presence from the nation in response to the sin of the golden calf, Moshe successfully entreats Him to reconsider.[1]

In the midst of these pleadings, however, Moshe suddenly seems to broaden his requests of God: "And now, if I have found favor in Your eyes, *let me know Your ways; that I may know You...*"[2]

A few sentences later Moshe again beseeches: *"Please show me Your glory!"*[3]

To this second request God responds:

> I shall make My goodness pass before you, and I will call in the name of the Lord before you; and I will show favor upon whom I will show favor, and I will bestow mercy upon whom I will bestow mercy...
>
> You cannot see My face, for no man can see Me and live...
>
> Behold! There is a place near Me; you will stand on the rock. And when My glory passes by, I will place you in a cleft of the rock and I will cover My hand over you until I pass. And I will remove My hand and *you will see My back; but My face may not be seen.*[4]

A paragraph later the Torah chronicles an event which appears to be the fulfillment of God's commitment to Moshe. When Moshe ascends

---

1. Shmot 33:12–23.
2. Ibid., 33:13.
3. Ibid., 33:18.
4. Ibid., 33:19–23.

Mount Sinai with the second set of tablets awaiting God's inscription, God appears to Moshe in a cloud, "calls out in the name of the Lord" and reveals to Moshe the Thirteen Attributes of Divine Mercy.[5]

Questions

No dialogue in the Torah text is potentially more significant than this conversation between God and Moshe in the aftermath of the *chet ha'egel*. Moshe, whose relationship with his Creator is closer than any individual who precedes or follows, *directly confronts God with questions about God's divine essence – and receives a reply!* One can scarcely imagine the wealth of information, concerning the most fundamental questions of existence, potentially embedded in these passages.

Our understanding of this foundational interaction, however, is severely hampered by the enveloping mysteries.

What exactly is the meaning of Moshe's pleas "Let me know Your ways" and "Please show me Your glory"? What aspect of God is this great leader trying to understand?

What is God's response? What does it mean to be able to see God's "back" but not His "face"?

In the sentence directly preceding Moshe's requests, the Torah clearly states, "And God spoke to Moshe face-to-face, as a man would speak to his friend…"[6]

The positioning of this declaration immediately before Moshe's questions of God cannot be coincidental; the Torah is clearly telling us something. But what? The inherent contradiction calls out for interpretation. If Moshe is granted prophetic vision of such clarity, if he "sees God face-to-face," what element of the divine does he still fail to understand?

Finally, why is this puzzling section recorded in the middle of the Revelation narrative? What are we meant to learn from this personal interaction between God and Moshe placed so prominently in the text, during the most critical moments of our nation's birth?

---

5. Ibid., 34:4–7.
6. Ibid., 33:11.

Approaches

The deep hesitation which should mark our approach to this pivotal section of Torah text is eloquently and movingly expressed by Rabbi Shimshon Raphael Hirsch:

> At no part of the Torah does translation and explanation have to tread with greater care and diffidence than at the contents of Shmot 33:12–23. For here we are led to the extreme limit of man's knowledge of God, and even that which lies beyond this limit is intimated to us, for the purpose of letting us know just this boundary line, beyond which the degree of our actual knowledge of God cannot extend during the period of our life here below. How fearful must we be that our attempts at understanding and our efforts at putting this understanding into words will miss the exact point of the truth.[7]

Cautiously, with this disclaimer to guide us, we will carefully discuss some possible approaches to this text.

—A—

We begin by turning two of our questions into answers.

1. The Torah specifically balances the clarity of Moshe's prophetic vision with his immediate admission of limited understanding in order to convey a simple, powerful message: even Moshe, whose contact with God occurred on a "face-to-face" level – as experienced by no other human being throughout history – was unable to fully penetrate the mysteries surrounding the divine. This truth is, at once, both frustrating and comforting. On the one hand, we are made acutely aware of our own limitations: if Moshe could not fully understand God, then how can we? At the same time, we are comforted in the knowledge that we share our limitations with the greatest figure of Jewish history. Even Moshe lived with unanswered questions; how could we expect otherwise for ourselves?

2. Moshe's quest for knowledge is included specifically at this point in the text because his personal search is an integral part of the Revelation narrative.

The Torah describes a process of Revelation that unfolds *on two levels*

---

7. Rabbi Shimshon Raphael Hirsch, Shmot 33:12.

simultaneously. Most prominently, at the base of Mount Sinai, an earth-shattering national unfolding takes place as the Israelites accept the Torah, en masse, and become God's eternal chosen people. At the same time, in quieter fashion, the individual struggle of one man, Moshe, is interwoven with the story of the nation. The Torah thus teaches us that Moshe's lonely, personal quest is as critical to *Matan Torah* (the giving of the Torah) as is the nation's experience.

From this time onward, in each era, *Revelation will unfold for the Jewish people on these two levels at once.* Each generation of Jews, like the Israelites, will be challenged, communally, to make Judaism their own – to accept an ancient legacy, study it, apply it and build upon it in ways appropriate for their time and their world. At the same time, like Moshe, each individual Jew will be challenged to a lonely, personal struggle with his tradition – as he determines the meaning of Judaism within his life, wrestles with un-answered questions of faith and belief, and determines the place he will assume in the unfolding story of his nation.

—— **B** ————————————————————

Having suggested principles upon which this dialogue is based, we now must answer the two fundamental remaining questions: what does Moshe ask and what is God's answer?

Some authorities choose to see this mysterious dialogue in narrow terms.

The Rashbam, for example, *pashtan* par excellence, maintains that Moshe's appeals to God do not actually break new ground at all. Moshe does not move beyond the parameters of the issues already being discussed.

Claiming that Moshe would not have the temerity to ask for a direct vision of God's essence, the Rashbam explains the requests as follows: "Let me know Your ways…" *Please, God, continue to invest Your presence among us. I ask that You, Yourself, show us the way and I will follow You.*

And then, once God agrees: "Please show me Your glory…" *Enact a covenant concerning that very issue; guarantee that Your presence will continue to journey directly with us.* This second request, says the Rashbam, is similar to the patriarch Avraham's request of God which immediately leads to the Covenant between the Pieces (see *Bereishit*: Lech Lecha 4).[8]

---

8. Rashbam, Shmot 33:13, 18.

— **C** —

In stark contrast, numerous scholars understand Moshe's search in much broader terms. Emboldened by God's reconciliation with the nation, Moshe truly attempts to probe the mysteries of the divine.

The Rambam is among those who suggest that Moshe requests personal revelation of two aspects of God. He asks to become knowledgeable of "God's ways" –that God reveal His traits and modes of interaction with the world. Moshe also requests direct knowledge of the divine – that he be able to clearly perceive the essence of God, as an entity separate from all other existing entities, in the same manner that he is able to perceive another human being.

God responds positively to the first request by revealing the Thirteen Attributes of Divine Mercy – a clear blueprint of God's interaction with His creations. God, however, refuses Moshe's second request. Mortal man cannot directly perceive God's essence. Our understanding of the divine is limited to our comprehension of God's impact upon the world. Thus God states, "You will see My back; but My face may not be seen." God wants man to study attributes of the divine, so that man will emulate those very attributes in his own life. God, Himself, however, remains beyond the boundary of human perception.[9]

Mirroring the Rambam's position, Rabbeinu Bachya quotes a supporting passage from Mishlei (Proverbs): "It is the glory of God to conceal a thing; but the honor of kings is to search out a matter."[10] Investigation into the "honor of kings" – that aspect of God which is revealed through the conduct of His realm – is desirable. Study of the "glory of God" – the actual essence of the divine – is futile and, often, dangerous. This tension, says Rabbeinu Bachya, can be compared to man's relationship with the sun. As long as an individual studies the sun by analyzing its effect upon the world, that study is worthwhile and productive. If an individual, however, attempts to examine the sun through a direct gaze, he will not only fail but suffer injury in the process.[11]

While following the same general approach as the Rambam and Rabbeinu Bachya, Rabbi Shimshon Raphael Hirsch is a bit more specific in his

---

9. Rambam, *Moreh Nevuchim* 1:54; *Mishneh Torah*, Hilchot Yesodei HaTorah 1:10.
10. Mishlei 25:2.
11. Rabbeinu Bachya, Shmot 33:13.

understanding of Moshe's requests and God's responses. Moshe's initial plea "Let me know Your ways" is premised upon God's threat to withdraw from the people as a result of the *chet ha'egel*. In light of the new relationship between God and the nation, Moshe wants to understand "the 'uniformity' behind the manifold ways of God." How can God pursue His original goal for the nation given a changed path? Moshe couches his request in terms of his leadership needs. In order to properly lead the nation under these changed circumstances, he must better understand God's ways.

God informs Moshe that he need not be concerned. Responding to the nation's repentance, God will return to a direct relationship with the people. Moshe's request for a greater understanding of God's ways, in addition, will nonetheless be granted due to Moshe's personal preciousness to God.

Encouraged by God's willingness to share this information on the basis of their relationship, Moshe pushes the envelope and asks that he be allowed to "see" God's glory. To this second request God responds that Moshe will, indeed, be allowed to "see" – but only the substance of his first request. He will gain a direct view into God's ways by being granted a vision of the "manifold diversity of ways in which the constant uniform goodness of God is given to His creatures."[12]

Moving in a different direction, Rabbi Yitzchak Arama suggests that with the words "And you will see My back," God informs Moshe: *You will perceive Me not by understanding what I am, but by comprehending what I am not. Study well your own limitations – all the weaknesses of mortal man – and recognize that I possess none of these limitations. In this way, by a process of exclusion, you will begin to piece together a picture of the divine.*[13]

In support of his position, Arama cites a parable from the Rambam's *Guide to the Perplexed*. There, the Rambam compares man's efforts to understand God to a group of individuals in a ship who attempt to determine the nature of the vessel in which they sail. Each individual notes a different exclusionary detail concerning the ship. One person notes, for example, that the vessel is not a living being. Another individual observes that it is not attached to anything else. Another passenger remarks that the ship's shape is not round. By piecing these and other observations together,

---

12. Rabbi Shimshon Raphael Hirsch, Shmot 33:13–20.
13. Akeidat Yitzchak Shmot, sha'ar 54.

those on the vessel are able to arrive at some approximation of the entity on which they find themselves.

So, too, while mortal man is unable to understand God directly, he can arrive at an indirect picture, by perceiving what God is not.[14]

—— D ——————————————————

Another interpretive layer is added to our understanding of the text by a famous Talmudic tradition, quoted by Rashi. Focusing on the statement "And God passed before him and he called...," Rabbi Yochanan states:

> Had this text not been written, we would never have been able to make this claim on our own – The Torah indicates that God wrapped Himself [in a *tallit*, "prayer shawl"], as would the leader of the communal prayer service, and showed Moshe the order of the prayers.
>
> God said to him, "Whenever Israel sins let them pray in this fashion and they will be forgiven."[15]

According to Rabbi Yochanan, God's esoteric, mysterious revelation to Moshe is eminently practical and concrete as well. *In effect, God opens the door to prayer.* He reveals to Moshe the power that man has to move divine will and demonstrates both the text and the method of the Jewish prayer service. So concrete is the Talmudic vision in this regard that the rabbis even claim that the phrase "And you shall see My back" midrashically indicates that God showed Moshe "the [rear] knot of the tefillin [leather boxes containing passages of the Torah text which are worn during the prayer service]."[16]

Even more importantly, the words that accompany God's revelation to Moshe – the Thirteen Attributes of Divine Mercy – eventually become central to Jewish liturgy (in the Ashkenazic tradition during the period of the High Holy Days and in the Sephardic tradition on a daily basis). Jewish tradition, thus, concretely follows God's message as understood by the Midrash: "Whenever Israel sins let them pray in this fashion and they will be forgiven."

---

14. Rambam, *Moreh Nevuchim* 1:60.
15. Talmud Bavli Rosh Hashana 17b.
16. Talmud Bavli Brachot 7a.

With this observation, the rabbis once again remind us that much of what we have come to accept as "given" actually had to be "given" to us by God. Only through God's beneficence is mortal man granted the gift of dialogue with the divine.

— E —

Without question, however, the most powerfully poignant commentary on Moshe's encounter with God is found in a Talmudic discussion in the tractate of Brachot concerning the nature of Moshe's requests and the extent of God's responses. Two clear positions are cited.

1. Based upon the text, Rabbi Yochanan maintains, in the name of Rabbi Yossi, that Moshe presented three requests to God, *all of which were granted*. He asked that God continue to invest the Divine Presence within the people; that God relate uniquely to the Israelite nation; and that God reveal "His ways."

Rabbi Yossi goes on to elaborate on the nature of Moshe's third request. Moshe said to God: *Master of the Universe! Why are there righteous individuals to whom good happens and righteous individuals to whom bad happens? Why are there evil individuals to whom good happens and evil individuals to whom bad happens?*

2. Rabbi Meir agrees with Rabbi Yossi concerning the content of Moshe's requests, but disagrees concerning God's responses.

Two of Moshe's pleas, this sage maintains, were granted. The third inquiry – relating to the issue of divine justice – was not![17]

Here, then, is the foundational rabbinic discussion one would expect in connection with Moshe's mysterious encounter with God. So pivotal is this event to the rabbis, that they relate it to the core question of theodicy (divine justice).

And yet, we must ask, how can the rabbis claim to know the exact nature of Moshe's third request? Moshe's first two appeals are clearly recorded in the text. Rabbi Yossi, however, makes a major philosophical leap from the vague phrase "Let me know Your ways" to the specific issue of theodicy. What gives him this right and why do none of his colleagues challenge this leap?

What, in addition, is the substance of Rabbi Yossi's and Rabbi Meir's

17. Ibid.

debate concerning God's answer to Moshe's third request? Why is Rabbi Meir so insistent that, to this specific inquiry, no direct answer is given?

Key to our understanding of this beautiful Talmudic passage, perhaps, is the personal stake which the sages have in the event before us. The encounter between God and Moshe represents the single closest historical interchange between God and a single individual. In effect, the rabbis, therefore, ask themselves: *placing ourselves in Moshe's place, given the opportunity to ask anything at all, what would we ask of God?*

To the rabbinic mind the answer is clear. Rabbi Yossi and his colleagues are certain of the substance of Moshe's last request because for them – as for us – theodicy is "the issue"! The single most perplexing philosophical problem confronting the man of faith is the problem of divine justice – or, in popular terms: Why do bad things happen to good people (and vice versa)? A number of years ago, in fact, a major contemporary scholar told a newly graduating cadre of rabbis (in which I happened to find myself) that "Almost any philosophical discussion which you may have with a congregant will eventually boil down to a discussion of the issue of theodicy."

From the perspective of the Talmudic sages, there is no question as to what Moshe asked God during their encounter.

What about Rabbi Meir, however? Why is he so insistent that Moshe never received an answer to that last query? Placing Rabbi Meir's assertion within the context of his life grants us deep and powerful insight into the Talmudic narrative.

Rabbi Meir emerges as one of the single most tragic figures in the annals of Jewish history. He endures the premature death of his two young sons[18] and, separately, the tragic loss of his brilliant wife, Bruria, under extremely difficult circumstances.[19] He alone remains loyal to – but agonizes deeply over the defection of – his revered teacher, Elisha ben Abuya, who, due to his apostasy, becomes known in the Talmud simply by the title *Acher* (Other).[20]

One can imagine Rabbi Meir turning to Rabbi Yossi, and for that matter to any of his other colleagues, and saying: *You might think that Moshe received an answer to that third and final query concerning the issue of*

---

18. Yalkut Shimoni, Mishlei 247:964.
19. Rashi, Talmud Bavli Avoda Zara 18b.
20. Talmud Bavli Chagiga 15b; Talmud Yerushalmi Chagiga 2:1.

theodicy. I, however, tell you that he did not! I know, from bitter experience, that no human being – not even Moshe – can lay claim to that knowledge. Sometimes the better part of wisdom is to admit what we do not know and will not know until our journey on this earth ends…

Points to Ponder

I don't know… I don't understand…

Simple words that, so often, seem so hard to say.

And yet, our inability – or our unwillingness – to admit our lack of knowledge and understanding can sometimes be extremely damaging.

It leads to philosophical justifications for inexplicable tragedies such as the Holocaust – justifications which demean the very memory of the innocent victims of that tragic horror.

It leads to the offering of facile, even hurtful, rationalizations to those who have endured the tragic loss of loved ones.

Sometimes the greatest evidence of wisdom is silence in the face of the inexplicable, and a humble admission that some things lie beyond our ken. Rabbi Meir reminds us that there are mysteries that even Moshe could not penetrate.

Vayakhel-Pekudei ויקהל־פקודי

Parsha Summary

Coming full circle...

The short parshiot of Vayakhel and Pekudei form a cohesive unit, chronicling the story of the Mishkan's construction as the book of Shmot comes to a close. After the complex digressions of Parshat Ki Tissa, surrounding the sin of the golden calf, the narrative comes full circle as God's directives concerning the Sanctuary – first recorded in the parshiot of Teruma and Tetzave – are now fulfilled.

Parshat Vayakhel opens as Moshe gathers the nation in order to convey God's instructions. After a brief digression outlining laws of Shabbat, Moshe commands the Israelites to collect material for the construction of the Sanctuary. The people, men and women, respond with great generosity and Moshe publicly appoints, as per God's prior directive, Betzalel and Oholiav to supervise the project. The remainder of Parshat Vayakhel outlines, in detail, the creation of the components of the Sanctuary.

In the opening section of Parshat Pekudei, a reckoning is given of the material collected for the construction of the Mishkan. The Torah then outlines the fashioning of the garments to be worn by Aharon in his role as Kohen Gadol.

Upon the completion of the Mishkan's components, Moshe blesses the people.

On the first day of the first month of the second year after the Exodus, upon God's instructions, Moshe erects the Mishkan, places the various utensils in their proper locations and sanctifies the Sanctuary and its components.

As the curtain falls on the dramatic book of Shmot, the Mishkan is miraculously invested with a covering cloud by day, a pillar of fire by night and the glory of God within.

1 Understanding Shabbat

Context

As the curtain rises on Parshat Vayakhel, Moshe assembles the nation in order to convey God's commandments concerning the construction of the Mishkan.

Suddenly, however, he opens his remarks with the following directives concerning Shabbat:

> Six days work may be done and the seventh day shall be holy for you, a Shabbat, a day of complete rest for God; whoever does work (*melacha*) on that day shall be put to death. You shall kindle no fire in any of your dwellings on the Shabbat day.[1]

Questions

As is evident from the body of Parshat Vayakhel, Moshe's clear purpose in assembling the nation at the beginning of the parsha is to launch the construction of the Mishkan.

Why, then, does Moshe abruptly insert the subject of Shabbat?

While Shabbat is certainly a hugely important topic, why must it be mentioned, apparently out of context, specifically at this historic moment?

Approaches

The abrupt, seemingly arbitrary pairing of Shabbat and the Mishkan at the beginning of Parshat Vayakhel is not an isolated phenomenon. Earlier, in Parshat Ki Tissa, on the summit of Mount Sinai, God follows His commandments to Moshe concerning the construction of the Sanctuary with the immediate warning "However, you must observe my Sabbaths…" This

---

1. Shmot 35:1–3.

301

admonition introduces a series of further directives concerning Shabbat.[2] In the book of Vayikra, Shabbat and the Sanctuary are again connected without explanation in the passage "My Sabbaths you shall observe and my Sanctuary you shall revere – I am the Lord."[3]

This repeated pairing of themes, clearly intentional, serves as the source for a series of foundational halachic observations on the part of the rabbis.

A

Commenting on the opening passage of Parshat Vayakhel, Rashi verbalizes the most immediate halachic lesson learned from the encounter between Shabbat and the Sanctuary: "[Moshe] prefaced the commandments concerning the work of the Mishkan with a warning concerning Shabbat – *to convey [that work within the Mishkan] does not supersede Shabbat*."[4]

B

The halachic decision granting Shabbat supremacy over the Sanctuary is more far-reaching than it may seem, playing a major role in the legal definition of Shabbat observance itself.

To understand, we must recognize the challenge created by an apparent omission in the Torah text.

Over and over again, the Torah prohibits the performance of "*melacha*" (usually translated as "work"; see *Points to Ponder*, below) on Shabbat. The problem is, however, that nowhere does the Torah directly define or quantify the term *melacha*. The list of activities prohibited on Shabbat is never cited within the text. Left to our own devices, with only the written text to guide us, we simply would not know what tasks to refrain from on this sanctified day. Shabbat observance would be impossible.

Thankfully, the Oral Law (see Yitro 5) comes to the rescue. Based upon the repeated juxtaposition of the themes of Shabbat and the Sanctuary in the text, the rabbis learn, not only that the tasks associated with the Sanctuary must cease on Shabbat, *but that the very definition of the activities*

---

2. Ibid., 31:1–17.
3. Vayikra 19: 30.
4. Rashi, Shmot 35:2.

prohibited on Shabbat is determined by the tasks that were connected to the
construction[5] (and, some say, the operation[6]) of the Mishkan.

Specifically, the rabbis delineate thirty-nine *avot melacha* – major categories of creative labor – associated with the construction of the Sanctuary, which are, consequently, prohibited on Shabbat. These thirty-nine general categories of *melacha* and their derivatives serve as the basis for the laws of Shabbat.[7]

The encounter between Shabbat and the Sanctuary, orchestrated by Moshe at the beginning of Parshat Vayakhel, is far from arbitrary. Emerging from the intersection of these two foundational phenomena are the laws which define the observance of Shabbat itself.

— **C** —————————————————————————

On a philosophical plane, the message which emerges from the encounter between Shabbat and the Mishkan is significant, as well.

Shabbat and the Sanctuary represent two different realms of potential sanctification within Jewish tradition: the *sanctification of time* (e.g., Shabbat, Rosh Chodesh and the festivals) and the *sanctification of space* (e.g., the Mishkan, the Temple, the Land of Israel and the city of Jerusalem). Through the observance of God's laws, man is challenged with the investiture of holiness into each of these central domains.

And yet, while both of these realms are clearly significant, when a choice between them must be made, *the sanctification of time reigns supreme.* That is why the observance of Shabbat supersedes the construction of the Sanctuary.

The primacy of time sanctification is indicated in other ways in the Torah, as well.

Not by chance, the phenomenon of *kedusha* (sanctity) is first mentioned in the Torah in conjunction with Shabbat, an example of the sanctification of time.[8]

As we have also seen, the first mitzva granted to the Jewish nation is

---

5. Talmud Bavli Shabbat 49b; Rashi, ibid.
6. Rav Hai Gaon; see introduction to *Iglei Tal* written by Rabbi Avrohom Bornstein (the Avnei Nezer) for a review of rabbinic positions on this matter.
7. Talmud Bavli Shabbat 49b; Mishna Shabbat 7:2.
8. Bereishit 2:3.

Kiddush Hachodesh (the sanctification of the new moon), an example of the sanctification of time (see Bo 3).[9]

While the clear transcendence of time sanctification over space sanctification remains unexplained in the text, a rationale may be offered from our own experience: *the single most precious and tenuous commodity we possess in life is time.* Our moments are limited; each moment exists…and before we know it, that moment is gone.

There could, therefore, be no greater expression of our belief in and our loyalty to God than the dedication of some of our limited moments specifically to His service. The sanctification of time – the dedication of time solely to our relationship with God – is one of the highest religious acts possible, transcending other acts of sanctification.

When Moshe, therefore, underscores the laws of Shabbat immediately before the launching of the construction of the Mishkan, he reminds the people to remember their priorities. As monumentally historic as the launching of the Mishkan may be; as overwhelmingly important as the Mishkan and all of its symbolism will be across the face of history; even more precious to God is the dedication of our own moments of time to His service.

— **D** —

Another message of prioritization may well be included in Moshe's words, as well.

By specifically stating, "You shall kindle no fire *in any of your dwellings* on the Shabbat day," Moshe underscores the primacy of that fundamental unit – the centrality of which is underscored, over and over again, at critical points in Jewish history – *the Jewish home* (see *Bereishit*: Vayechi 4, *Approaches* B, *Points to Ponder*; see, as well, Bo 4, *Approaches* A1).

Even as the nation congregates for the stated purpose of launching the central concept of the Sanctuary within Jewish tradition, Moshe cautions:

As central as the Sanctuary and Temple will be in your experience, their role will pale in comparison to that of your homes and your families. Within your homes, new generations will learn of their affiliation to our people and its traditions; observance will be taught through example; children will be

---

9. Shmot 12:1–2.

raised, deeply connected to their proud past and prepared for their challenging futures.

The Sanctuary is meant to inspire and to teach, but the lessons it teaches will reach their fulfillment only within your homes...

Never believe the Mishkan to be more important than your personal observance of a single commandment: "You shall kindle no fire in any of your dwellings on the Shabbat day."

Points to Ponder

What is the secret of Shabbat? What is the ultimate purpose of this all important, weekly holy day?

The answer, it would seem, should lie within the laws which define the day. As we have seen, however, approaching Shabbat through the law is a difficult task, a path shrouded in mystery. The Torah does not clearly classify the term *melacha*, the term used by the text to refer to the Shabbat prohibitions. The ultimate definition of *melacha*, derived through association with the Sanctuary, is technical, with no apparent philosophical base.

Popularly, the term *melacha* is often defined as "work" – and the logical claim is made that "work" is prohibited on the "day of rest." This explanation, however, is clearly insufficient. Using the classical definition of work – "an activity in which one exerts strength or faculties to do or perform something"[10] – we would be hard-pressed to explain why, for example, one is allowed to lift a book on Shabbat but prohibited from flipping a light switch; why one can move a chair or walk up stairs but cannot rip a paper towel.

In his short, classic work, *The Sabbath*, Dr. Dayan I. Grunfeld analyzes sources in the oral tradition and arrives at the following working definition of the term *melacha*: *an act which shows man's mastery over the world by the constructive exercise of his intelligence and skill.*[11]

We might, based upon those same sources, suggest a further refinement of Dr. Grunfeld's definition: *melacha* represents an attempt by man to transform his environment through a thought-filled act of physical creation.

The Torah tells us that, on the "seventh day" of the world's birth, God

10. Merriam-Webster Online Dictionary.
11. Grunfeld, Dayan Dr. I., *The Sabbath* (New York: Feldheim Publishing, 1959), p. 19.

stops creating in the physical realm.[12] To mark that divine cessation, we are commanded to cease physical creation, each week, on the "seventh day," as well.

What specifically, however, is accomplished by this mandate? Why would God commands us to commemorate His "day of rest" with our own?

The brilliance of the Shabbat concept can best be understood, I believe, by considering two dangerous philosophical extremes towards which each of us can easily gravitate.

At one end of the spectrum lies our tendency to develop, to use Torah terminology, a *kochi v'otzem yadi* complex. Towards the end of his life, Moshe warns that, upon successful entry into the Land of Israel, the Israelites should not falsely conclude, *Kochi v'otzem yadi asa li et hachayil hazeh*, "My power and the might of my hand made me all of this wealth."[13]

How easy it is, particularly in our era, to lose our way at this extreme. Mind-boggling scientific discoveries, ferociously fast-paced technological advancement, define the world in which we live. Our mastery over our physical surroundings grows exponentially with each passing day. Never before has man been as "powerful" as he is today.

At the same time, at the opposite end of the spectrum, lies our deep capacity for despair in the face of our "powerlessness" – the moments when, standing beneath the vault of the heavens, we contemplate the stars above and mark our own apparent insignificance. How many galaxies, suns, planets, stretch out around us? In the face of such unimaginable vastness, how can we even contemplate the notion that we are important or powerful?

Much of Jewish tradition is designed to place us exactly where we belong, *in the middle between these two extremes.*

Tefilla (prayer), for example, reminds the individual suffering from a *kochi v'otzem yadi* complex that he is dependent upon God for continued health, sustenance and so much more. At the same time, prayer addresses the individual in despair by sensitizing him to his own value. He is a unique, independent being of inestimable potential value, capable of discourse with a responsive God.

---

12. Bereishit 2:1–3.
13. Devarim 8:17.

Our weekly observance of Shabbat is carefully crafted to help us maintain a proper balance between power and limitation, as well.

One day a week, we remind ourselves of our creative limitations. Through the cessation of physically creative acts we testify to the true mastery of the Divine Creator. We recall the creation of the world on Shabbat and we recognize that only God has the power to create *yesh mei'ayin* (something from nothing), while man, at his best, can only create *yesh mi'yesh* (something from something).

During my college years at Yeshiva University, excitement ran high in the scientific community, which felt itself to be on the brink of the creation of life (specifically a virus) in a test tube. Such an accomplishment, many scientists proclaimed, would constitute an assault on the very heavens, proof of man's God-like powers to create life itself. Deeply concerned, we raised the issue to one of our teachers – a Talmudic scholar who possessed significant scientific background as well. "I see no issue," he responded. "If scientists could take an empty test tube and conjure life within, that would present a theological challenge. What they propose to do now, however, is to take God's hydrogen, God's oxygen, God's nitrogen, etc., and mix them together to create their virus. That does not make them, God forbid, God; it makes them good chefs."[14]

A *kochi v'otzem yadi* complex is impossible to maintain in the face of Shabbat. The observance of this day reminds us that, in the final analysis, only God is the true Creator.

At the same time, however, while Shabbat sensitizes us to the limitations of our power, this very same day reminds us how truly powerful we really are.

Throughout the week our lives are, in so many ways, controlled by the forces surrounding us. Work, school and other responsibilities pull us along at a frenetic pace. Cell phones, BlackBerries and e-mail keep us in constant contact. The demands on our time and energy, from all sides, are overwhelming. We feel out of control, powerless to set these pressures aside.

---

14. In July 2002 scientists were apparently successful in synthesizing the polio virus; the head of the team himself placed the accomplishment in perspective by stating, "I do not want to say that we created life in a test tube because we would be in deep trouble.... [The polio virus is merely] a chemical with a life cycle." *BusinessWeek* (July 22, 2002), accessed at http://www.businessweek.com/magazine/content/02_29/c3792082. htm.

And then…Shabbat arrives. The cell phones, computers and BlackBerries are shut down and put on the shelf. Work, school and other responsibilities are set aside for another day. Time is spent, at ease, with family and friends. We reconnect with community. We are given the opportunity to regain control of our lives. Our cessation of physically creative acts becomes a freeing experience, enabling us to truly recognize the power we possess to define and control the quality of our lives.

This empowering aspect of Shabbat was driven home to me many years ago through the example of a friend whom I will call "Bill." Bill was a chain-smoker who went through several packs a day. Come sundown each Friday night, however, he would lay down his cigarettes. He would light his first cigarette of the next week, Saturday night, from the Havdala candle (the candle used as part of the ceremony marking the end of Shabbat).

If you asked Bill at any point of the Shabbat day whether he missed his cigarettes, he would look at you as if you were crazy and say, "Of course not – it's Shabbat." He could not, however, replicate this abstinence on a weekday. Shabbat freed my friend from a habit that controlled him every other day of his adult life.

Tragically, Bill failed to learn the full lesson that Shabbat is meant to convey. The true power of this day lies in its potential effect beyond its borders. If on this one day of the week, we are successful in reaching proper perspective – in striking a healthy balance between our power and our limitations – then we can strike that balance on the other days of the week, as well.

The genius of Shabbat, in the final analysis, is evident from its laws. Through the cessation of *melacha*, this holy day teaches us how to reclaim proper life perspective.

2 Detail and Discrepancy

Context

As the parshiot of Vayakhel and Pekudei unfold, Moshe transmits detailed instructions concerning the construction of the Mishkan to the nation. Under the supervision of the chief artisans, Betzalel and Oholiav, Moshe's directives are carefully fulfilled, using materials generously donated by the people.[1]

Questions

Almost all of Parshat Vayakhel and much of Parshat Pekudei consist of information already fully recorded in the parshiot of Teruma, Tetzave and Ki Tissa, when God first issues detailed instructions to Moshe concerning the Mishkan.

Why does the Torah engage in such seemingly unnecessary repetition? As the Ralbag notes, the entire construction of the Mishkan could have been simply summed up with the statement "And Betzalel the son of Uri the son of Chur carried out the work of the Mishkan as God had commanded Moshe, and with him worked Oholiav the son of Achisamach…"[2]

On the other hand, a striking discrepancy does emerge when the text of Parshat Teruma is compared to that of Parshat Vayakhel.

In Parshat Teruma, God first instructs Moshe to fashion the utensils associated with the Sanctuary (e.g., the Aron, the Shulchan, the Menora, etc.) and only then does He turn His attention to the construction of the Mishkan itself.[3]

When Moshe commands the people, however, in Parshat Vayakhel, and when those instructions are fulfilled, the mandated order is reversed.

---

1. Shmot 35–39.
2. Ralbag, Shmot 35:39.
3. Shmot 25–26.

Moshe first instructs the nation to build the Mishkan and then to fashion the utensils. This second sequence, according to the text, is the one actually followed in the construction of the Sanctuary.

Why is the sequence of directives concerning the Mishkan so obviously reversed as the text moves from Parshat Teruma to Parshat Vayakhel?

Approaches

Many commentaries, including Rashi, are silent concerning the obvious textual repetition surrounding the construction of the Mishkan.

Others, however, directly address the issue through a range of approaches.

The Ralbag uses this narrative to launch a much broader question: is there a global pattern to all cases of repetition in an otherwise terse Torah text?

While admitting lack of success in finding a pervasive pattern, the Ralbag, known for his willingness to think "outside the box," offers a bold suggestion. Perhaps, he says, *recapitulation in the Torah is reflective of the writing style of the times.*

"It is possible to say that it was the practice of people at the time of the giving of the Torah to tell their stories in this [repetitive] fashion; and a prophet inevitably speaks according to the customs of the day."[4] (For a discussion of temporal context and its relationship to the Torah text, see Mishpatim 1, *Points to Ponder.*)

Nehama Leibowitz notes that, centuries later, the Ralbag's suggestion actually finds support among modern scholars, based upon a review of the written records from the time of Revelation.[5]

The Ralbag's approach, however, fails to explain the inconsistency in the Torah concerning the phenomenon of repetition. Why, at times, such as in the parshiot of Vayakhel and Pekudei, does the Torah repeat itself at length, while at other times it avoids such recapitulation entirely? The Ral-

---

4. Ralbag, Shmot 35:39.
5. Leibowitz, *Studies in Shemot*, p. 648.

bag himself apparently recognizes the insufficiency of his suggestion and offers a number of other solutions, as well.[6]

For his part, the Ramban delineates a series of five textual recapitulations in the narrative surrounding the Mishkan, some of which are detailed while others are general in scope. After analyzing the differences among these five sections and the significance of each, the Ramban states: "And in general, *all of this [repetition] is a reflection of the love and esteem* [with which the construction of the Mishkan is viewed by God]…and the numerous recapitulations are designed to *increase the reward* for those involved in this labor."[7]

According to the Ramban and to those who follow his lead, *recapitulation is a tool used by the Torah text to indicate the preciousness to God of the topic or event under discussion.* As proof of their position, these scholars cite the following Midrashic pronouncement:

> The conversation of the patriarchs' servants is more precious to the Holy One Blessed Be He than the Torah of their descendents – for, behold, the story of Eliezer covers two to three pages of text as the events occur and are repeated, [while critical aspects of the law are often only derived obliquely from the Torah].[8]

Representing those scholars who find allegorical meaning behind every detail of the Sanctuary's construction, Rabbi Shimshon Raphael Hirsch offers an original explanation for the repetition of these details, as well. He suggests that *an item designed to serve as a sanctified symbol must be created with specific intent towards its symbolic role.* Even a written word, by its very nature a symbolic entity, becomes an acceptable part of a Torah scroll, only when the scribe writes that word specifically for the purpose of "the sanctity of a Torah scroll." Through reiteration of the details of the Mishkan's construction, says Hirsch, the Torah conveys that the making, delivering, assembling and erecting of every feature of the Mishkan and its utensils was done with vivid awareness of and conscious intent to fulfill the mitzva involved.[9]

---

6. Ralbag, Shmot 35:39.
7. Ramban, Shmot 36:8.
8. Midrash Rabba Bereishit 60:8.
9. Rabbi Shimshon Raphael Hirsch, Shmot 36:8.

—— **B** ————————————————————————————————

The Abravanel deals with the textual issues surrounding the construction of the Mishkan by connecting the two questions with which this study opened. The repetition within the text, he claims, is an unavoidable result of the discrepancy in sequence between the order of God's commandments to Moshe and the actual order in which the Sanctuary was built.

The Abravanel explains that the relationship between the various components of the Mishkan is complex and multilayered. The Torah therefore records two distinct sequences relating to the construction of the Mishkan – one sequence referenced in God's original commandments to Moshe and the second reflected in Moshe's instructions to the people and in the actual construction of the Sanctuary. These two sequences mirror two different sets of lessons potentially derived from the interface of the Sanctuary's components with each other (lessons which the Abravanel proceeds to list, at length).[10]

The change in sequence from Parshat Teruma to Parshat Vayakhel, continues the Abravanel, might, however, lead us to the erroneous conclusion that additional alterations are made by the Israelites as they move to fulfill God's instructions. The Torah, therefore, lists and repeats every aspect of the Mishkan's construction, over and over again, to demonstrate that, other than the one mandated sequential change, God's words are faithfully followed.[11]

—— **C** ————————————————————————————————

The discrepancy between God's commandments and the order of the Mishkan's construction gives rise to a beautiful Midrashic narrative recorded in the Talmud and in other sources:

> Rabbi Shmuel bar Nachmani stated in the name of Rabbi Yonatan: Betzalel's name reflected his wisdom. When God said to Moshe, "Create for Me a Mishkan, Aron and utensils," Moshe reversed the order and stated: "Create an Aron, utensils and Mishkan."
>
> [Betzalel] responded: "Moshe, our teacher, the way of the world is that an individual first builds a home and then places utensils within

———————————————
10. Abravanel, Shmot 27.
11. Ibid., Shmot 35.

it – and yet you say create an Aron, utensils and Mishkan! These utensils that I am to fashion – where shall I place them?"

Moshe responded: "[Betzalel, you are correct!] Perhaps you were hidden *B'tzel E-l* – in the shadow of God [figuratively: on the summit of Mount Sinai when God spoke to Moshe], and you overheard."[12]

Betzalel's very name, suggests the Talmud, derives from the words *B'tzel E-l* (in the shadow of God) and reflects his natural understanding of and intuition into God's will.

While the Midrash justifies the change of sequence in the text, however, it fails to explain Moshe's original assumption. Why would this great leader originally reverse God's orders and why would that reversed sequence, if erroneous, be recorded by Moshe in the text as if commanded by God?

Confronted with these obvious questions, numerous commentaries struggle to explain the Midrash.

The Maharal, for example, suggests that Moshe views the construction of the Mishkan from a spiritual vantage point while Betzalel sees the project in technical terms. From Moshe's perspective, the sanctified utensils take precedence over the Mishkan, which he views simply as the structure for their housing. Betzalel, ever the artisan, however, gives precedence to the creation of the structure which, on a practical level, must precede the fashioning of the components.[13]

Numerous Chassidic sources offer a fascinating mystical approach to the dialogue between Moshe and Betzalel. Moshe desires, through the construction of the Mishkan, to return the world to its original state – before Adam and Chava sinned through the Tree of Knowledge of Good and Evil. In that earliest condition, content took precedence over form. Moshe, therefore, commands the fashioning of the "content" (the Aron and utensils) before the creation of the "form" (the Mishkan). Betzalel recognizes, however, that after the sin of the golden calf, such a return is impossible. He therefore insists that the Mishkan be created first as a "protection" for the Aron and utensils.[14]

---

12. Talmud Bavli Brachot 55a.
13. Gur Aryeh, Shmot 38:22.
14. Summarized in Nachshoni, *Hagot B'parshiot HaTorah*, pp. 383–384.

—— **D** ——————————————————————————————

Another approach to the Midrash can be suggested through consideration of a similar change of sequence emerging out of an earlier, dramatic moment in the nation's development. On the eve of the final plague in Egypt, God commands Moshe to instruct the Israelites to place the blood of the Pesach offering *on the doorposts and on the lintels of the entrances to their homes.*[15] When Moshe actually repeats this commandment to the people, however, he reverses the order and instructs them to place the blood *on the lintels and on the doorposts* of their homes.[16] Commenting on the discrepancy between God's commandment and Moshe's transmission, the rabbis explain that, in this instance, sequence is inconsequential; the doorposts and lintel are all equally important and any of them can be "anointed" first.[17]

At first glance, the conclusions reached in the two cases before us seem contradictory. In the case of the Paschal Lamb, the rabbis conclude that a sequential discrepancy between two textual passages implies that sequence is inconsequential. Concerning the Mishkan, however, the Midrash indicates that order matters a great deal, and that Moshe's "mistaken" sequence must be corrected.

Perhaps, however, the Midrashic traditions can be harmonized. In both cases, the Midrash teaches us that *the individual elements of the sequence are equally important.* Although a decision must be made as to whether the Mishkan or its utensils will be fashioned first, that decision is motivated not by intrinsic significance but by Betzalel's reference to "the way of the world." On a theoretical level, both the utensils and the Mishkan are of equal importance. *The Torah, therefore, records two sequences – one which mentions the utensils first and one which mentions the Mishkan first – in order to convey the fundamental equality between the Mishkan and its components.*

Points to Ponder

A profound symbolic lesson potentially emerges from our analysis of the Midrash.

Let us assume that the Mishkan represents the overall structure of

———————————————

15. Shmot 12:7.
16. Ibid., 12:22.
17. Mechilta, Shmot 12:22.

Jewish observance while the various utensils represent the details of that observance. The text then indicates that both the general structure and the details of Jewish practice are equally important.

To live Jewishly, on the one hand, we must be consistently aware of our tradition's overall goals. We cannot allow ourselves to be blinded by the intricacies of observance to the extent that our vision of the people that God wants us to be is lost. At all times, we must remember that our task on this earth is to sanctify God's name through our actions. How we observe the mitzvot – and how that observance affects those around us – is, therefore, often as important as the mitzvot themselves.

At the same time, however, the details of Jewish practice are absolutely essential. Attention to detail demonstrates a conscious, concrete commitment to God; infuses every aspect of our lives with connection to the divine; and creates the practical system of ritual that has maintained our identity as a people throughout our turbulent history.

The Mishkan would have been empty without its components, while the utensils would have been meaningless without the Mishkan. So, too, only by maintaining both detail and overall structure in our personal and communal lives will we succeed in fulfilling God's will.

3 Exalted or Humble Origins?

Context

Among the multitude of details recorded in the parshiot of Vayakhel and Pekudei, one specific feature is particularly eye-catching. As the Torah outlines the fashioning of the various Sanctuary components, the text of Parshat Vayakhel states:

> And he [Betzalel] fashioned the basin of copper and its copper stand *b'marot hatzovot asher tzavu petach Ohel Moed* (from the mirrors of the legions [of women]) who crowded at the entrance of the Tent of Meeting.[1]

Later, in Parshat Pekudei, when the Torah lists the various utensils fashioned out of the donations of copper, the basin and its stand are conspicuously omitted.

Questions

Why does the Torah single out the basin and stand, both by omitting these items from the general reckoning and by specifying the origin of the copper used in the fashioning of these utensils?

What is the significance of the fact that these items were created from the mirrors donated by the women?

Approaches

Diametrically opposed positions are adopted by the commentaries as they strive to interpret the unique origin of the basin and its stand.

---

1. Shmot 38:8.

— A —

Various scholars, including the Ibn Ezra and the Sforno, believe that the mirrors were suitable for use in the Temple specifically because their owners rejected those items' usual usage. Mirrors are used, then and today, for vain purposes, to cultivate personal beauty and attractiveness. The women who donated these mirrors, however, as evidenced by their contribution, rejected physical vanity and showed a deep desire to cultivate and focus on a continuing spiritual relationship with God.

Taking a radically different tack, but evidencing an equally negative attitude towards personal vanity, the Chizkuni and a number of the Tosafists maintain that the strange passage concerning the basin and stand refers, not to the *origin* of these items, but to their *placement*. The basin and stand were strategically placed, they say, between the Sanctuary and the Mizbeiach so that they *could be seen* by the women regularly congregating at the Sanctuary.

The water from the basin was used in the divine trial of a *sota*, a woman suspected of adultery.[2] The very sight of these utensils, therefore, would serve as a reminder of the dangers of licentious behavior.[3]

— B —

At the opposite end of the spectrum are those commentaries, represented by Rabbi Shimshon Raphael Hirsch, who not only maintain that the basin and its stand were fashioned out of mirrors, but that *the mirrors' normal usage actually recommended them for this purpose*. The Mishkan, says Hirsch, ultimately aims to influence the Israelites towards the sanctification of their lives. How appropriate, therefore, that specifically the basin, used by the Kohanim for the sanctification of their hands and feet as they enter the Mishkan, should be fashioned out of mirrors. The physical, sensual side of man is, thus, not excluded from the Sanctuary but is, instead, "the first and most essential object" of its sanctification.[4]

Hirsch's position is entirely consonant with Judaism's fundamental view that no aspect of human existence is inherently evil. The sensual side of man is a gift from God meant to be channeled into sanctified relationships

---

2. Talmud Bavli Sota 15b.
3. Chizkuni, Shmot 38:8; Da'at Zekeinim Miba'alei Hatosafot, Shmot 38:8.
4. Rabbi Shimshon Raphael Hirsch, Shmot 38:8.

of love and marriage. The very origin of the basin thus serves as a reminder that all aspects of our lives, properly directed, are potential mediums for holiness.

A beautiful tradition found in the Midrash and quoted by Rashi further reflects Judaism's position that no external object or human characteristic is inherently evil, but that value is ultimately determined by usage (see *Bereishit*: Bereishit 1 *Approaches* F).

During the period of Egyptian slavery, the Midrash relates, Pharaoh decreed that the Israelites should not sleep at home or have relations with their wives. Intent on perpetuating the nation in the face of this fearsome edict, the Israelite women went down to the fields of labor and, looking into their mirrors together with their husbands, aroused the men's desire. In this way the women succeeded in ensuring that the nation would "be fruitful and multiply."

Now, after the dramatic Exodus from Egypt and the powerful Revelation at Sinai, the newly formed nation begins to build the Mishkan. The Israelite women wonder: *What can we contribute to the Sanctuary?*

As one, they congregate outside the Mishkan and present their mirrors to Moshe. Moshe's reaction is swift and harsh: *What use have we for such mirrors – for items created to satisfy the evil inclination?*

God, however, intercedes: *These items are dearer to Me than all else! Through these mirrors the women raised up "countless hosts" in Egypt.*[5]

The Midrash informs us that, in the words of Nehama Leibowitz: "The same instinct or impulse which can lead man to perversions, filth and destruction can also lead him to creativity, the building of a house and the continuity of the nation."[6]

The basin and stand in the Sanctuary serve as a reminder that God grants us gifts. The value of these gifts, however, is determined by how we use them.

---

5. Midrash Tanchuma Pekudei 9; Rashi, Shmot 38:8.
6. Leibowitz, *Studies in Shemot*, p. 694.

4 A Retrospective: From Servitude to Sinai

Context

In retrospect, the book of Shmot reflects that the Jewish nation is born through a two-stage process, with the road to Sinai passing through Egypt. The Exodus and Revelation are both clearly portrayed in the Torah as critical components in the formation of our national character.

Questions

Why are the Exodus and Revelation both essential to the birth of the Jewish nation? Is there a philosophical continuum between these two events that might inform our lives today?

Approaches

—A—

At first glance, the questions raised seem clearly rhetorical. The Torah itself openly elucidates lessons to be learned from each of these monumental events – and rabbinic literature is replete with additional observations.

The existence of God; God's hand in history; our obligation to be kind to strangers; the equality of our personal origins; gratitude to God for our freedom; the recognition that true freedom carries obligations; the transience of seemingly powerful empires; the primacy of law – these are only a few of the foundational ideas so clearly conveyed by the two powerful experiences which shape the earliest moments of our national history.

—B—

And yet, perhaps an even more basic observation can be made about the nature of our early national journey, inspired by a parallel, yet quieter journey: the individual passage of the potential convert who wishes to join the Jewish nation today.

The question is raised in the Talmud: Where does the potential convert begin? *What is the first step along the path towards conversion to Judaism?*

One would assume the answer to be obvious: the journey should begin with elucidation of the mitzvot. After all, what defines Judaism if not the Torah and its laws? Shouldn't the initial requirement for entry into a nation forged at Sinai be the understanding and acceptance of the law given at Sinai? Nothing else would seem appropriate.

The rabbis, however, disagree. In a striking Talmudic passage they clearly outline the first step a potential convert must take:

> If a prospective proselyte comes to convert in this day, we say to him: "What did you perceive that prompted you to come? Did you not know that the Jewish people are afflicted, oppressed, downtrodden and harassed – and that hardships are regularly visited upon them?"
>
> If the individual responds: "I know, and I am unworthy [of sharing in their hardships]," we accept him immediately [as a potential convert worthy of education] and we inform him of some "minor" mitzvot and some "major" mitzvot...[1]

Apparently the rabbis feel that there is a prerequisite to the acceptance of mitzvot. Before an individual can begin to accept the Torah, he must first meet the *challenge of belonging*; he must first be willing to throw his lot in with the Jewish people, whatever trials that choice might produce, whatever difficulties might ensue.

— C ———————————————

What, however, is the basis of this rabbinic position? What source can the Talmudic scholars cite to support their confident claim that conversion to Judaism must begin with the choice to "belong"?

The answer, it would seem, is powerfully simple. The rabbis believe that the initial journey of an individual who wishes to join the Jewish nation must mirror the initial journey of the nation itself.

---

1. Talmud Bavli Yevamot 47a.

As stated above, the Jewish nation is born through a two-stage process. Before we could arrive at Sinai God challenged us with participation in the Exodus. Before we could experience Revelation we had to choose to "belong" to the Jewish people. Each of us had to throw our lot in with our fellow Israelites, to leave the familiar and travel into the unknown, to follow the leadership of a relative stranger towards a destiny shrouded in mystery. The Midrashic tradition that only a fraction of the Israelites actually followed Moshe into the wilderness[2] reflects a keen awareness of the difficulty of this decision.

The rituals of the conversion process, as we have seen, are derived from the experience of the Israelites immediately prior to and during the Revelation at Sinai.[3] (See *Bereishit*: Vayeishev 4, *Approaches* B; Yitro 1, *Points to Ponder*.) The first step towards conversion, however, like the first step of our national journey, is rooted in the Exodus.

Reaching across the ages, the journey of the book of Shmot speaks to us clearly. First you must choose to "belong."

Points to Ponder

Many years ago, I taught a young woman towards conversion. She was intelligent, diligent, unfailingly polite, and took her studies seriously.

I was, however, troubled. I could not put my finger on it, but something simply did not feel right. I was unwilling to dismiss my student as long as I could not quantify the problem. I moved very slowly, however, hoping that the issues would be clarified, one way or the other, over time.

Then, suddenly, one morning, I received a phone call. It was my student, in tears. "I just saw a television program last night concerning the Holocaust," she said, "I was up all night. *I'm sorry, but I could never become part of a people that the world could do that to.*"

I never saw her again.

It was then that I realized the brilliance of the rabbinic approach to conversion. My student had made a choice. Tellingly, she had *not* said, "I cannot be part of a world that could perform such atrocities." She was comfortable belonging to a society that gave rise to the Holocaust, yet unwilling to become part of a people who, by standing against that society,

---

2. Rashi, Shmot 13:18.
3. Talmud Bavli Kritot 9a.

might again, God forbid, become its victims. By making that choice, she had effectively terminated her own potential conversion.

The message involved, however, is directed not only towards potential converts, but towards all, Jews by birth or Jews by choice, who would be part of the Jewish journey.

The rabbis, the very architects and defenders of halacha, are reminding us that there is more to Judaism than the law – as important, essential and critical as they know that law to be.

To be Jewish means to choose – between right and wrong, between the perpetrators and the potential victims. To be Jewish means to belong to a people that is charged with the task of sanctifying God's name, no matter the cost, in good times and in bad; a people that has served as God's moral messengers to the world across a turbulent history. Only once that ethical choice is made, only when that foundation is laid, can God's law truly take root in our lives.

Two pivotal challenges, I believe, emanate from this conclusion.

1. Choosing to "belong" means that we are challenged to *examine our commitment to the Jewish nation, as a whole.* To meet this challenge we must raise a series of critical questions that we don't think about often enough:

Have we become so communally insular that any real interaction with Jews outside our walls is practically nonexistent? Charedi, Chassidic, Modern Orthodox, Conservative, Reform, Religious Zionist, Secular Zionist – have we reached the point where we see other Jews as somewhat "alien," if not as "obstacles" to the perpetuation of our own lifestyles?

I would challenge, for example, my own Modern Orthodox community: are we so blinded by our own successful growth that we no longer feel the danger of the rampant assimilation outside our walls? We are presiding, in our own day, over the swift disappearance of the largest Jewish community in the world. Do we feel a sense of responsibility towards that greater whole? Are we willing to join forces with other groups, despite our differences, to find ways to combat that tragedy?

Another case in point: there was a time in Israeli politics when, despite the stark philosophical differences between parties and politicians, all struggled to achieve their vision of the "common good." Today the proliferation of scores of single-issue parties, representing particular sectors of the population, intent only on protecting the rights of their own constituencies, reflects a growing societal fragmentation and the loss of a shared national vision.

How can we recapture a sense of "belonging" to the entire Jewish people?

2. Choosing to "belong" also means that we are challenged to *regularly assess whether the "Judaism" we practice is truly consonant with the eternal vision and values of our people.*

Judaism preaches, for example, that both Jews and non-Jews can be righteous. Why, then, are some "observant" Jews deeply prejudiced towards non-Jews?

Judaism preaches ethical behavior in all of our dealings. Why, then, are some "observant" Jews comfortable cutting ethical corners in their dealings with each other and, certainly, with an outside society?

Judaism preaches that we give others the benefit of the doubt. Why, then, are some "observant" Jews so quick to judge the actions of those around them?

Judaism preaches serving as a "light unto the nations." Why, then, are some "observant" Jews openly uncaring about the example that their behavior sets for others?

Judaism preaches *hakarat hatov* (gratitude for good bestowed). Why, then, do some "observant" American Jews fail to cultivate gratitude, in themselves and their children, towards the country that has afforded them rights undreamt of anywhere else in their long diaspora history?

We are so intent upon "perpetuating Judaism" that we rarely stop to analyze whether it's really Judaism that we are perpetuating.

First you have to choose to "belong" – to a people and to its vision...

"All the rest...," said Hillel to the potential convert, after informing him of the rule "What is hateful to you, do not do to your neighbor," "...all the rest is commentary; go and learn."[4]

---

4. Talmud Bavli Shabbat 31a.

5 A Retrospective: Putting Sinai in Perspective

Context

One of the indelible images of the book of Shmot is of the free-willed acceptance by the Israelites of the Torah at Sinai, captured in the people's proclamation "we will do and we will hear."[1] Yet a Midrashic tradition quoted in the Talmud shatters that image, painting a vastly different picture.

Rabbi Avdimi bar Chama bar Chasa maintains that the Torah passage "And [the Israelites] stood at the base of the mountain"[2] implies that during Revelation, "God held the mountain over them like a barrel and proclaimed: 'If you accept the Torah, fine – but if not, here will be your burial!'"

Rava agrees with Rabbi Avdimi but claims that, centuries later, at the time of the Purim story, the Jews finally freely accept what their ancestors had accepted at Sinai under duress. As proof he cites a passage at the end of Megillat Esther which closely parallels the commitment "we will do and we will hear" rooted at Sinai. The Megilla testifies that the Jews "fulfilled and accepted."[3] "They fulfilled," says Rava, "that which they had already accepted."[4]

Questions

Why do the rabbis transform the scene at Sinai so completely? Why is Rabbi Avdimi so intent upon adding an element of coercion to the Revelation narrative that does not seem to exist in the straightforward reading of the text?

---

1. Shmot 24:7.
2. Ibid., 19:17.
3. Megillat Esther 9:27.
4. Talmud Bavli Shabbat 88a.

Furthermore, how does the Purim story, according to Rava, relate to the Revelation narrative? Purim, a story of survival from the Persian period of Jewish history, occurs centuries later and would seem to be completely unrelated to the events at Sinai. Is Rava simply playing a word game, arbitrarily connecting two totally different tales on the basis of a linguistic nuance?

Approaches

Through a figurative, rather than literal, interpretation of this well-known Midrash, a powerfully significant lesson can be derived.

—A—

The rabbis demonstrate tremendous historical integrity as they ask us to put ourselves in the place of the Israelites at Sinai: *You have just witnessed the Ten Plagues, the Exodus, the parting of the Reed Sea, the battle with Amalek, the gift of the manna and more. And now, amidst the thunder, lightning and sounding of the shofar of Revelation, God turns to you and asks, "Will you accept my law?"*

Could your answer possibly be anything other than a resounding "Yes"?

On a technical level, of course the Israelites retained their free will during Revelation. In reality, however, they were faced with coercion of circumstance. It was as if "God held the mountain over their heads." Given the surrounding environment, they did not have the opportunity to freely choose.

—B—

In this light, Rava's puzzling observation suddenly makes abundant sense, as well.

Yes, he says, it is true that at Sinai the Israelites did not have the benefit of choice. Surrounded by the miraculous events of the moment, they could not choose a different path.

The time comes, however, when God withdraws; when His hand in the world is no longer open and He orchestrates events from behind a screen. Within the national era of Jewish history, that moment arrives at the time of the Purim tale. Purim marks the onset of the non-prophetic period of the national era. At no point does God speak directly to Esther or Mordechai, the heroes of the story. They must, instead, determine divine will during a time of God's silence and in the face of extraordinarily trying circumstances.

And when the Jewish community of that day accepts the story of Purim as divinely orchestrated, when they see the hidden miracle in a series of events that could have been interpreted as coincidental – only then, for the first time, the nation accepts with total freedom what their ancestors were forced to accept at Sinai.

As we have noted before, both the patriarchal era and the national era of Jewish history open with clear, direct communication between God and man. A point is reached, however, in each of these eras, when prophecy is silenced and God pulls back to allow us to find our own way. Just as a parent must let go of the child's hand if a child is to learn to walk on his own, so too God withdraws and challenges us to determine our path.

And when that moment arrives – during the patriarchal era at the time of the Yosef story, and during the national era at the time of Purim (see *Bereishit*: Vayeishev 1) – full free will is born and our challenge truly begins.

Points to Ponder

One of the common questions asked by children and adults alike as we consider the flow of Jewish history is, "Why did God limit the performance of miracles to ancient times?" With a sense of longing, we look back to a time when everything was open, when God's existence was obvious and His connection to our lives clear.

The rabbis, however, would have us understand that, on some level, this sense of longing is misplaced.

To live in a time when God is "hidden" is to face a trial that transcends the test of Sinai. When the thunder, lightning and shofar of the book of Shmot fall silent; when we are forced to find and appreciate God's existence in the quiet miracles that surround us each day, that is when the mature challenge truly begins.

Sources

Abravanel – Rabbi Don Yitzchak Abravanel; biblical commentator, philosopher, statesman, diplomat (Portugal, Spain, Italy, 1437–1508).

The last great figure of Spanish Jewry, the Abravanel served during his lifetime as finance minister to the kings of Portugal, Spain and Italy. The Abravanel used his high position and great wealth to benefit his brethren and spared no effort in petitioning the Spanish king and queen, at the time of the Spanish Inquisition, to reverse the edict banishing the Jews from Spain. Failing in that effort, the Abravanel himself suffered expulsion in 1492 with the rest of the exiles.

The Abravanel authored many works including major commentaries on the Torah, other books of Tanach, *Pirkei Avot*, the Hagada and the Rambam's *Guide to the Perplexed*. His commentaries are divided into chapters, each of which is introduced by the list of questions and problems which he intends to address in the chapter. The Abravanel often applied the lessons learned from Scripture to issues confronting the Jewish society of his day.

Alshich – Rabbi Moshe Alshich, scholar, halachist, commentator (Turkey, Israel, Syria, 1508–1593).

Born in Adrianople, Turkey, Alshich emigrated at a young age to Tzfat, Israel, where he studied under and was ordained by Rabbi Yosef Caro. Alshich gained such prominence as a teacher, orator, halachic authority and communal leader that he was granted the title *Hakadosh* (the holy one), a title reserved for a few select rabbinic figures across Jewish history. The Alshich's last years were spent in Damascus, Syria.

Among other works, the Alshich published volumes of his popular lectures and sermons relating to various sections of Tanach (Torah, Prophets and Writings). Particularly noteworthy is his commentary on the Torah, *Torat Moshe*, which follows a homiletic approach and is filled with practical lessons on ethics and morals.

Avi Ezer – A commentary on the Ibn Ezra authored by Rabbi Shlomo HaCohen of Lissa (Leszno), Poland, in the eighteenth century.

Through careful examination of the Ibn Ezra's commentary on the Torah, the Avi Ezer explores the foundations of the Ibn Ezra's positions, often connecting the latter's comments on disparate texts to reflect a cohesive approach.

Avnei Nezer – Rabbi Avraham ben Ze'ev Nachum Bornstein of Sochaczew; Chassidic Rebbe (grand rabbi), Talmudic scholar, halachist (Poland, 1839–1910).

The first Rebbe of the Sochatchover dynasty, Bornstein earned early fame as a child prodigy and, at the age of fourteen, married the daughter of the renowned Chassidic leader Rabbi Menachem Mendel of Kotsk.

Bornstein occupied a number of rabbinical posts before assuming, in 1883, the position of rabbi in the city of Sochaczew, where he remained until his death.

Emerging as one of the greatest halachic scholars of his generation, Bornstein founded a yeshiva and trained numerous disciples who became scholarly Chassidic leaders in their own right.

Bornstein's two major works were *Avnei Nezer*, his collection of responsa on the four sections of the *Shulchan Aruch* (which earned him the personal title the Avnei Nezer), and *Eglei Tal*, a study of the laws of Shabbat.

Avot D'Rabi Natan – An interpretive expansion on the Mishnaic tractate of *Pirkei Avot* (see below).

Apparently dating from the Mishnaic period, *Avot D'Rabi Natan* is essentially a companion piece to *Pirkei Avot*.

In many cases, *Avot D'Rabi Natan* acts as a commentary to the existing text of *Pirkei Avot*, elaborating on and enriching the Mishna through anecdotes and exegetical interpretation. On other occasions, each of these texts presents material not found in the other.

Beit HaLevi – Rabbi Yosef Ber Soloveitchik; Talmudic scholar, halachist (Belarus, Poland, Russia, 1820–1892).

The Beit HaLevi was the great-grandson of Rabbi Chaim Volozhiner and the great-grandfather of Rabbi Yosef Dov Soloveitchik.

Incisive, brilliant and determined in his approach to Talmud study, the Beit HaLevi also distinguished himself through extraordinary acts of kindness towards the poor and needy.

The Beit HaLevi's life was marked by numerous personal and professional transitions. In 1854, after years of study in the cities of Brody, Lemberg and Minsk, he assumed the position of co-rosh yeshiva of the Yeshiva of Volozhin, partnering with Rabbi Naftali Tzvi Yehuda Berlin (the Netziv). Over time, however, it became apparent that differences in approach and temperament precluded the ability of these great leaders to work together. After ten years of service to the yeshiva, therefore, the Beit HaLevi left Volozhin to become the rabbi of Slutsk. In 1875 he relinquished that position and in 1878 he became the rabbi in Brisk, where he remained until his death. His son Chaim (Reb Chaim Brisker) succeeded him.

His numerous published works, including commentary on the Talmud, responsa, sermons and halachic novella, were all printed under the title *Beit HaLevi*.

Caro, Rabbi Yosef – *Hamechaber* (the author); scholar, halachist, author of the *Shulchan Aruch* (Set Table), the universally accepted, authoritative code of Jewish law (Spain and/or Portugal, Turkey, Israel, 1488–1575).

Born either in Spain or Portugal, Caro fled to Turkey with his family upon the expulsion of Jews from Portugal, in 1497. Living successively in the cities of Istanbul, Adrianople, Nikopol and Salonika, Caro studied with numerous scholars many of whom shaped his mystical life perspective.

In 1522, at the age of thirty-four, Caro began to write his monumental *Beit Yosef*, a project which would occupy him for twenty years and which he concluded only after moving to Tzfat, Israel. With this work, Caro strove to create order out of the multiplicity of codes and halachic rulings that had developed in Jewish law over the centuries. Caro traced each law to its origins, discussed the law's development through an analysis of divergent opinions and rendered authoritative practical rulings. In order to avoid unnecessary duplication, Caro fashioned the *Beit Yosef* as a commentary to the *Arba Turim* of Rabbi Yaakov ben Asher.

While the *Beit Yosef* was considered by Caro to be his most important scholarly writing, it is the more succinct digest of that work, the *Shulchan Aruch*, for which this scholar was eventually immortalized. The *Shulchan Aruch*, with its ordered, succinct presentation of practical Jewish law, quickly became the authoritative legal code for world Jewry and the point of departure for halachic works that followed.

Among Caro's other contributions was the *Kesef Mishneh*, an extensive commentary on the Rambam's *Mishneh Torah*.

Chafetz Chaim – Rabbi Israel Meir HaCohen Kagan, Talmudic scholar, halachist, ethicist (Lithuania, Belarus, 1838–1933).

A towering figure in the development of Orthodox Judaism during the nineteenth and twentieth centuries, the Chafetz Chaim's continued influence is felt in many spheres of Jewish life to this day.

Of humble origin, the Chafetz Chaim was taught by his parents until the age of ten, when his father's death prompted the family to move to Vilna to allow for Israel Meir's continued studies. After his marriage at the age of seventeen, the Chafetz Chaim settled in the town of Radun where he and his wife subsisted on the proceeds of a small grocery store. The Chafetz Chaim's Torah teaching became so popular that students flocked to his side, leading to the eventual establishment of a yeshiva carrying his name.

At the age of thirty-five, he anonymously published his first volume, *Chafetz Chaim* (He Who Desires Life), devoted entirely to the laws surrounding the prohibitions of slander, talebearing and gossip. Eventually his authorship of this work became known and earned him the personal title the Chafetz Chaim. Among many other works, his greatest halachic contribution was the *Mishneh Berura*, an extensive commentary and elaboration on one section of Rabbi Yosef Caro's *Shulchan Aruch*. The *Mishneh Berura* is widely used as an authoritative halachic guide to this day.

The Chafetz Chaim played a major role in communal and religious affairs of his day and was universally known for his kindness, piety, humility and integrity.

Chaifetz, Rabbi Moshe – Teacher, philosopher, poet (Italy, 1663–1711).

Born in Trieste, Chaifetz moved to Venice, where he earned his livelihood as a private tutor. He was proficient in areas of Jewish scholarship as well as in mathematics, philosophy and the natural sciences.

In addition to poetry, Chaifetz's major work was a philosophical commentary on the Torah, *Melechet Machshevet*. He also wrote *Chanukat HaBayit*, a volume dealing with the construction of the Second Temple.

Chizkuni – Rabbi Chizkiya ben Manoach Chizkuni; biblical commentator (France, thirteenth century).

Almost nothing is known about the personal life of the Chizkuni, a classical biblical commentator who lived in Provence around the year 1250. The Chizkuni's commentary, which focuses on the *pshat* (simple meaning) of the text, is based, according to the author, upon a number of earlier sources. In particular, the Chizkuni often elaborates upon the observations of Rashi.

The commentary of the Chizkuni first appeared in print in Venice in 1524.

Da'at Zekeinim Miba'alei Hatosafot – A compilation of Torah commentary authored by the Tosafists (a large group of twelfth- to thirteenth-century medieval rabbis whose critical and explanatory glosses are basic to the study of Talmud).

The period of the Tosafists began after the completion of Rashi's commentaries; the first Tosafists were actually Rashi's sons-in-law and grandsons. The Talmudic commentaries of the Tosafists are characterized by lengthy analyses of difficult passages and by a willingness to critically review the positions of their predecessors, particularly Rashi.

Preserved in manuscript for centuries, the *Da'at Zekeinim Miba'alei Hatosafot* was first formally published in 1783.

Dubno Maggid – Rabbi Yaakov Kranz; rabbi, orator (Lithuania, Poland, 1741–1804).

The Dubno Maggid was born in Zeitel, Vilna, and educated in Mezerich.

Demonstrating powerful homiletical skill at an early age, he spoke in Zilkiew, Wlodawa, Kalicz and Zanosc. His true fame, however, was attained in the city of Dubno where he served for eighteen years.

Using the full breadth of Jewish ethical, halachic and kabbalistic teachings, the Dubno Maggid fashioned homilies that were readily understandable and accessible to the layman. Through the use of parables and fables he conveyed complex ideas and concepts in clear, memorable fashion.

The Dubno Maggid's works were published posthumously.

Epstein, Rabbi Baruch Halevi – Commentator, scholar, author (Russia, 1860–1942).

The son of Yechiel Michel Epstein, Baruch Halevi studied under the tutelage of both his father and his uncle, the Netziv.

Although he was offered numerous rabbinic positions in such major centers as Pinsk, Moscow and Petrograd, Epstein opted to earn his livelihood as a bookkeeper and to devote his free time to Torah study. The author of numerous volumes, he is best known for his monumental

Torah Temima. In this work, he connects passages of the Talmud and Midrash to their sources in the written text and comments extensively on the topics they raise.

Epstein, Yechiel Michel – Rabbi, halachist (Russia, 1829–1908).

Born in Bobruisk, Belorussia, Epstein reluctantly entered the rabbinate at the prompting of his own town rabbi, Eliyahu Goldberg. After serving the community of Novozpktov for over a decade, Epstein accepted the rabbinic position in Novogrudok in 1874 and remained there until his death.

Epstein's wife was the sister of the Netziv (Rabbi Naftali Tzvi Yehuda Berlin).

Epstein is most well known for his *Aruch Hashulchan*, an important halachic compendium which follows the structure of Rabbi Yosef Karo's *Shulchan Aruch*. In this work, Epstein carefully traces the origins of each law and custom to its source, discusses the positions of a wide range of halachic authorities and issues clear rulings concerning practical observance. In contrast to a number of his contemporaries, Epstein shows a marked tendency towards leniency in his rulings.

Feinstein, Rabbi Moshe – Reb Moshe; preeminent Torah sage and halachic authority of the twentieth century (Russia, America, 1895–1986).

After serving as Rabbi of Luban (near Minsk) for sixteen years, Reb Moshe immigrated to the United States in 1937. Settling in the Lower East Side, where he remained for the rest of his life, he assumed the position of rosh yeshiva at Mesivta Tiferes Yerushalayim. Under his guidance, this institution became a leading American yeshiva.

Reb Moshe was regarded by most rabbinic contemporaries as the *gadol hador*, the greatest Torah sage of his generation, and his decisions on Jewish law were accepted as authoritative by Orthodox Jews throughout the world. He played a major role in defining the continuing interface between halacha and issues of modernity, rendering decisions on a wide range of issues including artificial insemination, transplantation surgery, end-of-life medical care, abortion, financial ethics, business and labor disputes, etc.

Close to two thousand of Reb Moshe's responsa are contained in *Igrot Moshe*, a multivolume work arranged according to the sections of the *Shulchan Aruch*. His commentary on the Torah was published posthumously under the title *Darash Moshe*.

Grunfeld, Dayan Dr. I. – Rabbi, lawyer, author (Bavaria, England, 1900–1975).

The Bavarian-born Grunfeld practiced law in his native city before settling in England in 1933. He was appointed a member of the London Beit Din (Jewish court) and was active in many religious, cultural and social endeavors.

A recognized authority on the works of Rabbi Shimshon Raphael Hirsch, Grunfeld edited and translated many of Hirsch's works into English and presented, in his own original writings, new ideas based upon Hirsch's religious philosophy.

HaCohen, Rabbi Meir Simcha of Dvinsk – Rabbi, talmudic scholar, biblical commentator (Latvia, Lithuania, 1843–1926).

Renowned as a brilliant Talmudic scholar and beloved as a compassionate leader, Rabbi Meir Simcha served as rabbi of the city of Dvinsk for forty years. In 1906 he turned down a rabbinic position in Jerusalem as a result of the entreaties of the Dvinsk community who argued that his departure would "destroy" not only their community but the entire diaspora. During World War I when most of the Jewish community fled Dvinsk, leaving behind only the poorest inhabitants, Rabbi Meir Simcha remained, declaring that as long as there were nine Jews in the city he would be the tenth.

Among his most important works were the *Meshech Chochma* and *Or Sameach*, commentaries on the Torah and on the Rambam's *Mishneh Torah*, respectively.

Halevi, Rabbi Yehuda – Philosopher, scholar, poet, physician (Spain, Egypt, Israel? 1075–1141).

The most prolific, and according to many, the greatest of all medieval Hebrew poets, Yehuda Halevi was educated in traditional Jewish scholarship, Arabic literature and the Greek sciences and philosophy. Most of his life was spent in various communities within Christian and Islamic Spain where he earned great renown as a communal leader, physician and scholar. He enjoyed a close friendship with Rabbi Avraham Ibn Ezra and is often quoted in the latter's Torah commentary.

In spite of his success and honored position in Spain, in his later years Yehuda Halevi determined to embark upon a pilgrimage to the Land of Israel where he intended to spend the remainder of his days. After a perilous journey, he arrived on September 8, 1140, in Alexandria, Egypt, and from there traveled to Cairo. Greeted with admiration and honor

wherever he went, Yehuda Halevi successfully resisted the entreaties of
many who tried to convince him to remain in Egypt.

The last stage of Yehuda Halevi's journey is unfortunately shrouded in
mystery. While numerous scholars suggest that he never actually succeeded
in reaching the Holy Land, legend claims that he was murdered by an Arab
as he knelt to pray in Jerusalem, at the Western Wall.

In addition to hundreds of lyrical poems and other works, Yehuda
Halevi authored a major philosophical treatise, *Sefer Hakuzari*. The literary
framework for this text is the conversion to Judaism of the pagan king of
the Khazars, who, searching for truth, interviews scholars representing
different philosophies and religions. The Jewish scholar's dialogue with
the king provides the vehicle through which Yehuda Halevi presents his
foundational philosophical positions.

Hirsch, Rabbi Shimshon Raphael – Biblical commentator, rabbinic leader,
philosopher (Germany, 1808–1888).

In the wake of the emancipation, traditional Judaism was desperately
in need of a powerful leader to guide the transition of Orthodoxy into a
new world marked by greater freedom. Rabbi Shimshon Raphael Hirsch
successfully filled that role.

In 1851, Hirsch relinquished a prominent rabbinic post to become the
rabbi of eleven individuals who had separated from the general community
of Frankfurt-on-the-Main in response to that community's shift towards
Reform Judaism. From those humble beginnings, Hirsch built a model
Orthodox community of five hundred members.

Hirsch developed a philosophy of *Torah im Derech Eretz* (lit.: Torah and
the way of the land) which envisioned a relationship between traditional
observant Judaism and the modern world. Much controversy exists today
as to the exact dimensions of the relationship envisioned by Hirsch. There
is no question, however, that Hirsch's contributions were instrumental in
the development of German Orthodox Jewry and paved the way for the
development of today's Modern Orthodox community throughout the
Jewish world. Hirsch published many works including *Nineteen Letters*,
in which he brilliantly responds to the major philosophical questions of
his day; *Horeb*, a text outlining his approach to Jewish belief and practice;
and an extensive, thought-provoking commentary on the Torah.

Ibn Ezra – Rabbi Avraham ben Meir Ibn Ezra; biblical commentator, philosopher, poet, grammarian, physician, astronomer/astrologer (Spain, Egypt, North Africa, Italy, France, England, Israel, 1092–1167).

Over the course of an impoverished and itinerant life, the Ibn Ezra made a profound contribution to Jewish scholarship. A prolific poet, the Ibn Ezra produced treatises on Hebrew grammar, mathematics, astronomy/astrology and philosophy.

The Ibn Ezra's greatest contribution, however, was made through his renowned commentary on the Torah and other books of Tanach (an acronym for the biblical canon – Torah, Nevi'im, Ketuvim: the five books of Moses, the Prophets and the Writings). This work, which inspired numerous supercommentaries, is singular for its strong use of grammatical principles to uncover the *pshat* of the text. While the Ibn Ezra's commentary included a great deal of exegetical material authored by his predecessors, he did not shy away from offering his own original observations.

Jacob, Rabbi Benno – Biblical commentator (1862–1955).

Born in Breslau, Jacob attended the gymnasium, university and theological seminary of his native town, earning his PhD in 1889. He served as rabbi in Gottingen from 1891 to 1929 after which he retired to Hamburg to concentrate on his writing.

Jacob's biblical commentary is noteworthy for its use of literary analysis and modern scholarship.

Kli Yakar – Rabbi Ephraim Shlomo ben Chaim of Luntshitz; rabbi, biblical commentator, orator (Poland, Bohemia, 1550–1619).

At an early age, the Kli Yakar earned a reputation as a spellbinding speaker and traveled in that capacity through numerous cities and towns. Subsequently, he served as rosh yeshiva and *av beit din* (head of the Jewish court) in Prague.

His renowned commentary on the Torah, the *Kli Yakar*, is largely homiletic in style.

Leibowitz, Dr. Nehama – Biblical scholar and commentator, teacher (Israel, 1905–1997).

Born in Riga, Latvia, Nehama Leibowitz was awarded a doctorate from the University of Berlin in 1930 and emigrated that same year to the British Mandate of Palestine. Over the course of her career, Leibowitz taught for decades at a religious Zionist teachers seminary, lectured at Tel Aviv

University, where she was appointed full professor, delivered regular radio addresses on Voice of Israel radio and lectured in a multitude of settings throughout the country.

Leibowitz is best known for her *gilyonot* (lit.: pages), stencils on the weekly Torah reading which she distributed to all interested. Her incisive analytical approach to text made these *gilyonot* immensely popular and through their distribution she rekindled intense interest in the study of biblical text and commentary throughout the Jewish world. Later Leibowitz produced formal studies, which were eventually collected into books on the Torah. Leibowitz was awarded the Israel Prize for education in 1957.

Luzzatto, Shmuel David – Philosopher, scholar, biblical commentator, poet (Italy, 1800–1865).

Over the course of a prolific literary career, Luzzatto produced a great number of works in both Hebrew and Italian including a commentary on the Torah, commentaries on numerous books of the Prophets, a treatise on Hebrew grammar, a guide to the understanding of *Targum Onkelos*, essays and poems.

While deeply traditional, Luzzatto was unafraid to challenge established ideas. He subjected the commentary of the Ibn Ezra to scathing attack and, while he greatly admired the Rambam for the latter's halachic contributions, he did not hesitate to criticize that great scholar for adopting elements of Aristotelian philosophy.

In 1829, Luzzatto was appointed professor at the rabbinical college of Padua. He contributed to most of the Jewish periodicals of his time, corresponded voluminously with contemporaries and wrote on an extremely wide range of Jewish topics.

Maharal – Rabbi Yehuda Loew; rabbi, Talmudic scholar, philosopher, commentator (Poland, Bohemia, 1525–1609).

Born to a noble family that traces its lineage to King David, the Maharal was one of the most influential Jewish thinkers of the postmedieval period. So expansive was his influence that Rav Avraham Yitzchak HaCohen Kook (the first chief rabbi of Israel) once proclaimed that the Maharal was "the father of the approach of the Vilna Gaon on the one hand and the father of the Chassidic movement on the other."

After serving as Rabbi of Nikolsburg in the province of Moravia for twenty years, the Maharal moved to Prague in 1573, there opening a yeshiva and mentoring numerous outstanding disciples. After leaving for a brief period to serve as rabbi in the city of Posen, the Maharal returned to Prague in 1598 to assume the position of chief rabbi.

A renowned educator, the Maharal criticized his contemporaries for not heeding the advice of the Mishna which counsels that children should be taught subjects that are age appropriate. "The fools nowadays," he proclaimed, "teach boys Torah with the commentary of Rashi, which they do not understand and also Talmud which they cannot yet grasp." While clearly rooted in the world of Torah, the Maharal embraced the study of secular subjects, particularly mathematics.

A prolific writer, the Maharal was held in high esteem by Jews and non-Jews alike. His statue was erected in 1917 at the entrance to the province town hall by the municipal authority, and his synagogue, the Altneu Shul, stands to this day.

Malbim – Rabbi Meir Leib ben Yechiel Michael; biblical commentator, community rabbi (Poland, Romania, Russia, 1809–1879).

The Malbim served as the rabbi of a series of prominent communities including Bucharest, where, for a time, he assumed the position of chief rabbi of Romania. The Malbim's strong defense of traditional Judaism and his unwavering opposition to the new rites and practices promulgated by the Reform movement provoked the resentment of many wealthy German Jews. Repeatedly, the Malbim's persecutors managed to instigate his removal from rabbinic positions and, on one occasion, their accusations actually led to his imprisonment.

The Malbim's incisive commentary on the Torah, *Hatorah V'hamitzva*, is noteworthy for projecting the unity of the Written and Oral Law and for its strong foundation in linguistic analysis.

Mecklenberg, Rabbi Yaakov Tzvi – Rabbi, biblical commentator (East Prussia, 1785–1865).

Mecklenberg began his rabbinic career in 1829 when he became the assistant to the rabbi of Koenigsberg, the capital of the German province of East Prussia. In 1831, he graduated to the role of rabbi and remained in that position until the day he died.

Mecklenberg's major work was *Haktav V'hakabala*, a commentary on the Torah which stressed the indivisibility of the Written and Oral Law. Responding to the emerging claims of the Haskala (Enlightenment) movement that the traditional explanations of the Torah were outdated and far-fetched, Mecklenberg demonstrated the authentic textual and linguistic basis for traditional interpretation.

Meiri – Rabbi Menachem ben Meir Meiri; Talmudic scholar, biblical commentator, halachist (France 1249–1316).

The scion of a distinguished Provençal Jewish family, the Meiri was born in Perpignan, where he spent his entire life. Few details of his personal life are known but he apparently experienced a series of tragedies at a fairly early age.

The Meiri contributed greatly to Jewish scholarship through comprehensive works which summarized the teachings of his predecessors during the previous three centuries. He wrote on a vast spectrum of Jewish thought including ethics, Torah commentary, halacha, Talmudic interpretation, philosophy and customs. Most of his writings remained in manuscript form until the beginning of the twentieth century, possibly because of their extraordinary length.

Chief among his works was the *Beit Habechira*, a monumental interpretive summary of the contents of the Talmud with a focus upon both the substance of the text and the halachic conclusions.

Midrash Hagadol – Collection of Midrashim compiled in the late thirteenth century by the Yemenite scholar Rabbi David Ben Avraham Adani.

This work, culled from ancient Tannaitic (Mishnaic) sources, was preserved in manuscript for centuries and studied primarily within the Yemenite community. European scholars, within the last 150 years, have printed carefully edited versions of the text. The Midrash Hagadol serves as a significant record of many teachings from the Mishnaic and Talmudic period which are found in no other source.

Midrash Lekach Tov – A Midrashic commentary on the Torah and the five Megilla scrolls.

Also known by the title *Psikta Zutarta*, this work was compiled by the Bulgarian rabbinic scholar Tuvia Ben Eliezer in the late eleventh century.

Midrash Rabba – A collection of Midrashic anthologies on various books of Tanach.

Although the title "Rabba" is shared by all of these anthologies, they are not a cohesive work but a series of Midrashic texts edited in different centuries and in various locales. Bereishit Rabba (Midrash Rabba Bereishit) was compiled in the sixth century and consists of wide-ranging ethical teachings, homilies, maxims, parables and metaphors all connected (albeit sometimes loosely) to the text of Bereishit.

Midrash Tanchuma – A compilation of Midrashim, many of which are ascribed to the Talmudic sage Tanchuma bar Abba.

Rav Tanchuma bar Abba, who lived in Israel during the second half of the fourth century CE, was a student of the renowned sage Rav Huna and a major author of *aggadot* (Midrashic tales). The text ascribed to his name has appeared over the centuries in various versions.

Midreshei Halacha – A group of Tannaitic expositions on the Torah designed to identify the sources of the six hundred thirteen mitzvot within the Torah text.

In contrast to *Midreshei Aggada* (homiletical Midrashim such as the Midrash Rabba, Midrash Tanchuma, etc.), *Midreshei Halacha* are primarily halachic in purpose. Nonetheless, they contain much aggadic material, as well. While the contents of the *Midreshei Halacha* date to the Mishnaic period, the redaction of the extant texts apparently occurred much later. Numerous theories, in fact, concerning the categorization and dating of these Midrashim have been offered by scholars and historians.

Because practically no halachic legislation derives from the book of Bereishit, *Midreshei Halacha* are only found in connection with the books of Shmot, Vayikra, Bamidbar and Devarim. These Midrashim are referred to by various titles such as *Mechilta, Sifra, Sifrei* and *Torat Kohanim.*

Mirsky, Rabbi Yitzchak – Rabbi, halachist (Israel).

A contemporary halachist, Mirsky is the author of the well-received multivolume set *Hegyonei Halacha*, containing studies on the festivals.

Mishna – First official written summary of the Oral Law.

The editing of the Mishna by Rabbi Yehuda Hanasi at the end of the second century CE marked a major transformation in the mode of transmission of Jewish tradition. Until this time, the distinction between Written Law (Torah She'bi'chtav) and Oral Law (Torah She'b'al Peh) had been studiously maintained, the latter memorized and transmitted verbally across the centuries. Driven by the fear, however, that the Oral Law would be lost if not recorded in writing, Rabbi Yehuda developed the six "orders" of the Mishna. This pioneering sage, however, preserved the character of the Oral Law by recording the Mishnaic edicts in short, cryptic style which requires immediate further oral explication.

The sages of the Mishna are known as the Tannaim.

Mizrachi, Eliyahu – Talmudic scholar, biblical commentator, halachic authority (Turkey, 1450–1526).

Born and educated in Constantinople, Mizrachi rose to become the foremost rabbinic authority in the Ottoman Empire of his day. Mizrachi was firm and unbending in his legal positions and responded to halachic queries addressed to him from far and wide. His grueling daily schedule encompassed communal leadership, the stewardship of a yeshiva, extensive teaching, the rendering of legal decisions and scholarly writing.

In addition to his major achievements in the area of Jewish scholarship and communal leadership, Mizrachi also studied and wrote on secular subjects, particularly mathematics and astronomy.

Mizrachi's crowning achievement – and the project which he personally considered his most important – was his monumental supercommentary on Rashi. This extensive work became the basis for continued study and analysis by later commentaries.

Netziv – Rabbi Naftali Tzvi Yehuda Berlin; Talmudic scholar, rosh yeshiva, biblical commentator (Poland, Russia, 1817–1893).

For forty years beginning in 1854, the Netziv served as the rosh yeshiva of the Yeshiva of Volozhin. The Netziv's scholarship, coupled with a deep personal love for all of his students, transformed the yeshiva into the largest such institution of its time and a major spiritual center for the Russian Jewish community. His opposition to the secularization of the yeshiva eventually brought him into conflict with government authorities and, according to some versions, led to the yeshiva's closing in 1892 (others suggest that the closure was due to internal upheaval). The Netziv was one of the early supporters of Jewish settlement in the Land of Israel.

Among the Netziv's publications was his popular biblical commentary, the *Ha'ameik Davar*, in which he emphasized the consonance between Talmudic interpretation and the *pshat* of the Torah text.

A son of the Netziv's first marriage was Rabbi Chaim Berlin, who became chief rabbi of Moscow and subsequently chief rabbi of the Ashkenazic community in Yerushalayim; a son of his second marriage was Rabbi Meir Berlin (later Bar-Ilan), a leader of the religious Zionist Mizrachi movement who inspired the creation of Bar-Ilan University (named in his memory).

Ohr Hachaim – Rabbi Chaim Ibn Attar; biblical commentator, Talmudic scholar, kabbalist (Morocco, Israel, 1696–1743).

One of the most prominent rabbis in his native land of Morocco, the

Ohr Hachaim decided in 1733 to resettle in the Land of Israel. He was, however, detained along the way in Livorno, Italy, by leading members of the Jewish community who established a Talmudic academy for him. Finally arriving in Jerusalem in 1742, the Ohr Hachaim served as the head of the Beit Midrash Knesset Yisrael until his death.

The Ohr Hachaim's commentary on the Torah combines textual analysis with Talmudic and kabbalistic insights. Over the years, this commentary has become particularly popular within the Sephardic and Chassidic communities.

Onkelos – Convert to Judaism, scholar and author of the seminal Aramaic translation of the Torah, *Targum Onkelos* (Rome, Israel, 35–120 CE).

According to tradition, Onkelos was the nephew of the Roman emperor Titus (who, as a general, was responsible for the destruction of the Second Temple).

After his conversion, Onkelos authored *Targum Onkelos*, a monumental interpretive translation of the Torah into Aramaic. This translation, which received the approbation of Onkelos' teachers, the Mishnaic scholars Rabbi Eliezer and Rabbi Yehoshua, offers striking insights into the text. So authoritative did this work become that the rabbis of the Talmud decreed that the weekly reading of the Torah portion should include the reading of the *Targum*, as well. *Targum Onkelos* is included in almost all published editions of the Torah today.

Paneiach Raza – Midrashic work authored by the thirteenth-century kabbalist Isaac ben Yehuda Levi.

A continuous commentary on the Torah narrative, the Paneiach Raza employs *gematria* (numerological valuation of the Hebrew letters) and other exegetical tools to uncover hidden lessons embedded in the text.

Pesikta Rabbati – A medieval Midrashic compilation focusing on the special Sabbaths and festivals of the Jewish year.

Unlike most other Midrashic compilations, the *Pesikta Rabbati* is not a continuous commentary on the Torah, but, instead, consists of a series of separate sections dealing with the biblical and prophetic lessons emerging from the festivals.

While the earliest Midrashim within the *Pesikta Rabbati* apparently date to 845, the whole work is viewed as a composite reflecting several periods of editing.

Pirkei Avot – Mishnaic tractate containing the ethical pronouncements of the Tannaitic sages.

Pirkei Avot is singular within the Talmud in its focus upon ethical maxims as opposed to legal stricture. Many of Judaism's best-known proverbs and moral observations are contained within this tractate.

Elsewhere, the Talmud proclaims, "He who desires to be pious, let him practice the teachings of *[Pirkei] Avot*."

Pirkei D'Rabi Eliezer – Midrashic work on Bereishit, Shmot and portions of Bamidbar.

Pirkei D'Rabi Eliezer is ascribed to the Tannaitic (Mishnaic) sage Rabbi Eliezer ben Hyrcanus (first century CE). In spite of its early roots, the first authoritative version of this text apparently appeared in the ninth century.

Rabbeinu Bachya – Rabbi Bachya ben Asher; biblical commentator, rabbinic judge, preacher (Spain, 1263–1340).

A disciple of the renowned Talmudist Rabbi Shlomo ben Aderet (the Rashba), Rabbeinu Bachya served as a preacher and a *dayan* (rabbinical judge) in Saragossa, Spain. Rabbeinu Bachya is best known for his commentary on the Torah, which combines *pshat*, Midrash, philosophy and Kabbala. Each weekly parsha is introduced by an ethical discussion citing a verse from Proverbs.

Rabbeinu Chananel – Chananel ben Chushiel; Talmudic scholar, halachic authority, commentator (Tunisia, 990–1055).

Rabbeinu Chananel lived in the city of Kairouan, Tunisia, where he studied under the tutelage of his father, Chushiel ben Elchanan, head of the Kairouan yeshiva. Following in his father's footsteps, Rabbeinu Chananel eventually earned the title *Reish Bei Rabbanan*, chief among the rabbis, accorded by the Babylonian academies of his day.

Rabbeinu Chananel wrote the first authoritative commentary on the Talmud, great sections of which are preserved and recorded on the actual pages of specific Talmudic tractates. In contrast to the later commentary of Rashi, Rabbeinu Chananel's work is not a running interpretation of the entire text. Instead, he summarizes and explains the main arguments of the Gemara and issues halachic decisions on the matters in question. He relies greatly on the positions of the Babylonian Geonim, and thus serves as an important bridge between the teachings of the Geonim and the scholars of North Africa and those of the scholars of Europe and Israel. Many later commentaries cite his work extensively.

Rabbeinu Chananel also wrote a commentary on the Torah, only portions of which have been preserved.

Ralbag – Rabbi Levi ben Gershon; Talmudic scholar, commentator, philosopher, mathematician, astronomer/astrologer (France, 1288–1344).

Little is known about the life of this revolutionary Jewish philosopher who authored works ranging from biblical commentary to acclaimed philosophical and mathematical treatises. His major philosophical text, *Sefer Milchamot Hashem* (The Wars of the Lord), was composed over a twelve-year period and earned the Ralbag renown well beyond the Jewish community.

In opposition to the generally accepted position of classical Judaism, the Ralbag maintained that God deliberately limits his own omniscience with regard to his foreknowledge of human acts. By stating that God knows the choices available to us but consciously chooses not to know the specific decisions that we will make, the Ralbag addressed the age-old dilemma of how man's free will can exist in the face of God's omniscience.

Rambam – Rabbi Moshe ben Maimon, also known as Maimonides; widely recognized as the greatest post-Talmudic authority on Jewish law and thought (Spain, Morocco, Egypt, 1135–1204).

The Rambam's works include *The Guide to the Perplexed*, a philosophical work on Jewish theology; *Sefer Hamitzvot*, a compendium of the six hundred thirteen commandments of the Torah; a commentary on the Mishna; and his magnum opus, the *Mishneh Torah*, a masterful, comprehensive code of Jewish law. In his commentary on the Mishna, the Rambam delineated thirteen principles still considered to be the cornerstones of Jewish belief. His *Mishneh Torah* launched the course for halachic codification across the ages and served as the forerunner of other essential texts such as the *Arba Turim* and the *Shulchan Aruch*.

A royal physician and world-class philosopher, the Rambam made a monumental impact upon the development of Jewish tradition and law, reflected in the well-known dictum inscribed on his tomb: "From Moshe (Moses) to Moshe (Rambam) no one arose like Moshe."

Ramban – Rabbi Shlomo ben Nachman, also known as Nachmanides; biblical and Talmudic commentator, scholar, physician (Spain, Israel, 1194–1270).

The Ramban's commentary on the Torah combines *pshat*, Midrash and kabbalistic insights. A towering figure in the history of Jewish scholarship, the Ramban authored numerous works on the Talmud as well as Jewish law and thought. His vigorous defense of Judaism in the face of Christian attack culminated in a public disputation with the Jewish apostate Pablo Christiano, in the presence of King James of Spain in 1263.

The Ramban's deep love for the Land of Israel is manifest in his writings and in his philosophy of Jewish law. In 1267, at the age of seventy-two, the Ramban settled in the Land of Israel and worked vigorously to rebuild Jerusalem's Jewish community.

Ran – Rabbi Nissim ben Reuven; Talmudic scholar, halachist, philosopher, physician (Spain, 1290–1380).

Widely recognized as the greatest rabbinic authority of his time, the Ran served as rabbi of Barcelona and responded to thousands of halachic inquiries from across the Jewish diaspora. The Ran is best known for his practical commentary on the halachic work of Rabbi Yitzchak ben Yaakov Alfasi (the Rif). Through this commentary, the Ran achieved a revered position in the world of Talmudic scholarship. The Ran's compendium of sermons, *Drashot HaRan,* provides insight into many of the basic tenets of Jewish faith.

Rashbam – Rabbi Shmuel ben Meir; biblical commentator, Talmudic scholar (France, 1080–1158).

The Rashbam, Rashi's grandson, was a leading member of the Tosafists (a large group of medieval rabbis whose critical and explanatory glosses are basic to the study of the Talmud). The Rashbam's commentary on the Torah is remarkable for its bold adherence to *pashut pshat* even when the *pshat* leads to controversial conclusions. The Rashbam took issue with his renowned grandfather's periodic Midrashic interpretation of the text and, in fact, claimed, "I debated with him [Rashi] and he admitted to me that, if he had the time, he would be obligated to author other commentaries based upon the straightforward explanations of the text…."

So great was the storm concerning some of the Rashbam's views that his commentary on the first chapters of Bereishit was omitted in many earlier editions of the Bible.

Rashi – Rabbi Shlomo Yitzchaki; arguably the greatest of all biblical and Talmudic commentators (France, 1040–1105).

Rashi's commentary on the Torah, considered an essential companion to the study of the text, combines *pshat* with the periodic referencing of Midrash (when he feels such referencing is necessary for textual comprehension).

In addition to commentaries on the Prophets and Writings, Rashi also authored an indispensable running commentary on the Talmud, known for its brevity and clarity.

No course of study in the Torah or Talmud is considered complete without the accompanying study of Rashi's commentary.

Rema – Rabbi Moshe Isserles; Talmudic scholar, *dayan* (judge), preeminent halachic authority for Ashkenazic Jewry (Poland, 1520–1572).

Born in Cracow, Poland, the Rema studied in Lublin where he married the daughter of Rabbi Shalom Shachna, the rosh yeshiva. Upon his wife's untimely death at the age of twenty, the Rema honored her memory with the building of a synagogue which stands in Cracow to this day. The Rema's second wife also came from a scholarly family.

The Rema distinguished himself as an outstanding scholar at an early age and by 1550 was a member of the Cracow Beit Din (religious court). He established a yeshiva in Cracow, supported its students through his own resources and earned a worldwide reputation as a brilliant and effective *posek* (halachic arbiter). Humble and self-effacing, the Rema was, nonetheless, so confident and incisive in his halachic positions that he became known to his contemporaries as the "Maimonides of Polish Jewry." Like Maimonides, the Rema also pursued secular knowledge through the study of history, astronomy and philosophy.

While the Rema authored many works, he is best known for his *Mapa* (Tablecloth), a series of annotations inserted into the body of Rabbi Yosef Caro's halachic compendium, the *Shulchan Aruch* (Set Table). These glosses append the legal positions and customs of Ashkenazic Jewry to Caro's Sephardic-oriented work, thus transforming the *Shulchan Aruch* into the primary universal code of law for the entire Jewish nation.

Saadia Gaon – Talmudic scholar, philosopher, halachist (Egypt, Babylonia, 882–942).

Arguably the greatest scholar of the Geonic period (late sixth–eleventh centuries), Saadia Gaon is also considered by many to be the "father of Jewish philosophy." Sensing the twin dangers posed to rabbinic Judaism by Karaism (a movement that accepted the Written but not the Oral Law) and rationalistic thought, Saadia developed a systematic philosophy of Judaism which examined its truths and teachings in the light of reason.

Saadia played a major role in a calendar controversy between the Jerusalem and the Babylonian scholarly communities which threatened to create a dangerous schism concerning the fixing of festival dates. At the request of the Babylonian scholars, Saadia effectively refuted the position of Aharon ben Meir, the head of the Jerusalem Academy, and solidified the supremacy of the Babylonian rabbinate. Both as a result of this effort and in the merit of his extraordinary abilities, Saadia was appointed head of the famed Babylonian Academy of Sura in 928, at the age of forty-six.

So important were Saadia's contributions to Jewish thought that, centuries later, the Rambam proclaimed in his *Iggeret Teiman*: "Were it not for Saadia, the Torah would almost have disappeared from among Israel."

Sefer Hachinuch – Systematic analysis of the six hundred thirteen commandments of the Torah, published anonymously in thirteenth-century Spain.

Following the order of the Torah text, the Ba'al Hachinuch (as the anonymous author of the *Sefer Hachinuch* is called) links each mitzva to the parsha in which it is found and discusses both the philosophical underpinnings and halachic parameters of that mitzva.

Sforno – Rabbi Ovadia Sforno; biblical commentator, Talmudic scholar, philosopher, physician (Italy, 1470–1550).

The Sforno's broad-based education earned him recognition in many fields including law, philosophy, mathematics, medicine, Hebrew language and Hebrew literature. When the famous German humanist Johan Reuchlin desired to perfect his knowledge of Hebrew literature, Cardinal Domenico Grimani advised him to approach the Sforno. A prolific writer, the Sforno is best known for his clear commentary on the Torah and many books of Tanach. These works reflect great respect for the *pshat* of the text and are written in a beautiful, almost lyrical style.

Siddur – The Jewish prayer book.

The Siddur mirrors the historical journey of the Jewish people. While the earliest prayers were primarily spontaneous, prayer services became codified over time, stemming from various sources.

Biblically mandated prayers include the Shma Yisrael, the Birkat Kohanim (priestly blessing) and the Birkat Hamazon (grace after meals). The central prayer of the Jewish liturgy, known as the Amida (the standing [prayer]), was edited by Rabbi Gamliel and his colleagues in Yavne, after the destruction of the Second Temple.

The earliest true Siddur was drawn up in the ninth century by Rav

Amram Gaon, at the request of the Jewish community of Spain. One hundred years later, Rav Saadia Gaon compiled a Siddur, as well. Critical to the development of the Jewish prayer book was the Machzor Vitri, edited in the eleventh century by Simcha ben Shmuel, a student of Rashi. The Machzor Vitri contained all the regular prayers according to the custom of northern France.

The Siddur continues to evolve to this day, as evidenced by prayers included in many contemporary prayer books relating to the welfare of the State of Israel and its armed forces.

Soloveitchik, Rabbi Yosef Dov – The Rav; pioneering spiritual leader of the Modern Orthodox movement in America and throughout the Jewish world (Lithuania, America, 1903–1993).

Scion of a two-hundred-year-old rabbinic dynasty, the Rav arrived in America in 1932 armed with an education that combined traditional Lithuanian Talmudic studies and a PhD in philosophy from the University of Berlin. He assumed a rabbinic position in Boston where he established the Maimonides School and played a major role in many facets of the community's development. In 1941, he succeeded his father, Rabbi Moshe Soloveitchik, as the head of the Rabbi Isaac Elchanan Theological Seminary rabbinic school of Yeshiva University. For decades thereafter he commuted weekly between Boston and New York.

The Rav combined vast Torah and secular knowledge, a deeply analytical mind, powerful teaching ability and majestic oratorical skill with a magnetic leadership personality. Through his classes, widely attended public lectures, writings and policy decisions he furthered the philosophy of encounter between the highest form of Torah knowledge and the best secular scholarship of Western civilization. Adviser and teacher to tens of thousands, the Rav shaped the course of Modern Orthodox philosophy through the twentieth century and beyond.

Sorotzkin, Rabbi Zalman – Rabbi, Talmudic scholar, communal leader (Lithuania, Poland, Israel, 1881–1966).

After beginning his studies under the guidance of his father, the rabbi of Zakhrina, Russia, Sorotzkin continued his education in the yeshivot of Slobodka and Volozhin. His renown as a brilliant student earned him the hand of the daughter of Rabbi Eliezer Gordon, the rosh yeshiva of Telz.

Sorotzkin served as the rabbi of the Lithuanian towns of Voronova and Zhetel, where he established educational institutions. The outbreak of World War I forced him to flee to Minsk. During the war years, he devoted himself to communal activities. Shortly after the end of World War I, Sorotzkin was appointed rabbi of Lutsk, Poland. He remained in Lutsk until World War II, when he escaped to Israel.

Sorotzkin helped found numerous communal institutions and served in many leadership capacities. He enjoyed personal relationships with other Torah luminaries of his day including the Chafetz Chaim, the Chazon Ish and Rabbi Chaim Ozer Grodzenski. He authored the works *Oznaim LaTorah*, a commentary on the Torah, and *Moznaim LaTorah*, concerning the Jewish festivals.

Sperber, Rabbi David – Rabbi, *dayan* (religious court judge) (Rumania, Israel, ?–1961).

A renowned scholar, Sperber was accorded the title "the Gaon (genius) of Barshov" by his contemporaries. He served as a *dayan* and rabbi in Rumania before emigrating to Israel where he passed away in 1961.

Sperber's works included *Michtav L'David*.

Talmud Bavli – Babylonian Talmud; foundational compilation of the halachic (legal) and aggadic (ethical-homiletical) discussions of the sages of the Babylonian academies from the second through the fifth centuries CE.

The scholars of the Talmud, known as the Amoraim, expound at great length upon the concise teachings of the Mishna, often digressing to discuss loosely related issues and ideas. Structurally, the style of the Talmud Bavli can best be described as "conversation in suspended animation," reflecting the origin of its subject matter, which was memorized and transmitted orally for centuries before its eventual written recordation.

Together with the Mishna, the Talmud Bavli serves as the basic source for the continually developing Oral Law.

Talmud Yerushalmi – Jerusalem Talmud; collection of the teachings of the sages of the Israeli academies from 200 to 350 CE.

Like the Talmud Bavli, the Talmud Yerushalmi centers on the discussions of the Amoraim (Talmudic scholars) concerning the Mishna. The Talmud Yerushalmi, however, is smaller in scope, more fragmented, and more difficult to study than its Babylonian counterpart; consequently, over the centuries, the Yerushalmi has exerted less influence upon the development of Jewish law. The return to the land of Israel in recent years has given birth to a renewed interest in the Talmud Yerushalmi and the laws it contains pertaining to the land.

Trunk, Rabbi Yisrael Yehoshua of Kotno – Rabbi, halachist (Poland, 1820–1893).

Born in Plock, Trunk was a child prodigy who quickly earned a reputation as a great scholar. After serving as rabbi in Szrensk, Gabri, Warka and Poltusk, he assumed the rabbinic position in Kotno where he remained until the end of his life.

Trunk was an involved member of the *Chibbat Tzion* (lovers of Zion) movement, which promoted Jewish settlement of the Land of Israel. In 1886 he personally visited Israel to encourage the pioneers, who were facing the great challenges involved in the initial settlement of the land.

Trunk's works, some of which were published posthumously, included the halachic volumes *Yeshuot Yisrael*, *Yeshuot Malko* and *Yavin Da'at*, and a commentary on the Torah, *Mikra Meforash*.

Vilna Gaon – Rabbi Eliyahu ben Shlomo Zalman (Lithuania, 1720–1797).

Also known by the acronym the *Gra* (Gaon Rabbi Eliyahu), the Vilna Gaon is considered one of the greatest Talmudic scholars of the past two centuries and is recognized as the "founding father" of the Lithuanian (non-Chassidic) yeshiva movement.

The Gaon demonstrated extraordinary ability as a youngster, delivering a learned discourse in the Great Synagogue of Vilna at the age of six and a half.

A man of iron will, the Gaon devoted every waking moment of his life to all facets of Torah study. He reportedly never slept for more than two hours in a twenty-four-hour period and studied in an unheated room in the winter, placing his feet in cold water to prevent himself from falling asleep.

The Gaon's Talmudic methodology was sharp and incisive, standing in stark contrast to the lengthy *pilpul* (discussion) approach of the Polish yeshivot. He was a harsh opponent of the Chassidic movement, believing that the Chassidim replaced serious intellectual search with a superficial emotional approach.

The Gaon's influence upon the trajectory of modern Jewish scholarship cannot be overstated. He reframed the approach to Talmud study, authored over seventy works on wide-ranging aspects of Torah thought and mentored select students who became foremost Torah scholars in their own right.

Yalkut Reuveini – An anthology of nearly five hundred years of kabbalistic thought, compiled in 1660 by Reuven Hoeshke of Prague.

The first edition of this work was organized topically while a second, enlarged version was framed as a commentary on the Torah.

Yalkut Shimoni – An important, comprehensive Midrashic anthology compiled in the twelfth or thirteenth century.

The *Yalkut Shimoni* contains over ten thousand aggadic and halachic observations on the entire Torah text. Both the authorship and the exact date of the *Yalkut's* publication are the subject of dispute.

Zohar – Central work in the literature of Kabbala (Jewish mysticism).

The Zohar consists of several disparate sections containing Midrashim and discussions on a wide array of topics.

The Zohar's main section is arranged according to the parshiot of the Torah text, although the latter part of the book of Bamidbar and the book of Devarim are not completely covered. Other portions of the work include the teachings and experiences of the second-century Tanna Rabbi Shimon bar Yochai; mystical studies on specific sections of the Torah and other books of Tanach; and discourses on a variety of topics including the nature of God, the origin and structure of the universe, good and evil, man's relationship to God, etc.

While the authorship of the Zohar is subject to dispute, many traditionalists have, for centuries, traced its origins to Rabbi Shimon bar Yochai.

Index